D1435134

the
HOLY SPIRIT

debt. These chapters make no claims to originality. Of the modern writers I have used R. C. Sproul, Arthur Pink, Sinclair Ferguson, Christopher Wright, and Donald Macleod. Of course I have been influenced by Dr. Martyn Lloyd-Jones, even more by hearing him preach with the Holy Spirit sent down from heaven than by reading his sermons. Of the older writers John Owen is superb, especially his *The Holy Spirit* and *The Spirit and the Church* (Banner of Truth paperbacks). After reading them one wonders what need there was of anyone writing anything else.

So my thanks to my wife, Iola, who has kept me in the ministry and been patient with me both at times when I have been away and again at home when I have been ensconced in my upstairs study. Thanks also to the congregation in Aberystwyth that I have loved since 1965. Joel Beeke has encouraged me more than any other minister in the world. Yet most thanks is to the Spirit of the living God, who came into my life, convicting me, making me alive, giving me a new heart, illuminating and sanctifying me, gifting me to preach the riches of the Lord Christ. I possess with every Christian the privilege of illimitable access to the indwelling Spirit. Thanks be to God.

Geoff Thomas
September 2011

CHAPTER ONE

The Holy Spirit: The Infinite, Personal God

As they ministered to the Lord, and fasted, the Holy Ghost said, Separate me Barnabas and Saul for the work whereunto I have called them.

—Acts 13:2

In the book of Acts, the thriving congregation of Antioch is led by gifted men who are ministering to the Lord Jesus Christ. They speak warmly of Christ to one another, singing His praise, praying to Him and temporarily denying themselves earthly comforts so they may fix their minds more on their Savior. In the midst of this, a voice from heaven is heard. We do not know exactly how that occurred, but I believe there could have been an audible voice just as the one heard at the baptism and transfiguration of Jesus or at the conversion of Saul of Tarsus on the road to Damascus or during the vision John had on the Isle of Patmos.

During redemptive history such supernatural manifestations of God's voice have occurred. However, it might also have taken the form of a clear conviction that suddenly rooted in every mind of the church leaders as a word from God. Whatever the delivery of those words, all who heard them had the absolute certainty that the Holy Spirit was saying, "Separate me Barnabas and Saul for the work whereunto I have called them." Thus the extraordinary ministry of the apostle Paul was launched. The Spirit of God was calling these two men to a special work. The leaders of the church had been worshiping the Lord Jesus Christ, but the response in the midst of worship came from the Holy Spirit. It did not come in the form of strong feelings or a heightened sense of the Lord Jesus' presence, but as the Spirit actually speaking and telling listeners that they must obey Him in the practical details of ordaining and commissioning Barnabas and Saul to missionary service. This too was the Almighty God's response, for it was God who heard their prayer. God, who is omniscient and omnipresent but also personal, was there. The God who is is not silent speaks, and He says, "Set apart for me these two men. I have called them to do a work for me." The God who speaks is the Holy Spirit. The Holy Spirit Himself says those words.

Many people today are ignorant about the person and work of the Holy Spirit, both theologically and experientially. Still, there is much talk about Him, and many claim that He is at work in special ways in individuals and congregations. Such claims can intimidate us, but they have no more authority than the men and women who make them. Our consciences are not bound by human claims, but at the same time we dare not underestimate the crucial importance of the work of the Spirit of God. We know that the Son of God became incarnate, died on the cross, rose from the grave, and ascended to the throne of heaven so that He might pour out His Spirit at Pentecost and continue pouring Him out on the church everywhere. Without the gift of the Holy Spirit, the earlier accomplishments of the Savior would not have profited us. The essential, vital, central element in the life of every congregation is the person and work of the Spirit of God as illuminated and structured and judged by the Spirit-breathed Word.

The climax of Jesus' ministry takes place in the upper room, where He teaches the Twelve about the coming of the Spirit. There is no good in any of us that is not a result of the Spirit's work. Every virtue we possess, every victory we win, and every thought of holiness are due to the Spirit. Whatever God calls us to do in life can be accomplished only by the Holy Spirit. Without Him we can do nothing. We cannot do any spiritual good without the Spirit. Every new Christian becomes a believer through the sovereign work of the Holy Spirit. Every Christian who finishes the race of life and enters glory has been kept and prepared for heaven by the power of the Spirit. The only sin for which there is no forgiveness is one committed against the Spirit.

Still, what errors and heresies have crept into the church in the last two thousand years in relation to the Holy Spirit! How diligent we must thus be in studying and knowing about the person and work of the third person of the Godhead, the Holy Spirit. If a seminary turned out a hundred times more preachers than it does now, the church would not be one whit better off unless God is pleased to give a fresh outpouring of the Holy Spirit.

THE HOLY SPIRIT IS A PERSON

Hershey was the originator of wrapped chocolate bars; Hoover, of modern vacuum cleaners; Kellogg, of cornflakes; Ford, of affordable motor cars; and Dr. Scholl, of exercise sandals. Real persons produced materials that we use every day with scarcely a thought of their originators. We have even depersonalized the men who gave their names to what they made by saying we "hoover" the floor or eat a Hershey bar or drive a Ford.

We must be careful not to do that with the Holy Spirit. He is not merely a background influence in the church like the heating system, or a crowd rouser like a band at a rock concert or an agent of raw power such as electricity or an extraordinary means of communication like the World Wide Web. The Spirit may be heat and influence and power and communication, but before He is any of them, He is a person. He is as much a divine person as is God the Father or Jesus the Son. Many cults deny this. To support their views, they say, "Consider Acts 2, which says the Holy Spirit is *poured out* (v. 18) and *shed abroad* (v. 33). How can you pour out a person? You cannot pour out a prime minister or a president. The Spirit is an influence of God, not a person." That is one way they deny the personal nature of God the Spirit. Having rubbished the doctrine of the Trinity, they must then reject the Spirit as a divine person or confront a rival deity who has all the attributes and titles of God.

We respond to them by saying that the language of Acts 2 is figurative. Just as water can be poured down in a severe cloudburst, so the Holy Spirit descended on believers on the day of Pentecost. He affected 120 disciples of Jesus, filling them with Himself, and He regenerated three thousand unbelievers. He did not change one person here and another there; He came like Niagara Falls, cascading down upon the multitude. He shed Himself abroad like a monsoon on Jerusalem as crowds heard Peter preach. Sinners who were as spiritually dry as old sticks and dusty stones were drenched by the Spirit as He was "poured out" and "shed abroad." The true hermeneutic affirms the personality of the Spirit.

We insist that the Spirit is a person who has intelligence, will, understanding, affection, intentionality, and individuality. All the elements of personality are ascribed to the Spirit and are found in Him. He is not deficient in any moral quality such as kindness, patience, gentleness, wisdom, restraint, joy, and goodness. He has life in Himself just as the Father and the Son have life. Let us consider a number of ways in which the Spirit is a person.

1. *The Scriptures use personal pronouns in referring to the Holy Spirit.* Scripture does not refer to the Spirit as "it," as if talking about energy or power; Scripture uses "he." The Spirit also refers to Himself as a person. In Antioch the Spirit says to believers, "Separate me Barnabas and Saul for the work whereunto I have called them" (Acts 13:2). The Spirit of God uses the personal pronouns "me" and "I." The Lord Jesus Christ also refers to the Spirit as a person. In John 15:26, Jesus says, "But when the Comforter is come, whom I will send unto you from the Father, even the Spirit of truth, which proceedeth from the Father, he shall testify of me." What is grammatically interesting is that "Spirit of truth" uses the neuter gender for Spirit but is immediately followed by the word "he." If John wanted us to believe that the Spirit of God was an impersonal and neuter force, this would be the perfect place to do so, but John says "he."

The personhood of the Spirit is also evident in John 16:13–14, where the pronouns "he" and "him" are used eight times each: "Howbeit when he, the Spirit of truth, is come, he will guide you into all truth: for he shall not speak of himself; but whatsoever he shall hear, that shall he speak: and he will shew you things to come. He shall glorify me: for he shall receive of mine, and shall shew it unto you." There is no grammatical reason to use the masculine pronouns, but Jesus does so, thus offering the cults no excuse to deny the personality of the Holy Spirit. The Lord Christ says, "But if I depart, I will send him unto you" (John 16:7).

2. *The Scriptures ascribe personal traits to the Holy Spirit.* The Spirit can be lied to, Peter says in Acts 5:3. The apostle asks Ananias, "Why hath Satan filled thine heart to lie to the Holy Ghost, and to keep back part of the price of the land?" You wouldn't say, "I told a lie to the electrical current or to the water fountain or to the food-vending machine." You deceive people. Likewise Paul tells the Ephesians to "grieve not the holy Spirit" (Eph. 4:30). You cannot grieve an abstraction or a force. Astronauts do not weep in shame because they grieved the law of gravity, but you should weep when you have caused grief to someone who loves you and whom you also love. Scripture tells us the Holy Spirit is a person, whom we may please or offend, obey or defy. He loves and can be loved. He is a person to whom we personally relate.

3. *The Scriptures ascribe personal tasks to the Spirit.* Scripture says the Spirit has the power of speech; He thus speaks to the leaders of the church in

Antioch. In 1 Timothy 4:1, Paul says to Timothy, "Now the Spirit speaketh expressly, that in the latter times some shall depart from the faith." Likewise, Jesus says to the seven churches, "He that hath an ear, let him hear what the Spirit saith unto the churches" (Rev. 2:7). The Spirit also teaches, for Jesus says, "He shall teach you all things" (John 14:26). What impersonal power could teach us everything? We might learn elementary lessons from hurricanes or microwave ovens or electricity, but hardly "all things." Only a personal God could teach us "all things."

In addition, Jesus tells His disciples not to worry when they are put on trial and face accusations, "for the Holy Ghost shall teach you in the same hour what ye ought to say." (Luke 12:12). The Spirit's teaching does not move toward us in some mechanical way. It is not like a telephone answering machine that infuriates us by telling us to enter all kinds of numbers before getting an answer. The Spirit interacts with us individually and personally, telling us how to respond to a crisis or what to say to those who interrogate us. The Spirit intercedes for us and actually prays for us. As Romans 8:26 says, "Likewise the Spirit also helpeth our infirmities: for we know not what we should pray for as we ought: but the Spirit itself maketh intercession for us with groanings which cannot be uttered."

We have a personal God in glory; the man Christ Jesus, who is our great high priest and who lives to make intercession for us; and a personal God here with us on earth, the Holy Spirit, who prays for us. He is not like a Tibetan prayer wheel going round and round in the wind. He has a distinct holy personality. How could we cope with cross-bearing and the opposition of the world without the Spirit interceding for us? As Alfred H. Vine writes:

> Christ is our Advocate on high:
> Thou art our Advocate within;
> O, plead the truth, and make reply
> to every argument of sin.

4. *The Scriptures ascribe personal characteristics to the Spirit.* On four recorded occasions, Jesus refers to the Spirit as the "paraclete." The word is derived from the prefix *para* and the root *kalein*. Together they mean "one who is called alongside." In Jesus' day, a paraclete was summoned to give assistance in a court of law. He was a barrister or counsel who pleaded a person's case in court. *Paraclete* is the term Jesus uses in the opening

verse of 1 John 2:1: "We have an advocate with the Father, Jesus Christ the righteous." At the tribunal of God on judgment day, the judge will be the Savior who died for our sins. The defense lawyer who speaks for us will also be the Savior, who paid the cost of our redemption. In addition, the Holy Spirit will be our paraclete, for He helps us in our weakness and intercedes for us according to the will of God. He defends us and convicts those who would destroy us. He comforts and consoles us just like the Father, who will wipe away tears from our eyes. He is the Comforter, who is the most tenderhearted source of solace the church could ever know. A Christian may say about some aspect of ministry, "That is not my forte," meaning that he feels inadequate in something like witnessing or counseling or perhaps writing. But the Holy Spirit is the forte of every Christian. We can do all things through the Spirit, who strengthens us. We must go wherever God places us and do whatever tasks He gives us to do, for if we do not, we insult the Holy Spirit, who strengthens us when we come to the front line of Christian service. As Acts 1:8 says, "But ye shall receive power, after that the Holy Ghost is come upon you."

So the Holy Spirit is a person; He is not an influence or quality or force or power or some emanation from God. He is as much a person as Jesus, but like the angels and the Father, the Holy Spirit does not possess a body. He is spirit. R. C. Sproul says he was planning to marry his wife, Vesta, when he was converted in 1957. He was excited about telling her that he had become a Christian; however, her response was not warm. She was unhappy and fearful of this change, and remained so for months. Then one night she was persuaded to accompany him to a prayer meeting. Sproul had been praying for her at length. There, in the middle of the prayer meeting, she felt her heart strangely warmed. After the meeting was over, she said to Sproul, "Now I know who the Holy Spirit is." Unlike the years before that time, when she had merely heard about the Holy Spirit, she now knew who the Spirit was. Her first response to the Spirit, who gave her birth from above, was that He as a person had been dealing with her.

THE HOLY SPIRIT IS GOD

In the history of the church, there have been few disputes about the deity of the Holy Spirit. There have been significant debates about whether Christ was God. Through such controversies people minutely examined the Scriptures and came to agree that the Scriptures taught that Jesus Christ was God. The church concluded in its confessions that Jesus has all the attributes of God, all the names of God, all the prerogatives of God. Christ the Son is as much God as the Father is God.

Disputes about the divinity of the Holy Spirit are unusual, but they have occurred because there is no statement in Scripture that says, "The Spirit is God." However, the Bible does declare that the Spirit possesses divine attributes and exercises the sovereign authority of God. Such teaching is clear and unchallengeable. Let's examine some of the evidence substantiating this claim.

1. *The Holy Spirit is expressly called God.* In Acts 5:3–4, Peter says to Ananias, "Why hath Satan filled thine heart to lie to the Holy Ghost, and to keep back part of the price of the land? Whiles it remained, was it not thine own? and after it was sold, was it not in thine own power? why hast thou conceived this thing in thine heart? thou hast not lied unto men, but unto God." Peter says in verse 3 that Ananias has lied to the Holy Spirit. In verse 4, he says Ananias has lied to God. Peter, who had been raised as a Jew who confessed "Hear, oh Israel, the Lord your God is one God," had a deep hatred of idolatry. Yet he had spent three years in the presence of one he now knows as Lord and Christ, and he now identifies the Spirit as God.

The apostle Paul likewise grew up as a Jew, yet he calls Christians the "temple of God." He does this because, as he says in 1 Corinthians 3:16, "The Spirit of God dwelleth in you." Because a Christian is the temple of the Holy Spirit, he must therefore glorify God in his body. Paul goes on to say Christians are "the temple of the living God" (2 Cor. 6:16). In this he refers to the Holy Spirit as the living God. Again in 1 Corinthians 12, the apostle speaks of the three persons of the Godhead as "the same Spirit" (v. 4), "the same Lord" (v. 5), and "the same God" (v. 6). Notice the priority of the persons: first the Spirit, then the Lord, and then God.

2. *The Holy Spirit is the author of Old Testament verses spoken by Jehovah.* In the Old Testament the expressions "God said" and "the Spirit said" are used interchangeably. The activity of God in revealing truth to the prophets is also acknowledged as the activity of the Holy Spirit. There is no membrane of separation between the Spirit and Jehovah God. What is fascinating in the New Testament is that when the apostle Paul quotes the words of the LORD, he tells us that the Holy Spirit was speaking those

words. For example, in Acts 28:25, Paul speaks of the commission the prophet Isaiah received in the temple. Isaiah 6:9 says it is the LORD who speaks to the prophet and says, "Go, and tell this people," but when Paul quotes Isaiah in Acts he says, "Well spake the Holy Ghost by Esaias the prophet unto our fathers" (Acts 28:25). So what Jehovah said was also what the Holy Spirit said. They are one. We know from other passages in the Old Testament that Jehovah spoke by the mouth of the prophets, yet when Peter refers to these passages he says that holy men of old spoke "by the Holy Ghost" (2 Peter 1:21). So when Jehovah spoke, the Holy Spirit was also speaking.

3. The Holy Spirit displays all the perfections of God. The Holy Spirit is omniscient; He knows everything. The glory of that truth is not His knowledge of creation but the Holy Spirit's knowledge of the infinite God Himself. In other words, nothing in God is unknown to the Spirit. I will never know God exhaustively. For all eternity I shall have the mind of a creature, which, however enlightened and cleansed of sin and glorified, will still be a finite mind. By contrast, the Godhead is measureless and infinite. When Paul writes of the Holy Spirit, he says, "The Spirit searches all things, yea, the deep things of God. For what man knoweth the things of a man, save the spirit of man which is in him? even so the things of God knoweth no man, but the Spirit of God" (1 Cor. 2:10–11). No part of God is closed to the Spirit. God has no secrets that he withholds from the Spirit. The Holy Spirit may go into the deep things of God, such as how God can be one and yet three persons. He searches all things. All the unspoken thoughts of God, whatever they may be, are known to the Spirit. The Father keeps no secrets from the Son or the Spirit. Jesus once said, "All things are delivered unto me of my Father: and no man knoweth the Son, but the Father; neither knoweth any man the Father, save the Son" (Matt. 11:27). No one knows Father and Son save the Spirit. So, the Holy Spirit is omniscient because He knows God exhaustively; all the things of God have been committed to the Spirit because He is God.

The Holy Spirit is also omnipresent in our lives as believers; He is present where two or three gather together in His name. He is everywhere: in Tierra del Fuego, in Alaska, in China. He is in the heart of the atom, in the ocean's depths, at the core of the earth, in the Milky Way, in the furthest recesses of space from which faint radio signals emanate, and in the great silence beyond that. So there is nothing men may discover in cosmic exploration that is absent from the Spirit of God. What is yet to be discovered will bear evidences of God the Spirit's creative and sustaining energy. So Psalm 139:7–12 says, "Whither shall I go from thy spirit? or whither shall I flee from thy presence? If I ascend up into heaven, thou art there: if I make my bed in hell, behold, thou art there. If I take the wings of the morning, and dwell in the uttermost parts of the sea; even there shall thy hand lead me, and thy right hand shall hold me. If I say, Surely the darkness shall cover me; even the night shall be light about me. Yea, the darkness hideth not from thee; but the night shineth as the day: the darkness and the light are both alike to thee."

Wherever the Spirit is, God is. There is no place for rebel sinners or fugitives to hide that is outside of the presence of the Holy Spirit; He is ubiquitous. Such an attribute belongs to the being of God; it is not shared by any creatures. Mary the mother of Jesus does not have attributes like that. Neither do the archangels, who cannot be in more than one place at a time. Like the angels, we are all finite, created spirits. We are creatures bound by space and time. That is not so for the Holy Spirit; He is omnipresent.

The Holy Spirit is also the Creator. To create is a divine attribute. No one can create anything out of nothing except God. The Holy Spirit was active before the first day of creation. Genesis 1:1–2 tells us, "In the beginning God created the heaven and the earth. And the earth was without form, and void; and darkness was upon the face of the deep. And the Spirit of God moved upon the face of the waters." That theme is repeated time after time in the Bible. Psalm 104:30 says, "Thou sendest forth thy spirit, they are created: and thou renewest the face of the earth." Job 33:4 says, "The spirit of God hath made me, and the breath of the Almighty hath given me life." What is more, the Holy Spirit was the miraculous power that begat God the Son in the womb of the Virgin Mary. As Luke 1:35 says: "And the angel answered and said unto her, The Holy Ghost shall come upon thee, and the power of the Highest shall overshadow thee: therefore also that holy thing which shall be born of thee shall be called the Son of God." The Holy Spirit creates life where there is none. Jesus Christ was raised from the dead by the Spirit, for Romans 8:11 says, "But if the Spirit of him that raised up Jesus from the dead dwell in you, he that raised up Christ from the dead shall also quicken your mortal bodies by his Spirit that dwelleth in you."

The Spirit is also the absolutely holy One. The properties of power and might are His, but so are the moral qualities. God is the holy One.

The seraphim cover their eyes before Him and cry to one another, "Holy... holy.... Isn't He so holy?" (see Isaiah 6). He is described as "glorious in holiness." One time Jonathan Edwards was riding in the woods, contemplating God. He became so overwhelmed with the total perfection and righteousness of God that he had to lie down until he had the strength to stand up and mount his horse. The third person of the Godhead is addressed most frequently as the "Holy Spirit" or "the Spirit of holiness." He has all the moral perfections of God. So what the Spirit creates and sustains in those He indwells are all fruit of righteousness, which, according to Galatians 5:22–23, is "love, joy, peace, longsuffering, gentleness, goodness, faith, meekness, temperance." The Spirit is like God, but of course He is not like God at all; He *is* God, and so all the perfections of God are His. The Spirit of God is love, joy, peace, patience, kindness, goodness, faithfulness, gentleness, and self-control.

4. The Holy Spirit displays the sovereignty of God. Salvation is of the Lord and is applied to men and women by the Spirit of the Lord. Jesus makes that clear to Nicodemus in their dialogue in John 3:8: "The wind bloweth where it listeth, and thou hearest the sound thereof, but canst not tell whence it cometh, and whither it goeth: so is every one that is born of the Spirit." You cannot say, "Come here, wind, on this hot day, and blow on my cheek." The wind blows wherever it pleases, not as you direct. Likewise, you cannot say you will go and preach in such a place, and nine people will be converted. You cannot say, "I am going to talk to my erring daughter and convert her." Regeneration is not yours to perform. It is the Spirit's grand prerogative.

You cannot say you will perform a miracle tonight where a man with Down's syndrome will be delivered of that syndrome when you lay your hands on him. That is the work of the Spirit, and those works are done at His sovereign discretion. He does not inform us of His plans. We recognize that from our own experience.

The sovereignty of the Spirit is most powerfully seen in His relationship with God the Son. The Spirit formed the incarnate Son in Mary's womb. Who but God could do that? The Spirit anointed Christ at His baptism for public ministry. Who but God could anoint God the Son? The Spirit led Jesus into the wilderness. Who but a divine person had the right to direct the Mediator in the way He should go? Do the sheep direct the Shepherd, or the Shepherd direct the sheep? Where does authority lie? To whom but God would the Redeemer have submitted? What a sovereign Spirit He is!

The Holy Spirit is a person, and the Holy Spirit is God. So when our Lord commissioned the church to go into all the world and make disciples of all nations, He stipulated that they should be baptized "in the name of the Father, and of the Son, and of the Holy Ghost" (Matt. 28:19). The Father is God, the Son is God, and the Spirit is God. These three are one God. You realize how unacceptable it would be to say we are to baptize in the name of the Father and the Son "and the apostle Paul" or "the Virgin Mary." But when you see that the Spirit is as much a person as the Father and the Son and that He has all of the divine attributes and prerogatives and perfections, then it is essential that we say, "Father, Son, and Spirit." God is a triune God, and you have been joined to Him in that Trinity. You have been united with the Holy Spirit, the infinite-almighty and yet personal God, and you are one with Him forever. What hope that should give you for the future!

When you hear the apostolic benediction spoken at the end of every worship service, "The grace of the Lord Jesus Christ, and the love of God, and the communion of the Holy Ghost, be with you all" (2 Cor. 13:14), you will know that they are equal in their love for you and their power to redeem and sanctify you. You know that it is utterly unacceptable for a Roman Catholic to hear a benediction speaking of Christ's grace and God's love and the intercession of Mary. The phrase *fellowship of the Holy Spirit* sets the Spirit in right relationship with the Father and the Son, who are all co-essential, co-eternal, and co-equal. You are not alone; you are in daily communion with God the Holy Spirit. May He be with us all forevermore.

"That is how I must be known." He will allow no breach between Himself in the Old Testament and New Testament Scriptures.

Some people think the Holy Spirit was a stranger to believers in the Old Testament. But the Spirit of God is more evident in the Old Testament than is Jesus Christ, the second person of the Godhead. The Spirit is called by name more frequently than is the Son of God. About seventy-five references are made to the Spirit of God in the Old Testament. The opening verses of the Bible state, "In the beginning God created the heaven and the earth. And the earth was without form, and void; and darkness was upon the face of the deep. And the Spirit of God moved upon the face of the waters" (Gen. 1:1–2). The Holy Spirit makes His appearance already in the second verse of the Bible.

THE SPIRIT OF GOD WAS PRESENT AT CREATION

The opening verses of the Bible are the most widely read words of all literature. Perhaps they were the first sentences ever written. These simple, yet profound statements provide a clear understanding of the truth of Christianity against any challenges. The words "in the beginning *God*" refute *atheism*, which claims there is no God. In saying that God existed before the universe, these words also refute *pantheism*, which claims that everything is God. In saying that God created everything, these words refute *polytheism*, which claims there are many gods. And these words refute the *big bang* theory of the beginning of the universe because they say the living God created it all. There is God, and there is the Holy Spirit. There is one God, and yet very soon the Lord will say, "Let *us* make man in *our* image" (v. 26).

In the beginning was chaos and darkness. God looked out upon a bleak empty wasteland, a trackless waste, an enormous void. It was like being in the midst of the Irish Sea, halfway between Wales and Ireland, on a pitch-black night, without the light of a single star. The initial step of creation resulted in a totally bleak scenario. It was not at all like our cosmos today; it was utter chaos. Yet over it all was the Spirit of God. Some scholars have argued that "Spirit of God" (*ruach elohim*) should be translated as "mighty wind," but two arguments constrain us to reject that translation. First, everywhere else that the word *elohim* appears in Genesis 1, it is translated as "God," never as "mighty wind." Second, a wind, especially a mighty one, does not hover; it blows and howls. Wolfhart

Pannenburg, a German professor, considers the translation "mighty wind" as "grotesque."[2] The word "moved" can also mean to brood or hover. To help us better understand the word, we should look at how it is used in Deuteronomy to describe an eagle rising above her nest, her wings outspread as she glides and flutters over her young (Deut. 32:11).

So the first step of creation ushers in black chaos, an utter wasteland void of anything. Yet over it all hovers the Spirit, moving above the face of this primordial abyss as if tending His young. Like an eagle, He is protecting and keeping His fledglings. The Spirit was tending creation before the creation of the garden and the fall of man. The Spirit not only hovers over the manicured fields of Kent (known as "the Garden of England"), the beautiful landscaped farms of Cornwall, or the magnificent arboreta of Kew Gardens in London. Yes, He is present in the magnificent Swiss Alps and American Rockies, but He was also present at the beginning, when there was nothing remotely beautiful in creation and when it was a black discordant abyss of terror. The Spirit of God was there, loving, caring, and tending what first was made. Specifically, He was involved in two ways: in the ecology and theology of creation.

1. Ecology. What environment do you most fear? Being in the midst of an Arctic winter with no light or warmth? Stuck in the midst of the Sahara with no water or protection from the baking heat? Being trapped by a methane gas explosion in a coal mine, leaving you in total blackness half a mile underground? Living within range of the Chernobyl radiation, or in a labor camp in China? How about being locked up in a cellar for fifteen years without any natural light? We all fear certain places, yet here in the Bible we are told that in the darkest place this universe has ever known, the Spirit of God was present, caring, brooding, and loving it.

A Christian view of ecology must start with Genesis 1, where the Spirit of God was present in the darkest, bleakest of all places. Does this not tell people not to despair of dustbowls or spreading deserts or dried-up inland seas? What can we who care about God's creation do about such situations? We must do what we can. If the tenants of the house you buy left the garden like a chemical waste dump, you should do what you can to clean up the mess and restore the land. The late John Marshall of

---

2. Wolfhart Pannenburg, *Systematic Theology*, trans. G. W. Bromiley (Grand Rapids: Eerdmans, 1994), 2:77.

Hemel Hempstead preached every Saturday afternoon in the market in that town. Yet he also did everything he could to tend nature. We read, "He supported the Woodland Trust and loved to try and plant trees wherever he could. His friends driving with him would sometimes be surprised to see him throwing flower seeds out of the car window onto grass verges and sometimes he actually planted bulbs in empty spaces." His son Jeremy says, "There is a bridge on the road to Cambridge which now has masses of daffodils which Dad planted."[3] There is a link between John's declaring the Word of God and the planting of trees and plants; it hearkens back to the opening words of Genesis. God spoke creation into being, and His Spirit hovered over it.

2. *Theology.* The Spirit of God was present in and above creation. He created the sun that would be worshiped both in Egypt and in Babylon. He created the heavenly bodies that people would think of as deities controlling their destinies. Millions of people today still consult the stars for guidance on how to live. They read horoscopes based on the movement of the stars when they were born. They may publicly joke about such readings, thinking them foolish, but the next day they're checking their horoscopes again. They think that heavenly bodies control our daily destinies, but the first chapter of the Bible lists the stars almost as a divine afterthought. Genesis 1:16 says, "He made the stars also." The God of the Bible is in control of the world. There is no reason for any Christian to be influenced by astrology.

The sea that God created was considered a god in Canaanite mythology. People called this powerful god Yamm. But Genesis tells us God created the sea, and the Spirit of God is hovering over it. The Canaanites also worshiped a god of the earth, named Baal, son of El, who supposedly provided fertility to the soil. But the opening chapter of the Bible says the living God made everything. The sun, moon, stars, ocean depths, and the earth itself are the results of God speaking these things into being; they are the handiwork of the Creator God.

By the Holy Spirit, Jehovah spoke the universe into existence. By the Spirit, God brought into creation the light, order, and fullness that now surrounds us. The Spirit of God is the Lord and the giver of life. When

---

3. John J. Murray, *John E. Marshall: Life and Writings* (Edinburgh: The Banner of Truth Trust, 2005), 31–32.

"through the woods and forest glades we wander and hear the birds sing softly in the trees," our souls burst forth in praise to the Spirit, "My God, how great Thou art." If we long for deeper experiences of God's Spirit, we may find it through a deeper understanding of the God of the Old Testament and of His creation. What Christian farmer has not stopped driving his tractor to consider the glory of the creation around him and to simply worship the Lord? The prophet Isaiah heard the seraphim crying out, "The whole earth is full of his glory" (Isa. 6:3).

We must defy the dogmatic naturalism that is all around us, which teaches that the material realm is all there is. The Christian knows that behind the physical world is the divine mind of God the Father, Son, and Spirit. This world is not just a self-sustaining biosystem. Nature did not simply happen. God was actively involved in the creation and sustaining of all things in nature. The fullness of His glory is evident in everything God has made. So we cry with the psalmist, "The glory of the LORD shall endure for ever: the LORD shall rejoice in his works" (Ps. 104:31).

THE SPIRIT OF GOD WAS PRESENT IN THE CREATION OF MAN

You are unique as a human being, according to Genesis, in three ways.

1. You are made in God's image and likeness. Genesis 1:26–27 says, "And God said, Let us make man in our image, after our likeness: and let them have dominion over the fish of the sea, and over the fowl of the air, and over the cattle, and over all the earth, and over every creeping thing that creepeth upon the earth. So God created man in his own image, in the image of God created he him; male and female created he them."

2. God gave man the mandate to subdue the earth and rule over it. Genesis 1:28 says, "Be fruitful, and multiply, and replenish the earth, and subdue it: and have dominion over the fish of the sea, and over the fowl of the air, and over every living thing that moveth upon the earth."

3. God made man a unique way. "And the LORD God formed man of the dust of the ground, and breathed into his nostrils the breath of life; and man became a living soul" (Gen. 2:7). With no other creature is God so intimate; He virtually embraces man and breathes into him the breath of life.

So every person is made by God and for God. When we ask little children, "Who made me?" they answer, "God made me." We ask, "What else did God make?" They respond, "God made all things. Why did God make all things? For His own glory." We belong to God by right of creation; His Spirit is at work in us in our conscience and in creating within us a sense of God. Job says, "The Spirit of God hath made me, and the breath of the Almighty hath given me life" (Job 33:4). He also says, "But there is a spirit in man: and the inspiration of the Almighty giveth them understanding" (Job 32:8). And Job professes, "All the while my breath is in me, and the spirit of God is in my nostrils; my lips shall not speak wickedness" (Job 27:3–4). Job and his four companions all had the Spirit of God. Through His influence, they could look at Job's life and ask why God made him suffer so many losses. All great literature depends upon the influence of the Spirit of God. That is why no animals can produce works of art.

Yet we cannot avoid the horror story of Genesis 3, which tells how man fell into sin. We who were made in the image of God, in whom God breathed the breath of life so that we could know and love God, *rebelled*. We who were made by the Spirit of God defied God, we did things our own way, rejecting the authority of the one who had given us the kiss of life. So by our own choice we came under the sentence of death. A new relationship between man and the Spirit of God began with our sin. From that time on, the Spirit of God contended with man, restraining his sin and striving to convict him of his need of the grace of God. We are warned that God will not always graciously restrain us from sin. In Genesis 6:3 God says, "My spirit shall not always strive with man, for that he also is flesh: yet his days shall be an hundred and twenty years."

How long will you live? You do not know. But you do know it will be as long as God's Spirit gives you life. All people are energized by the Spirit of God. We live and move and have our being in God. But only while the Spirit strives within us will we live. When we have filled up our iniquities we will die, and when God withdraws His Spirit from us, we will return to dust. Ecclesiastes 12:7 says, "Then shall the dust return to the earth as it was: and the spirit shall return unto God who gave it."

THE SPIRIT OF GOD WAS PRESENT IN OLD TESTAMENT PEOPLE

The Old Testament often tells about the Spirit of God coming upon or filling a person. As a result, the person received a God-given ability, charisma, competence, power, or strength to do certain things for God or His people. The first example Scripture mentions of people who were filled with the Spirit of God were Bezalel and Aholiab. Did they prophesy as a result? Speak in tongues? No. The Spirit enabled these men to become *craftsmen*. Let us examine that first indwelling.

1. The Spirit in craftsmen. The Spirit of God filled Bezalel and Aholiab to become master artisans in metal, wood, and precious stones to build the temple of God. Exodus 35:30–36:1 says:

> And Moses said unto the children of Israel, See, the LORD hath called by name Bezaleel the son of Uri, the son of Hur, of the tribe of Judah; and he hath filled him with the spirit of God, in wisdom, in understanding, and in knowledge, and in all manner of workmanship; and to devise curious works, to work in gold, and in silver, and in brass, and in the cutting of stones, to set them, and in carving of wood, to make any manner of cunning work. And he hath put in his heart that he may teach, both he, and Aholiab, the son of Ahisamach, of the tribe of Dan. Them hath he filled with wisdom of heart, to work all manner of work, of the engraver, and of the cunning workman, and of the embroiderer, in blue, and in purple, in scarlet, and in fine linen, and of the weaver, even of them that do any work, and of those that devise cunning work. Then wrought Bezaleel and Aholiab, and every wise hearted man, in whom the LORD put wisdom and understanding to know how to work all manner of work for the service of the sanctuary, according to all that the LORD had commanded.

Chris Wright comments, "There is something so wonderfully creative (and therefore God-like) in what this passage describes: craftsmanship, artistic design, embroidery with rich colours, carving wood and stone. I fondly wish I had some of these skills and greatly admire the work of artists who do. We should take seriously that these things are said to be marks of the filling with God's Spirit."[4]

A man at my church was filled with the same Spirit of God who was in Bezalel and Aholiab. Ron Loosley worked on the plans to renovate our manse. He transformed Plas Lluest into a Christian home for people with learning difficulties, and drew the blueprints for the Christian book shop. He saved the church tens of thousands of pounds, but the beautiful skill

---

4. Wright, *Knowing the Holy Spirit*, 38–39.

of his work was what made it so memorable. The same Spirit who came upon Bezalel and Aholiab also filled Ron Loosley, and our congregation rejoices in the goodness and loveliness of all that he has so wonderfully designed and executed.

2. The Spirit in the judges. A refrain throughout the book of Judges is the achievements of Israel's leaders, whom they called judges. The task of a judge was to sort out disputes between people, give judgments on local problems, lead people into battle against oppressors, and to summon the tribes of Israel to act against a sudden threat. Consider the judge Gideon, for example. Judges 6:34 says, "Then the Spirit of the LORD came upon Gideon." If we read those words carelessly, we might conclude that Gideon stood up abruptly, shook off his lethargy, and seized his weapons to do battle against the Mideonites, who were oppressing Israel. But what we actually read in these beautiful words is something different.

The Hebrew word for "came upon" that we find there is the same one that is used when a man puts on his jacket. When it's time to go off to work, many people put on their work clothes. The doctor has his white coat, the flight attendant her uniform, the banker his suit. Yet the act of putting on work clothes does not signify that the uniform will do the work; rather, it indicates the moment at which a person puts on those clothes to begin working. The patient does not look to a white coat to heal him; yet when he sees the doctor has put on that white coat, he knows he means to get to work. Likewise, Judges 6:34 says the Spirit of the LORD clothed himself with Gideon. God's Spirit put Gideon on like a coat. Gideon was to the Spirit what overalls are to a worker. He was only a set of work clothes. The one doing the work was the Spirit.

Thus, the one who springs into action is not Gideon but the Spirit. The Lord rises to do battle. What we get here, then, is not the story of the great deeds of a certain person but a report about the mighty deeds of the Lord. So when you read about the Spirit coming upon a judge in Judges, remember it is God who arises to vindicate His name among the people.

3. The Spirit in the kings. Saul is the last judge of Israel and her first king. He is a mixture of them both. We are told the Spirit of the Lord came upon Saul in 1 Samuel 11:6. But later the Spirit of the Lord departed from Saul (1 Sam. 16:14). In its place came a spirit of dark moods, depression, and murderous jealousy. So the Spirit may give someone ability, leadership, and courage, but the Spirit may also remove Himself from those who grieve Him and defiantly persist in their folly. In the New Testament John tells us to test the spirits (1 John 4:1) to see whether they are from God or from the Devil. Jesus also warns us that men may have the gifts of prophesying and may even work miracles but in the great day may be told by Christ, "Depart from me. I never knew you."

4. *The Spirit in Moses.* The gifting ministry of the Spirit is more fully described in His dealings with Moses than with the judges and kings. The merit of examining how the Spirit prepared and used Moses is recognized by the prophet Isaiah. Looking back to the wilderness wanderings of Israel, Isaiah says the children of Israel "rebelled, and vexed his holy Spirit" (Isa. 63:10). We are told that their leader, Moses, was "very meek, above all the men which were upon the face of the earth" (Num. 12:3). That is a staggering testimony to one of the greatest leaders of human history.

Yet Moses was not always like that. As a young man he had killed an Egyptian officer who was whipping an Israelite. For this he was sent to the wilderness for forty years, where he tended his father-in-law's sheep. Finally, God revealed Himself to Moses in a burning bush and asked him to redeem Israel from slavery and lead them into the Promised Land. God did not choose Moses because of his natural gifts but because of what the Spirit of God had done in him over the past decades.

The Spirit of God then served Moses in a remarkable way. We are told in Numbers 11:16–17: "And the LORD said unto Moses, Gather unto me seventy men of the elders of Israel, whom thou knowest to be the elders of the people, and officers over them; and bring them unto the tabernacle of the congregation, that they may stand there with thee. And I will come down and talk with thee there: and I will take of the spirit which is upon thee, and will put it upon them; and they shall bear the burden of the people with thee, that thou bear it not thyself alone." Moses' greatness was evident in his dependence upon the Spirit and his willingness to accept God's Spirit in others. Moses trusted the seventy elders. He did not regard them as potential rivals to his leadership. He recognized their abilities as gifts that the Spirit had given to them. Moses knew that more people who were gifted by God for leadership in the church would enrich the life of the people of God. Numbers 11:24–30 offers another example of Moses' humility:

And Moses went out, and told the people the words of the LORD, and gathered the seventy men of the elders of the people, and set them round about the tabernacle. And the LORD came down in a cloud, and spake unto him, and took of the spirit that was upon him, and gave it unto the seventy elders: and it came to pass, that, when the spirit rested upon them, they prophesied, and did not cease. But there remained two of the men in the camp, the name of the one was Eldad, and the name of the other Medad: and the spirit rested upon them; and they were of them that were written, but went not out unto the tabernacle: and they prophesied in the camp. And there ran a young man, and told Moses, and said, Eldad and Medad do prophesy in the camp. And Joshua the son of Nun, the servant of Moses, one of his young men, answered and said, My lord Moses, forbid them. And Moses said unto him, Enviest thou for my sake? would God that all the LORD's people were prophets, and that the LORD would put his spirit upon them! And Moses gat him into the camp, he and the elders of Israel.

The Spirit in Moses made him secure in his relationship with God. He could exercise power and leadership without jealousy. He could wield power with humility because he held power without jealousy. Moses' longing that the Lord would put his Spirit on all people was eventually fulfilled in the outpouring of the Spirit on the day of Pentecost and has been experienced in the church ever since. The Lord has put His Spirit on every believer; no Christian goes without the indwelling and fruit and gifts of the Spirit.

Moses probably had the most critical, rebellious, awkward, ungrateful, unreasonable congregation that any leader could ever have. He coped with them by the power of the indwelling Spirit of God. Let no minister grumble about the problems of church members until he has read the book of Numbers and seen what Moses had to endure.

Consider some of the problems Moses had to deal with: administrative overload, food-catering problems, charismatic outbursts, family feuds, criticism of his own marriage, refusal to follow the vision God had given through him, rejection of his authority to speak for God, attacks from outside the community, sexual immorality within the community. Moses coped with all of that through the power of the Spirit of God.

Doesn't Moses remind you of the Lord Jesus? Jesus remained committed to His disciples, even when one betrayed Him to death, another denied Him with profanity, and the rest ran off and abandoned Him. Yet

Jesus affirmed to His Father that He had lost no disciple except Judas. The Spirit of God had come upon Christ at the beginning of His ministry. That is why He was so patient with His disciples. Or think of the apostle Paul dealing with the church at Corinth, which gave him endless problems. He wrote to them that he was their bond slave for Jesus' sake. Who was Paul? A mere servant, he said. What drove his work? As Chris Wright says, it was his utter foot-washing dedication to "the real, gritty, grainy people whom God had entrusted to him."

The paradox of the power of Moses is that the greatest evidence of the *presence* of the Holy Spirit in him was the *absence* of those things commonly linked with great and powerful people: pride in one's self-sufficiency, jealous defense of one's own prerogatives, driving ambition for one's own legacy. The Holy Spirit empowers people through humility.

"The church needs leaders," Chris Wright says. "And leaders need power, if they are ever to get anything done (or, more properly, if God is ever to get anything done through them). But the kind of power they need is not the kind of power by which the world generally assesses leadership. For as Zechariah 4:6 says, 'Not by might nor by power, but by my Spirit, says the LORD Almighty.'"

Wright goes on to say," Pray for those whom God has called into positions of leadership among his people, including yourself, if appropriate, that there will be much greater evidence of the empowering Spirit of God, and much less evidence of the ambiguous and dangerous power of our fallen human weaknesses. May we be filled with the power of God's Spirit, in the likeness of Moses, and of Jesus."[5]

5. *The Spirit in all Old Testament believers.* The Holy Spirit indwelt true Old Testament believers. No one can be born again, believe, repent, or make one step of spiritual progress without the inward work of the Holy Spirit. In fact, no one can persevere in faith for one second without the ongoing internal work of the Holy Spirit–neither in the Old Testament nor in the New Testament. Without the Holy Spirit constantly in and at work in their hearts, believers will immediately apostatize.

But having laid that foundational continuity between the two Testaments, we must also ask, "In what ways did the indwelling work of the Holy Spirit differ in the Old Testament from the New, especially

---

5. Wright, *Knowing the Holy Spirit*, 60–61.

post-Pentecost?" Everyone accepts there was a difference. But what was it? The Spirit's indwelling in the Old Testament was like a water dropper continually dripping a little water onto a sponge on a hot summer day. The Spirit's indwelling in the New Testament is like a pressure washer jetting water into a sponge with excess water pouring out everywhere.

Think of a dry sponge on a hot day. Now imagine a water dropper. The dropper drips water so slowly onto the sponge that while it gets wet, it never fills up so much that the water begins to run out of the sponge. This was the Old Testament believers' and the New Testament disciples' experience of the Spirit. Christ kept them supplied with a continual "dripping of the Spirit" that kept them spiritually alive and fruitful, but rarely so much that their spiritual life overflowed into the lives of others. The same was true of the Old Testament church as a whole. But now imagine someone takes a pressure washer and starts jetting the sponge. Almost immediately it would not only fill with water, but water would be flowing out of it in every direction. Welcome to Pentecost. Welcome to what Jesus was predicting in John 7:37–39.

But why the delay? John says because "Jesus was not yet glorified" (v. 39). Prior to the New Testament, the Spirit had relatively little truth to work with. But when Christ was glorified—when He died, rose again, and ascended—then the Spirit had much more truth to work with.

When the fullness of God's revelation of Christ had come, then the fullness of the Spirit could be poured out. At Pentecost we see a new plenitude, perpetuity, pervasiveness, and publicity about the Holy Spirit. We see His work more intensively, extensively, and obviously. Narrow Jewish hearts would be so filled with Christ and the Spirit that they would burst their banks and overflow out into the nations with spiritual blessing as Peter did in Acts 2, for example.

In conclusion, then, we can say that while the Holy Spirit indwelt all Old Testament believers, their experience of the Holy Spirit was usually limited to a degree of personal filling, but they were rarely fully filled, and even more rarely did they overflow to others in witness, evangelism, and mission. That filling full and overflowing awaited the apex of the person and work of Christ, when the Holy Spirit was poured out on Him without measure and on His church in an overflowing way.

CHAPTER THREE

The Inspiration of Old Testament Prophets

Knowing this first, that no prophecy of the scripture is of any private interpretation. For the prophecy came not in old time by the will of man: but holy men of God spake as they were moved by the Holy Ghost.
—2 Peter 1:20–21

Peter was the disciple of Christ whom Jesus appointed to lead the rest of the disciples after His ascension. Peter had spent three years in our Lord's presence, learning from His teaching during His public ministry. Later Peter was appointed as an apostle to speak in the name of Christ, with our Lord's authority behind his words. Thus those who received Peter received Peter's Lord.

Peter's special calling was to feed Christ's sheep and lambs. Peter was filled with the Spirit on the day of Pentecost and preached the gospel so faithfully that God converted three thousand people. Peter was later inspired to write two letters. In the first letter, he offers his view (and the Lord Jesus') on the nature of Old Testament Scripture. He is most earnest on this matter, saying, "Knowing this first, that no prophecy of the scripture is of any private interpretation. For the prophecy came not in old time by the will of man: but holy men of God spake as they were moved by the Holy Ghost."

WHO WROTE SCRIPTURE

Peter stresses that prophetic portions of Scripture, or, indeed, the entire body of Scripture (I favor the latter interpretation), were not the result of individuals having hunches and feelings and convictions about God and the world, then writing those down. The Scriptures are not the product of human investigation and reason; they are not "of any private interpretation." To make that point clear, Peter says, "Prophecy came not in old time by the will of man."

Peter thus begins by clearing away erroneous attitudes. First, he tells us that Old Testament prophecy did *not* come by the will of man. It was not by human will that Moses, Samuel, David, Elijah, the three major prophets, and the twelve minor prophets wrote Scripture. The writings of those men have not come to us because they deeply believed they had a message from heaven, which they eventually committed to writing. The origin was not in the hearts and minds of any men.

Having cleared away that misunderstanding, Peter tells us the origin of prophecies of Scripture. He says, "Men of God spake as they were moved by the Holy Ghost." That conviction about the Old Testament is what he is teaching the New Testament church. The church's attitude about the Old Testament is therefore not optional; it cannot either take those words or leave them. Peter binds believers to all of Scripture. If Jesus Christ is our God and has appointed Peter to be His spokesman, we must also have this conviction about the spiritual nature of the Old Testament. Peter's language is as clear as Paul's in 2 Timothy 3:16 in saying that all Scripture is given by the inspiration of God.

Peter tells us that men spoke from God. What God said, they said; and what they said, God had said. Their words were only possible because "they were moved by the Holy Ghost," Peter says. Scripture is not a magical book that descended from heaven. It is not just a religious book, either. It is the book of the Holy Spirit, given to the church by God through men who spoke from Him. Edward J. Young of Westminster Seminary, Philadelphia, explains:

> If we examine closely the language of Peter, we shall note that it was while they were in this condition of being borne by the Spirit that men spoke from God. The source of their words is said to be God, and they spoke these words while they were being borne of the Holy Spirit. While they spoke they were passive, and God was active. It was he who bore them, and as he bore them, they spoke. It was, therefore, not in the void, but rather through the instrumentality and medium of men who were borne by the Spirit, that God spoke.
>
> Peter thus makes it clear that human beings actually spoke from God. That is, there were human writers of the Scriptures. The things which they uttered were not their own, but, since they had been borne by Him, were of God Himself. Since God gave His word

through human writers, we may truly speak of a human side to the Bible. The message of God was communicated by means of the instrumentality of men who were under the influence of his Spirit.[1]

You might ask how the Spirit controlled the writers of Scripture so that they wrote exactly what He desired, without stifling their individual styles and personalities. I cannot explain how that was so. How could Amos write, "The words of Amos...which he saw" (Amos 1:1), yet write words that were from Jehovah? If God was the author of those words, how could Amos also be their author? We can only say what Scripture itself says about these seemingly irreconcilable doctrines. As with the sovereignty of God and the responsibility of man, Scripture confronts us with a seemingly irreconcilable tension between two doctrines that can only be viewed as two parallel lines of truth that meet in infinity. So it is with Scripture's authorship; it stands in the light that the Word of God casts upon it. Our responsibility is to believe Scripture and to trust God in the apparent anomalies of its authorship. God has spoken. Let us hear His voice. Beyond that we should not go.

HOW THEIR TESTIMONY IS CONFIRMED

Let us consider the testimony of Israel's leaders from two perspectives: the testimony of leaders who followed them and their own experience of the inspiration of the Holy Spirit.

1. The testimony of leaders who followed. During the Old Testament, people of the exile looked back to the time of the prophets and acknowledged that they spoke courageously and faithfully under the inspiration of the Holy Spirit. Consider Nehemiah, for example, who led the Jews back to Israel after seventy years of exile in Babylon. In Nehemiah 9, this man of God tells how God sustained Moses during the years he and his people were exiled in the wilderness. "Thou gavest also thy good spirit to instruct them," Nehemiah says (Neh. 9:20). Moses taught the people, but it was by God's good Spirit that the word came through Moses to the people in Egypt and in the wilderness. Nehemiah reinforces the same point that Peter makes in the New Testament.

---

1. Edward J. Young, *Thy Word Is Truth* (Edinburgh: The Banner of Truth Trust, 1963), 225–26.

Later in his prayer, Nehemiah comments on the hard-heartedness and disobedience of the Israelites. In Nehemiah 9:30, he says, "Yet many years didst thou forbear them, and testifiedst against them by thy spirit in thy prophets: yet would they not give ear." Moses exhorted and rebuked the people, yet Nehemiah says those admonitions came by the Spirit of God. That is the same conviction of the New Testament apostles who said the Word of God came through the prophets by the Spirit of God.

Zechariah 7 includes a similar lament, for Zechariah also met resistance to his message summoning the people to live in obedience to the God of Israel. Zechariah preached to the people from the scriptures of Moses and the earlier prophets, but his words were rejected. He writes,

> And the word of the LORD came unto Zechariah, saying, Thus speaketh the LORD of hosts, saying, Execute true judgment, and shew mercy and compassions every man to his brother: and oppress not the widow, nor the fatherless, the stranger, nor the poor; and let none of you imagine evil against his brother in your heart. But they refused to hearken, and pulled away the shoulder, and stopped their ears, that they should not hear Yea, they made their hearts as an adamant stone, lest they should hear the law, and the words which the LORD of hosts hath sent in his spirit by the former prophets: therefore came a great wrath from the LORD of hosts (Zech. 7:8–12).

Eight hundred years after the death of Moses, leaders like Nehemiah and Zechariah could look back to their fathers, acknowledging how those men were led by the Spirit of God to speak His words.

2. The experiences of the prophets. The prophets knew by experience that their messages came through the illumination and authority of the Spirit of God. The prophet Micah says, "But truly I am full of power by the spirit of the LORD, and of judgment, and of might, to declare unto Jacob his transgression, and to Israel his sin" (Mic. 3:8). Likewise, the prophet Isaiah says, "And now the Lord GOD, and his Spirit, hath sent me. Thus saith the LORD, thy Redeemer, the Holy One of Israel; I am the LORD thy God which teacheth thee to profit, which leadeth thee by the way that thou shouldest go" (Isa. 48:16–17).

Or consider the last words of David, king and psalm-writer of Israel: "Now these be the last words of David. David the son of Jesse said, and the man who was raised up on high, the anointed of the God of Jacob, and the sweet psalmist of Israel, said, the Spirit of the LORD spake by me, and his word was in my tongue. The God of Israel said, the Rock of Israel spake to me" (2 Sam. 23:1–3).

When Solomon built the temple, did he precisely follow the plans left by David out of reverence for what the king had written or out of obedience to God? Scripture's reply is clear: "Then David gave to Solomon his son the pattern of the porch, and of the houses thereof, and of the treasuries thereof, and of the upper chambers thereof, and of the inner parlours thereof, and of the place of the mercy seat, and the pattern of all that he had by the spirit, of the courts of the house of the LORD" (1 Chron. 28:11–12). The prophets themselves and later leaders in Israel were convinced that the words they preached were delivered by the inspiration of the Spirit.

HOW SCRIPTURE WRITING DIFFERS FROM DICTATION

The Muslims claim that the Koran was fully written in Arabic in heaven before it came to earth. For this reason Muslims have been slow to grant permission for a new translation of the Koran, since no other form is admissible but the flawless one given to Mohammed. We reject such a theory of the inspiration of the Bible. God did not disregard the personalities of Moses, Samuel, David, Isaiah, and others in the writing of Scripture. Their styles and temperaments and personal feelings are apparent in all they wrote. We reject the suggestion that the prophets were little better than human Dictaphones who mechanically recorded the words God spoke to them. We do not believe in such parrot-like reproduction.

Critics of this view refuse to believe that God could supervise the upbringing, education, and experiences of a man and shape his composition of the written prophecy so that what he wrote was exactly what God intended. No Protestant theologian believes that Jeremiah, for example, was a mere typewriter. Rather, the Spirit of God adapted His inspiring activity to the cast of Jeremiah's mind, outlook, temperament, interests, literary habits, and stylistic idiosyncrasies, which God had prepared for this very purpose. The New Testament shows how the disciples were schooled by Christ for three years, yet each retained his distinctive personality. Peter, for example, retained his fervent impetuosity; John remained a sanctified son of thunder; and James showed his practical genius. When Isaiah wrote Isaiah 53, he did so in wonder, love, and praise. When Jeremiah composed the book of Lamentations, he did so with tears of empathy for his broken people. When David wrote some psalms, he could scarcely contain his joyful cries of doxology. We do not believe that God simply dictated the Bible, as some critics assert, for this view is stiff and mechanical. It is, and always has been, an imaginary view, and one which true Christians do not profess.

Let me describe how the process of divine dictation worked in the writing of Scripture. Jeremiah 36 says, "And it came to pass in the fourth year of Jehoiakim the son of Josiah king of Judah, that this word came unto Jeremiah from the LORD, saying, Take thee a roll of a book, and write therein all the words that I have spoken unto thee against Israel, and against Judah, and against all the nations, from the day I spake unto thee, from the days of Josiah, even unto this day" (vv. 1–2). But Jeremiah was bound and could not write, so he asked his servant to come to him. Jeremiah 36 continues:

> And Baruch wrote from the mouth of Jeremiah all the words of the LORD, which he had spoken unto him, upon a roll of a book. And Jeremiah commanded Baruch, saying, I am shut up; I cannot go into the house of the LORD: Therefore go thou, and read in the roll, which thou hast written from my mouth, the words of the LORD in the ears of the people in the LORD's house upon the fasting day: and also thou shalt read them in the ears of all Judah that come out of their cities. It may be they will present their supplication before the LORD, and will return every one from his evil way: for great is the anger and the fury that the LORD hath pronounced against this people. (vv. 4–7)

Baruch, son of Neriah, did everything Jeremiah the prophet told him to do; at the LORD's temple he read the words of the LORD from the scroll (Jer. 36:4–8). The great officials of Jerusalem then questioned Baruch, asking, "How didst thou write all these words at his mouth? Then Baruch answered them, He pronounced all these words unto me with his mouth, and I wrote them with ink in the book" (Jer. 36:17–18).

Jeremiah, who was in chains, was moved by the Holy Spirit to dictate the message he had received from God to Baruch. The servant unrolled a skin or sheet of papyrus and wrote on it with a reed pen, which he dipped into an ink horn to write the words that Jeremiah gave to him. When the work was finished, it was sacred because it was precisely what God wanted written.

When the people heard these words, they did not debate the method or timing of the composition. They gave their attention to what God was saying to them. However, when Jehoiakim, king of Israel, heard the words on the scroll, he cut the scroll apart and threw it bit by bit into a fire. The king could not accept the words of Jeremiah as words from God, inspired by the Holy Spirit. His heart was repulsed at such words of judgment. So he totally rejected the prophecy and destroyed the scroll on which it was written.

Jeremiah 36:27–32 goes on to say:

> Then the word of the LORD came to Jeremiah, after that the king had burned the roll, and the words which Baruch wrote at the mouth of Jeremiah, saying, Take thee again another roll, and write in it all the former words that were in the first roll, which Jehoiakim the king of Judah hath burned. And thou shalt say to Jehoiakim king of Judah, Thus saith the LORD; thou hast burned this roll, saying, Why hast thou written therein, saying, The king of Babylon shall certainly come and destroy this land, and shall cause to cease from thence man and beast? Therefore thus saith the LORD of Jehoiakim king of Judah; He shall have none to sit upon the throne of David: and his dead body shall be cast out in the day to the heat, and in the night to the frost. And I will punish him and his seed and his servants for their iniquity; and I will bring upon them, and upon the inhabitants of Jerusalem, and upon the men of Judah, all the evil that I have pronounced against them; but they hearkened not. Then took Jeremiah another roll, and gave it to Baruch the scribe, the son of Neriah; who wrote therein from the mouth of Jeremiah all the words of the book which Jehoiakim king of Judah had burned in the fire: and there were added besides unto them many like words.

God did not treat lightly King Jehoiakim's "pick and choose" attitude to Scripture in accepting some of His Word and destroying the rest. For in doing so, this king pushed God off the throne of his life and put himself on it.

This incident, which describes how Jeremiah's words were taken down via Baruch, may seem very much like dictation to us. However, this method of recording God's words here in the life of Jeremiah was not what happened during the rest of his life or in the life of other prophets and writers of other Old Testament Scripture. Moses was trained for decades to write the first five books of the Bible. His elementary education was in Pharaoh's palace. He did his graduate studies for forty years in a wilderness, at the back side of the desert, with sheep and herdsmen as his companions. God prepared him to write the Pentateuch over a period of some years as the amanuensis of God.

PROTECTING SCRIPTURE FROM ERROR

Numbers 24:2 tells us that the Spirit of God came upon a prophet named Balaam, and he uttered his oracle. The man was not an Israelite; he was a diviner who lived in Mesopotamia. He was hired by the king of Moab to put a curse on the nation of Israel, which was passing through Moab on its way to the Promised Land. Numbers 22:3 tells us, "And Moab was sore afraid of the people, because they were many."

Balaam accepted the job, but when he tried to curse the Israelites, God prevented him from doing so, saying, "Thou shalt not curse the people: for they are blessed" (Num. 22:12). King Balak tried to force the prophet again to curse Israel, promising the prophet great gifts if he would do so. Balaam replied: "I cannot go beyond the word of the LORD my God, to do less or more" (Num. 22:18). He traveled to Moab to explain that to the king, but the king was angry that the prophet had still failed to curse the Israelites. He said to the prophet, "Did I not earnestly send unto thee to call thee? wherefore camest thou not unto me? am I not able indeed to promote thee to honour?" (Num. 22:37).

"And Balaam said unto Balak, Lo, I am come unto thee: have I now any power at all to say any thing? the word that God putteth in my mouth, that shall I speak" (Num. 22:38). Can a prophet who speaks from God and is carried along by the Holy Spirit change the words that God gives him? Can he discard the divine message and give his own instead? Balaam says, "God is not a man, that he should lie; neither the son of man, that he should repent: hath he said, and shall he not do it? or hath he spoken, and shall he not make it good? Behold, I have received commandment to bless: and he hath blessed; and I cannot reverse it" (Num. 23:19–20).

By this time King Balak was desperate, for the prophet was actually blessing the people of God rather than cursing them. He pleaded with the prophet to just drop the whole thing. When Balaam responded, "Told not I thee, saying, All that the LORD speaketh, that I must do?" (Num. 23:26), the king exploded. He ordered the prophet to go home without being paid. Balaam responded, "Spake I not also to thy messengers which thou sentest unto me, saying, if Balak would give me his house full of silver and gold, I cannot go beyond the commandment of the LORD, to do either good or bad of mine own mind; but what the LORD saith, that will I speak?" (Num 24:12–13).

Balaam's conviction was indicative of the devotion of true prophets in the Old Testament, such as Micaiah. When Micaiah was hauled before Ahab and Jehoshaphat to give the Lord's blessing on their armies before going into battle, he refused to parrot what false prophets had said to the kings, affirming their battle plans. "And Micaiah said, As the LORD liveth, what the LORD saith unto me, that will I speak" (1 Kings 22:14). When pressed time after time to change his mind, he finally said what the Lord had told him to say: "I saw all Israel scattered upon the hills, as sheep that have not a shepherd: and the LORD said, These have no master: let them return every man to his house in peace" (1 Kings 22:17). The prophet could not speak error when speaking in the name of the Lord, even if it meant facing the wrath of two kings.

We have sought to prove to you the truth of Peter's words: "Knowing this first, that no prophecy of the scripture is of any private interpretation. For the prophecy came not in old time by the will of man: but holy men of God spake as they were moved by the Holy Ghost" (2 Peter 1:20–21). The minds and souls of writers of Scripture were controlled by the Spirit of God; they were conscious of the brevity of life and the judgment that would follow death, when they would have to give an account to God of every word they spoke, especially in God's name. Had they been faithful to the great commission God had given to them when he called them to be his prophets? Of course they were sinners, and there were times when they might lie or lose their tempers. For example, David, who wrote Psalm 23, once wrote a letter to his general, asking him to put a man in the front line of battle, then to withdraw from him so he would be killed (2 Sam. 11:15). David was not being carried along by the Spirit when he wrote that letter; he was ordering a murder to cover his sin of adultery. David spoke and wrote in the name of the Lord only when he was in the Spirit. Apart from that, he was a sinner like any other person.

CONCLUSION

The Old Testament Scriptures are infallible. They are holy. They are powerful. They are consistent. They are the appointed means of salvation. We are begotten by their truth, enlightened by their truth, sanctified by their truth, and saved by their truth. The Old and New Testaments contain all the revealed words of God that this fallen world needs. They are enough to thoroughly equip a believer for every possible good work. They are plain, so that everyone can understand what God says. They are the light of the world, the fountain of life, and the treasure store of God.

You should grieve if you go to a church that only sporadically preaches from the Old Testament. If you have the Spirit of God, you will recognize the Spirit as the one who inspired the prophets to write exactly what they wrote. A truly Spirit-filled minister preaches frequently on the Old Testament. If you are unfortunate to not have such a ministry, then make sure that you study these Scriptures for yourself and believe the truths they affirm. Study the Scriptures and apply them to your life. Read them as if God were speaking to you, and answer Him with words of gratitude, reverence, faith, joy, and fear as you apply those words to your life.

CHAPTER FOUR

The Anointing Spirit of God

[David] was ruddy, and withal of a beautiful countenance, and goodly to look to. And the LORD said, Arise, anoint him: for this is he. Then Samuel took the horn of oil, and anointed him in the midst of his brethren: and the Spirit of the LORD came upon David from that day forward.
—1 Samuel 16:12–13

The Old Testament often describes the anointing of a king or priest with oil at his coronation or consecration. People who lived in the baking heat of the Middle East regularly anointed their skin with perfumed oil. When the Good Samaritan found a half-dead man, he bandaged the man's wounds and poured oil and wine on them. In Jesus' time, throughout the countries of the Mediterranean basin, a guest would have his feet washed and his face anointed with fragrant oil. Even David Livingstone, while mapping the African continent 150 years ago, daily protected his skin with oils. So Psalm 23:5 repeats a common practice when it says, "Thou anointest my head with oil."

Oil has cosmetic and medicinal qualities. Yet we will go beyond these qualities to discuss how God took the ordinary act of anointing with oil and gave it an important symbolic function.

ANOINTING IN THE OLD TESTAMENT
Anointing with oil had several symbolic functions in the Old Testament. Here are some of them.

1. Anointing set apart the anointed one. The first example of anointing in the Bible is striking. The patriarch Jacob was on his way to Paddan Aram. He stopped along the way to rest, using a stone as his pillow. While sleeping, he dreamed about a staircase reaching from earth to heaven. Angels moved up and down the ladder. As Genesis 28:13 says, the Lord was also present. He said to Jacob, "I am the LORD God of Abraham thy father, and the God of Isaac: the land whereon thou liest, to thee will I give it, and to thy seed." It was such an unforgettable dream that when Jacob woke up, he said, "Surely the LORD is in this place; and I knew it not" (v. 16). He was also awestruck, saying, "This is none other but the house of God, and this is the gate of heaven" (v. 17). Early the next morning Jacob took the stone he had slept on, set it up as a pillar, and poured oil over it. He then named the place where he had dreamed "Bethel," meaning "house of God" (v. 19).

There were many stones where Jacob slept, and the stone he chose for a pillow was no different from any other in composition, size, or shape. Yet, this is the stone he chose to sleep on, and the stone on which he dreamed of heaven. It was also the stone on which he received God's mighty promise. So Jacob set that stone apart from others by standing it on end and anointing it with oil. Henceforth it was a special stone, forever marking the place where God communicated with Jacob. That is one of the functions of a sacred anointing.

Many years later, God told the prophet Samuel that He had set apart one of the sons of Jesse to be the next king of Israel. "I will send thee to Jesse the Bethlehemite: for I have provided me a king among his sons" (1 Sam. 16:1). Jesse had many sons, however. The first one Samuel met was Eliab. As Samuel looked at this tall, well-educated, battle-ready man, he thought, "Surely the LORD's anointed is before him" (1 Sam. 16:6). But God said no. "Look not on his countenance, or on the height of his stature; because I have refused him," God told Samuel, "for the LORD seeth not as man seeth; for man looketh on the outward appearance, but the LORD looketh on the heart" (1 Sam. 16:7).

Shammah was the next son Jesse presented to Samuel, but the prophet rejected him as well. Five more sons passed before the prophet, but none was right. So Samuel asked Jesse, "Are here all thy children? And he said, There remaineth yet the youngest, and, behold, he keepeth the sheep. And Samuel said unto Jesse, Send and fetch him: for we will not sit down till he come hither" (1 Sam. 16:11). The boy who eventually appeared was ruddy, with handsome features. The Lord said to Samuel, "Arise, anoint him: for this is he" (1 Sam. 16:12). So Samuel took the horn of oil and anointed David in the presence of his brothers. We read in 1 Samuel 16:13, "And the Spirit of the LORD came upon David from that day forward."

This plain teenage shepherd was officially set apart from his brothers by the sacred act of anointing. None of the others was to be the king of Israel—only David. He was the anointed one. He did not appoint himself; God chose David and set him apart through his chosen instrument, Samuel. God used the pouring of oil to symbolize the anointing of the Spirit. With this anointing, David was set apart for his life's work. Likewise, the anointing of the Spirit sets each one of us apart so that we may say, "For me to live is Christ."

2. *Oil was a symbol of the Holy Spirit.* No one claims that the trickle of oil running down a man's hair and forehead is what makes him a prophet or king. The oil is a symbol of the spiritual gifts of wisdom and authority that came upon David at his anointing. As real as the oil that poured over his head was the Holy Spirit's transformation of David's inner man. That is evident in verse 13, which says, "And the Spirit of the LORD came upon David from that day forward."

Walter Chantry comments, "At that hour, the youngest son of Jesse's family entered a new phase of development for his inner life. For the most part, David would keep in step with the Spirit. At every single moment of his life he wouldn't be conscious of the Spirit stirring within him, but there would be times when he would be profoundly self-conscious that he was unlike any other man, because he was full of the Spirit. He would grow to cherish the inward operations of the Spirit. After his fall into adultery and murder, he would give this anguished cry, 'Cast me not away from thy presence; and take not thy holy spirit from me' (Ps. 51:11)."[1]

3. *Anointing signified the spiritual graces of a king.* When believers in the Old Testament thanked God for the privilege of serving "an anointed king," they were not referring to the amount of oil or formula of oil used at his coronation. They were referring to the God-honoring life of their king. They weren't talking about their king's status and privileges, either. Rather, they were referring to the tasks that their king would faithfully perform. No one could doubt that David had been chosen and anointed by God to do the work the Lord wanted him to do, and that their king would tirelessly labor at his calling. He was the best king the children of

---

1. Walter J. Chantry, "A Man after God's Own Heart," *The Banner of Truth* 474 (March 2003): 32.

Israel would ever know. He was enabled by God's Spirit to serve God and the people. So the people cried, "Bless God for an anointed king!"

They could sing what Psalm 72 said about their king: "He shall judge thy people with righteousness, and thy poor with judgment.... He shall judge the poor of the people, he shall save the children of the needy" (vv. 2, 4). They might continue: "For he shall deliver the needy when he crieth; the poor also, and him that hath no helper. He shall spare the poor and needy, and shall save the souls of the needy. He shall redeem their soul from deceit and violence: and precious shall their blood be in his sight. And he shall live, and to him shall be given of the gold of Sheba: prayer also shall be made for him continually; and daily shall he be praised" (vv. 12–15). The doxology from a joyful congregation rose from being governed by an anointed king.

The prophet Jeremiah echoes the righteousness of David's reign when he tells King Zedekiah: "Hear the word of the LORD, O king of Judah, that sittest upon the throne of David, thou, and thy servants, and thy people that enter in by these gates: Thus saith the LORD; Execute ye judgment and righteousness, and deliver the spoiled out of the hand of the oppressor: and do no wrong, do no violence to the stranger, the fatherless, nor the widow, neither shed innocent blood in this place" (Jer. 22:2–3). A genuine spiritual anointing produces genuine spiritual fruit. The following are more notable examples of anointed kings:

- King Cyrus conquered Babylon and reversed its policy by allowing captive peoples to return to their native lands. According to Isaiah, God says this about Cyrus: "He is my shepherd, and shall perform all my pleasure" (Isa. 44:28). Cyrus, the king of Persia, wasn't aware that he had been anointed by Jehovah to shepherd God's people and send them home. Cyrus didn't know that the Lord was taking hold of his right hand and leading him to do his will, yet Cyrus fulfilled God's purpose in history. He was an anointed ruler who did what God required. He had the gift of spiritual leadership, though he was not a true believer.

- As King Josiah listened to the words of the Book of the Law that had been rediscovered in the temple, he tore his robes. He sent his servants to inquire of the Lord what should be done in response to the Law. He then instituted a pervasive reformation in the land, destroying idols, restoring the temple, and reinstituting worship. Josiah had been anointed by the Lord to be a reforming king and to call the people of God back to the Lord. He was twenty-eight years old when he began that mighty work. Only by the Spirit of God could he have done so much. The fruit of the Spirit was evident throughout Josiah's life, though the Spirit's anointing is not recorded in Scripture. The fruit of the anointing Spirit was evident in the actions of the king.

- Saul's anointing. In 1 Samuel 10 we read how the prophet Samuel took a flask of oil and poured it on Saul's head. Then he kissed Saul, saying, "And the Spirit of the LORD will come upon thee, and thou shalt prophesy with them, and shalt be turned into another man" (v. 6). When Samuel and Saul went to Gibeah, a procession of prophets met them. The Spirit of God then came upon Saul in power, and he joined the prophets in testifying.

  Anointing was a sign of being chosen by God to do a special task; the flask of oil was unscrewed and poured over Saul's head to show that he was to be king. Anointing was also the reality of God's equipping a person to do that task; the Spirit of the Lord would come upon him with power. It authorized Saul for his work as king. However, the spiritual gift that he received at his anointing did not guarantee his success as a leader. It did not keep Saul faithful or sanctify him forever. And it did not result in his long-term effectiveness. Saul eventually became proud, disobedient, presumptuous, jealous, and finally self-destructive, even though he had been anointed with the Spirit. The anointing of the Spirit is no guarantee of perseverance in faith.

Most of the kings of Israel in those shadowy times of the Old Testament were failures. More were like Saul than like David. They failed to do what God told them to do. They lacked the anointing of the Spirit. They had all been anointed with oil by the correct officials, but most of them did evil in the eyes of the Lord. That is the great refrain in the Old Testament. So what would give the people of God hope for the future? If what was to come was like what had happened in the past, hope was lost.

THE ANOINTED ONE OF THE NEW TESTAMENT

In light of the failure of most of the kings of the Old Testament, the people of Israel could look to the future with hope only because of the promise of a Messiah who would exceed even David in restoring the nation of Israel. The prophet Isaiah promised, "Our kings have almost always let us down, but God in the last days will send us a glorious ruler who will never let us down. The Messiah, *the* Anointed One, is coming." God's people received three great prophecies about the coming ruler who would be uniquely anointed with the Spirit.

1. Isaiah 11:1–5 offers the first promise:

> And there shall come forth a rod out of the stem of Jesse, and a Branch shall grow out of his roots: and the spirit of the LORD shall rest upon him, the spirit of wisdom and understanding, the spirit of counsel and might, the spirit of knowledge and of the fear of the LORD; and shall make him of quick understanding in the fear of the LORD: and he shall not judge after the sight of his eyes, neither reprove after the hearing of his ears: but with righteousness shall he judge the poor, and reprove with equity for the meek of the earth: and he shall smite the earth: with the rod of his mouth, and with the breath of his lips shall he slay the wicked. And righteousness shall be the girdle of his loins, and faithfulness the girdle of his reins.

The Messiah King was coming. He would arise from the stump of Jesse, David's father, but He would be greater than David. He would be a branch that would spring forth from the roots of David. What's more, the Spirit of the Lord would not simply give this king a boost at the beginning of His life. The Spirit would permanently rest on this king forever and ever. This king would be faithful and true to God all His days and would deal righteously with all of His subjects.

2. Isaiah 42:1–7 gives the second promise:

> Behold my servant, whom I uphold; mine elect, in whom my soul delighteth; I have put my spirit upon him: he shall bring forth judgment to the Gentiles. He shall not cry, nor lift up, nor cause his voice to be heard in the street. A bruised reed shall he not break, and the smoking flax shall he not quench: he shall bring forth judgment unto truth. He shall not fail nor be discouraged, till he have set judgment in the earth: and the isles shall wait for his law. Thus saith God the LORD, he that created the heavens, and stretched them out; he that spread forth the earth, and that which cometh out of it; he that giveth breath unto the people upon it, and spirit to them that walk therein: I the LORD have called thee in righteousness, and will hold thine hand, and will keep thee, and give thee for a covenant of the

people, for a light of the Gentiles; to open the blind eyes, to bring out the prisoners from the prison, and them that sit in darkness out of the prison house.

Matthew, the first book in the New Testament, quotes these very words of Isaiah, saying they have been fulfilled in the Lord Jesus Christ (Matt. 12:17–21).

3. *The third promise, in Isaiah 61:1–3,* is given in the first person, for the Messiah Himself is speaking:

> The Spirit of the Lord GOD is upon me; because the LORD hath anointed me to preach good tidings unto the meek; he hath sent me to bind up the brokenhearted, to proclaim liberty to the captives, and the opening of the prison to them that are bound; to proclaim the acceptable year of the LORD, and the day of vengeance of our God; to comfort all that mourn; to appoint unto them that mourn in Zion, to give unto them beauty for ashes, the oil of joy for mourning, the garment of praise for the spirit of heaviness.

Jesus quoted these very words in Nazareth, the town where he had lived for thirty years, and in the synagogue where He and his family had worshiped every Sabbath. Jesus stood up to read this passage, then rolled up the scroll, gave it back to the attendant, and sat down. While everyone stared at Him, He said, "This day is this scripture fulfilled in your ears" (Luke 4:21). He couldn't have made a clearer claim to be the promised Messiah, for the word *messiah* is the Hebrew word for "anointed one." Likewise, the word *Christ* is the Greek word for "anointed one." Jesus was saying, "I am the Spirit-anointed one of whom Isaiah wrote."

That was not the only time Jesus quoted Isaiah in reference to Himself. When John the Baptist was in prison, he sent messengers to Jesus, asking if He was the Messiah or if they should look for another. Jesus quoted from Isaiah, saying, "The good news is preached to the poor." Then He told the disciples to go back to John to report what they heard and saw (Matt. 11:4). Isaiah's prophesy had already been fulfilled, for Jesus was preaching the gospel to the poor. There was no need to look for another Messiah.

All the acts of anointing kings with oil in the Old Testament were symbols and shadows of the Anointed One to come. They said to the people who observed them, "Wait until you see the glorious reality represented by these types: the Messiah, the Anointed One. He will be truly anointed when the Holy Spirit comes upon Him without measure."

CHRIST'S ANOINTING

Christ was anointed by the Spirit at His baptism. Matthew 3:16–17 tells us, "And Jesus, when he was baptized, went up straightway out of the water: and, lo, the heavens were opened unto him, and he saw the Spirit of God descending like a dove, and lighting upon him: and lo a voice from heaven, saying, This is my beloved Son, in whom I am well pleased." Now we know that Jesus was begotten by the Holy Ghost when His mother was overshadowed by the Spirit. His birth was from above, and He was filled with the Spirit from that time. There was no time when He was not filled with the Spirit. Why, then, did He need to be anointed with the Spirit at His baptism?

The Spirit's coming upon Christ in the form of a dove signifies the certainty of the new kingdom that Jesus is about to bring in. After God drowned the earth with the flood at the time of Noah, only those who were in the ark were saved. They must have wondered when the watery judgment on the earth would end. Many months went by before Noah finally dared to open the window of the ark. He sent out a dove twice, but only after the second time did the dove return with an olive leaf in its beak. Noah then knew that the waters had abated, and the full judgment of the Lord had been exhausted. Likewise, when Jesus emerged from the waters of the Jordan after His baptism, the Spirit, in the form of a dove, settled on Him, affirming that God's new kingdom was about to begin through the work of Christ. "The cosmic work will be completed that I have begun," God was saying. Christ would bring forth justice to the nations, but He would not use His omnipotence to break a bruised reed or quench a smoldering wick. He would be tender with the weak and lame. He would be like a dove, not a hawk.

The Holy Spirit rested upon Jesus to bear witness to His anointing. "He shall testify of me," Jesus said, and the Spirit did this by coming down on Jesus and remaining on Him. The Spirit found no sin in Jesus to grieve Him or drive Him away. The Spirit remained with Christ throughout His ministry as prophet, priest, and king.

The Holy Spirit also came upon Jesus to anoint Him for His ministry. Immediately after the anointing, Jesus was led by the Spirit into the wilderness to be tempted by Satan. After that, Jesus worked day and night for three years. The demands of teaching and healing and saving were enormous. He became so weary that He would fall asleep on a cushion in a little boat in a storm. He was exhausted, yet He would spend all night in prayer.

So, in the Jordan River, in all the frailty of His human flesh, Jesus is baptized and receives an unprecedented endowment of the Spirit, who comes without measure upon Jesus. One day Christ would pour out His Spirit upon all the church, so at His baptism He would receive an unmeasured possession of the Spirit. Doesn't the church today also need the outpouring of the Spirit of God? What a dismal future would lie before us if I said to you, "We already have the Spirit in all His fullness, so there is no reason to ask for additional outpouring. Let us simply plod on and be faithful."

I believe Christ continues to pour out His Spirit in abundance on the church. At times that outpouring transforms lukewarm preachers and congregations into shining lights. A man can go to bed like a lamb and get up like a lion to do extraordinary things in the name of Christ. In a single day, many people may come under great conviction of sin, and thousands may be converted. For example, a friend in County Tipperary in Ireland has labored for twenty years to a small congregation. Usually the church includes twenty or so people, but this past year, it has had unusual and inexplicable growth. Every seat is now taken by ninety people. When I asked the friend if he had done anything different, he said no, "I just close my eyes in the pulpit as I sit and pray at the beginning, and when I open them the church is full."

Let us pray for the Holy Spirit to come upon us, just as the Spirit came upon Christ at the beginning of the most extraordinary three years this world has ever seen.

THE ANOINTING OF THE CHURCH

On the day of Pentecost, the exalted Messiah anointed the entire church with His Spirit. The believers were all filled with the Spirit. When Peter preached to the wondering crowds, explaining what they were experiencing, he pointed them to the Lord Jesus. They could never understand the birth and extraordinary growth of the church without considering the Messiah. Where is Jesus of Nazareth, who was crucified in shame and weakness? Peter says, He is "by the right hand of God exalted" (Acts 2:33).

Jesus is not with Jacob and the patriarchs; He is higher up. He is not with Samuel and the prophets; He is higher up. He is not with the martyrs; He is higher up. He is not with the twenty-four elders; He is higher up. He is not with the four living beings that surround the throne; He is higher up. He is not with Michael and Gabriel the archangels; He is higher up. He is at the right hand of God, in the very midst of the throne of God. He is not on what is referred to as the throne of God and the prophets or the throne of God and the martyrs or the throne of God and the angels. He is seated on what will evermore be called the throne of God and the Lamb.

Peter also says Christ has "received of the Father the promise of the Holy Ghost, he hath shed forth this, which ye now see and hear" (Acts 2:33). No longer does the old frail Samuel unscrew his horn of oil and pour it on the head of one young man. It is no longer appropriate for us to live in the shadowlands of the anointing but in the reality of what those shadows anticipated. The reality is that the Father so loves His Son that He has given Him all authority in heaven and earth. Christ will build His church, and the gates of hell will not prevail against it.

Furthermore, God has given to Lord Christ the privilege of anointing His people with His Spirit. At Pentecost the Spirit was poured out by the God-man Christ Jesus from the midst of the throne of God, and from that time onwards He has not ceased to do this. In giving believers the birth from above and the fruit and the gifts of the Spirit, Christ anoints all believers with His Spirit. So from this time on, the anointing is not only for kings and prophets but for every Christian, both young and old, manservant and maidservant. Christ Jesus has made all who are saved and washed, sanctified and justified, free from the law of sin and death.

Paul stands in solidarity with the church as he tells Titus: "But according to his mercy he saved us, by the washing of regeneration, and renewing of the Holy Ghost; which he shed on us abundantly through Jesus Christ our Saviour" (Titus 3:5–6). All the signs and symbols of the pouring out of oil in the Old Testament pointed to Christ anointing us with His Spirit today.

We may be comforted that Jesus Christ is in the midst of the throne of God. From that very height, He will draw by His Spirit all people to Himself. The church is often very low, and, sadder still, doesn't recognize how low she is, but the highest place in heaven belongs to Christ. There He is pouring out the Spirit upon His people, and no power in earth or hell can resist Him. O blessed, irresistible grace that the exalted Christ should be all our comfort!

A Christian farmer kept a few pigs on his small farm. One Sunday morning before coming to church, the farmer discovered all his pigs had picked up some disease and died. He was destitute; they were his entire livelihood. He went to church, where the minister preached an excellent sermon. The people who heard it said to one another, "Wasn't that helpful?" Someone asked the farmer, "Wasn't that good?"

"I wish he'd said a few words about my pigs," the farmer said. You know what he meant. I don't know what your problem is today, but my message is directly relevant for you. Jesus Christ your Savior is in the midst of the throne of God. He knows all about you and your difficulties. He anoints us daily with His Spirit so that through Him we can do all things. We can handle any problem, carry any burden, and overcome any trial. We can do all things through Christ who daily anoints us with His Spirit. That is our only comfort in life and death.

CHAPTER FIVE

Blaspheming the Holy Spirit

Wherefore I say unto you, All manner of sin and blasphemy shall be forgiven unto men: but the blasphemy against the Holy Ghost shall not be forgiven unto men. And whosoever speaketh a word against the Son of man, it shall be forgiven him: but whosoever speaketh against the Holy Ghost, it shall not be forgiven him, neither in this world, neither in the world to come.
—Matthew 12:31–32

The glory of the Christian gospel is the work that Jesus Christ completed for full atonement of countless sinners. In anticipation of this, Isaiah declared: "Come now, and let us reason together, saith the LORD: though your sins be as scarlet, they shall be as white as snow; though they be red like crimson, they shall be as wool" (Isa. 1:18).

Thus the Lord offered forgiveness to King David for his sins of adultery, dishonesty, and murder. He offered forgiveness to the adulterous woman of Luke 7, to the prodigal son who wasted his life in riotous living in a distant city, and to Simon Peter who swore three times that he did not know Christ. He offered forgiveness to the Jewish leaders who nailed the Son of God to a cross and left Him to die. He offered forgiveness to Saul of Tarsus, who mercilessly persecuted new Christians, and to the member of the Corinthian church who slept with his father's wife.

God offers you forgiveness, too, no matter how great is your sin. You may be a modern minister who has led people astray for years by preaching error and calling your humanist ideas the gospel; yet the Lord also offers you forgiveness. If you abused children, God offers you forgiveness. If you ruthlessly destroyed companies or broke up family firms, putting people out of work, God offers you forgiveness. Consider the serial killer dubbed "Son of Sam," who murdered many young women in New York. The killer found forgiveness in prison by confessing his sins to the Savior and begging for mercy. He now works for Christ in the jail that he will never leave.

The blood of Jesus Christ, God's Son, cleanses us from all sin. Some might argue it's not fair to forgive people who have committed terrible sins. Forgiveness has nothing to do with fairness. It has everything to do with the vastness of God's pity, for He freely offers forgiveness to the vilest offenders—even you! In an old cartoon, Dennis the Menace and his little friend Joey are leaving Mrs. Wilson's house with their hands full of cookies. Joey says, "I wonder what we did to deserve this." Dennis answers, "Mrs. Wilson gives us cookies, not because *we're* nice, but because *she's* nice." God gives pardon even to a depraved monster, not because he does anything to deserve it, but because God's mercy is breathtaking.

The hallmark of divine mercy is that it is immeasurable. God's love extends to the heavens. He abounds in steadfast love to all who call upon Him. The writer of Psalm 130 was overwhelmed by God's mercy, saying, "If thou, LORD, shouldest mark iniquities, O Lord, who shall stand? But there is forgiveness with thee" (vv. 3–4). In a letter to Timothy, the apostle Paul soothed the young man's fears that he might out-sin the grace of God by reminding Timothy of Paul's wretched history of persecuting Christians. Paul had formerly blasphemed and insulted Christ, yet Christ showed him mercy (1 Tim. 1:13). God has enough forgiveness for all the sins and blasphemies of men.

John Wesley was converted May 24, 1738, in Aldersgate Street in the city of London. Two weeks later, the vice chancellor of Oxford University invited Wesley to preach at an official university service in St. Mary's Church. Before a crowd of faculty and students, Wesley began preaching on the text "By grace are ye saved." He told the crowd how the sublime mercy of God in Jesus Christ was sufficient to cover all their past sins and deliver them from guilt, fear, and the power of sin. Then Wesley paused. Envisioning the objections some listeners might have, he said,

> Some will say this forgiveness is an uncomfortable doctrine. Nay! It is very full of comfort to all sinners, that whosoever believeth in him shall not be shamed. That same Lord over all is rich in mercy unto all that call upon Him. Here is comfort high as heaven, strong as death!
>
> Others might say, "What? Mercy for all? For Zacchaeus, a public robber? For Mary Magdalene, a common harlot?" I hear someone asking, "Then, may even I hope for mercy?" So you may, you who

are afflicted. Be of good cheer, thy sins are forgiven thee, so forgiven that they shall reign over thee no more, yea, and the Holy Spirit shall bear witness with the Spirit that thou art a child of God.

O glad tidings; tidings of great joy which are sent unto all people! Ho, everyone that thirsts, come ye to the waters. Come ye, buy without money and without price. Whatever your sins are, though red like crimson, though more than the hairs on your head, return to the Lord, and He will have mercy on you, and to our God, for He will abundantly pardon. The foundation of all our preaching is that forgiveness must be preached first.

Wesley preached that all men were sinners, but through the love of God in Jesus, they were offered full forgiveness which they might receive by faith. That preaching was the foundation of the Great Awakening, for the theme of divine forgiveness is the very heart of the good news about Jesus Christ. If anyone is obsessed by the sin he has committed, he may be comforted to know that forgiveness from heaven is offered to him. For you who listen to preaching week by week, yet for many years have been distrusting Christ and now are beginning to think that it is too late and that the day of mercy is past, I say no! To you forgiveness is also offered in Jesus' name. The good news of mercy is offered to all creatures, however enormously defiling their sins, no matter how great the grief and pain they have caused others.

If all that is true, what is the Lord Jesus talking about when He warns in Matthew 12:31, "The blasphemy against the Holy Ghost shall not be forgiven unto men"? Why does He say this in such urgent tones? Is there a particularly heinous sin among those that we commit? Which one is it? Is it one of the Ten Commandments? Does a violation of one of those commands forever plunge a sinner into the despair of unforgiveness? Our Lord says there is a sin that will not be forgiven. He speaks of it here in Matthew 12 and again in Mark 3 and Luke 12. All three gospels refer to Jesus' words about the eternal sin. This is a warning against the heresy of universalism, which presumes that the sin of every person will be forgiven. It is to warn us not to think of forgiveness lightly and as something it is God's job to do.

This warning is also put into Scripture three times to help us resist sin more earnestly. Remember these are the words of Jesus, not me. I know the identity of the sin that can never be forgiven, and so do many of you. There is no mystery about what the unforgivable sin is. We have the biblical data to speak with such confidence. He who has ears to hear, let him hear what we have to say about the unforgivable sin.

WHAT THE UNFORGIVABLE SIN IS NOT

Many gross sins are sins against the Holy Spirit, yet they are not the sin of blasphemy against the Holy Spirit that is unpardonable.

1. The unpardonable sin is not blasphemy. You might think that this unpardonable sin is blasphemy because our Lord says in verse 31, "The blasphemy against the Holy Ghost shall not be forgiven unto men." But go back to the first of the verse, which says: "All manner of sin and blasphemy shall be forgiven unto men." The Heidelberg Catechism says in answer to Question 100: "No sin is greater or more provoking to God than the profaning of His name." Perhaps that is true, but we must affirm even for that sin God offers forgiveness. Saul of Tarsus in his rage against the first generation of Christians tells us, "And I…compelled them to blaspheme" (Acts 26:11). He brought terrible pressure upon the early Christians to make them curse the name of Jesus, but the God who pities His children certainly forgave them for that.

In his book *Spiritual Depression*, Dr. Lloyd-Jones recounts an incident that occurred in Port Talbot when he was pastor of Bethlehem Forward Movement. A man who had lived a very evil life was converted at the age of seventy-seven. He became a member of the church and experienced great joy at his first communion service. It was the greatest thing that had ever happened to him. Yet Lloyd-Jones says, "Next morning, even before I was up, that poor man had arrived at my house. There he stood, looking the picture of misery and dejection, and weeping uncontrollably. I was amazed and astounded, especially in view of what had happened the previous night, the greatest night of his life, the climax of everything that had ever happened to him."

Eventually Lloyd-Jones succeeded in calming the man. He asked what the trouble was. The man said that after the communion service, he remembered something that had happened thirty years ago. He was with a group of men drinking in a public house and arguing about religion, when he said in contempt and derision that Jesus Christ was a bastard. Now he remembered the occasion with fear and trembling. Surely there was no forgiveness for what he had said about the Son of God, the Savior of the world!

"He could not be consoled, he could not be comforted," Lloyd-Jones said. "This one thing had cast him down to utter hopelessness. (I thank God that by the application of the Scriptures I was able to restore his joy to him.) But that is the kind of thing I am referring to, something a man has once said, or done, that haunts him and comes back to him, and makes him miserable and wretched, though he still subscribes to the full Christian faith."[1]

A student once told me he was troubled with blasphemous thoughts. He was so distressed. We looked together at other men in the history of the church who had also been troubled like that, such as John Bunyan. Such thoughts are the fiery darts of the wicked one. We read and prayed together, and those troublesome thoughts dissipated in the student, never to return. They were not the unpardonable sin. I do not know whether Peter's swearing at a fireside that he didn't know Jesus was accompanied by blasphemies, but Christ offered full pardon to Peter.

Blasphemy is not the sin that cannot be forgiven. Be cheered if you have blasphemed, for if you seek mercy in God through Christ, your sin will be covered.

2. It is not a sexual sin. There are all sorts of sexual aberrations today, which are hideously and blatantly trivialized. The results of sexual sin should not be minimized, for it destroys people, peace, and purity. It spreads sexual disease and breaks apart families and causes much pain. But sexual sins are not unpardonable sins.

In his first letter to the Corinthians, Paul responds to the news that a church member has gone to a prostitute by saying: "Flee fornication. Every sin that a man doeth is without the body; but he that committeth fornication sinneth against his own body" (1 Cor. 6:18). This statement is somewhat mysterious, but we believe Paul is saying that in sexual union we sin in a unique way against our bodies, which are joined with Christ and destined for heaven and the presence of God. Thus to the church member who has sinned against his own body, Paul says, "Know ye not that your body is the temple of the Holy Ghost which is in you, which ye have of God" (1 Cor. 6:19).

---

1. D. Martyn Lloyd-Jones, *Spiritual Depression* (Grand Rapids: Eerdmans, 1965), 67–68.

When Joseph was tempted by Potiphar's wife in Egypt, his response was: "How then can I do this great wickedness, and sin against God?" (Gen. 39:9). Joseph knew that sexual morality was more than sin against his own body; it was also a sin against Almighty God. Yet there is nothing to suggest that any form of sexual sin is the unpardonable sin. The passages that tell us about sin against the Spirit make no reference to the seventh commandment. So if you have sinned sexually, please do not think that you have committed the unforgivable sin.

3. It is not suicide. I spent a day with a man who had spent thirty years without Christ, living for the world. He made a million dollars, but he was in utter despair. He had wanted to be a millionaire, and now that he was, his life was no sweeter. He contemplated suicide, but he was raised Roman Catholic and the Jesuits had told him suicide would send him to hell. The fear of hell kept him from suicide, but it did bring him in repentance to the Savior. After some time, he met my friend Dave Dykstra, who gently befriended him. They talked for some months before the man came to Dave's church. I met him a few years after he came to know the Lord, and his darkness turned to light.

Self-murder is not the unforgivable sin against the Holy Ghost. The jailer in Philippi intended to kill himself before Paul cried to him, "Do yourself no harm!" That is also our message to people of despair who live around us. We have good tidings of great joy for them. We have a Savior who offers forgiveness and an abundant life. Saul of Tarsus convinced new Christians that suicide would be better than the torture he could inflict upon them, yet Saul's sins were pardoned. There are no biblical grounds for us to believe that suicide is the unforgivable sin. People who take their own lives when their minds are disturbed are not inevitably lost.

There are other examples in the Bible of what that unforgivable sin might be. Some people think it might be the kind of increasing apostasy Solomon exhibited in taking wife after wife and raising temples and idols to strange gods. But even that wickedness is not blasphemy against the Holy Spirit. For you who fear you have committed such a sin are these words of Christ: "I tell you the truth, all the sins and blasphemies of men will be forgiven."

WHAT THE UNFORGIVABLE SIN IS

Let us look at the context in which Jesus speaks these words. He has begun His public ministry and set the nation of Israel on fire. By the power of the Holy Spirit, He has healed all kinds of sickness and disease. He has preached with authority, wisdom, and graciousness. He has delivered people from demons, which fled over a cliff or back to hell. Tens of thousands of people walk to Galilee to meet Christ and touch Him. By the Holy Ghost, Christ is doing great works. The kingdom of God has come. It has been established in Capernaum by the King from heaven.

The leading theologians in the land, the teachers of the law in Jerusalem, are not impressed with what Jesus is doing. They travel north up the Jordan Valley to Galilee to examine what Jesus says and does. After seeing the power of Christ exhibited in the works of God the Holy Spirit, the band of inquisitors declares: "This fellow doth not cast out devils, but by Beelzebub the prince of the devils" (Matt. 12:24).

Jesus responds to the accusation by saying, "And whosoever speaketh a word against the Son of man, it shall be forgiven him: but whosoever speaketh against the Holy Ghost, it shall not be forgiven him, neither in this world, neither in the world to come" (v. 32). The setting for those words is the abundant presence of the mighty accomplishments of the Spirit, which Christ's opponents utterly pervert. They deny what is divine and express hellish rage against Jesus and the testimony of the Spirit. In that context we can begin to understand what the unpardonable sin is: attributing to the devil what is the work of the redeeming Holy Spirit.

1. The unforgivable sin during Christ's ministry on earth. Matthew 12 records these words of Jesus, "And whosoever speaketh a word against the Son of man, it shall be forgiven him: but whosoever speaketh against the Holy Ghost, it shall not be forgiven him, neither in this world, neither in the world to come" (v. 32). So, blasphemy against Jesus is forgiven, but blasphemy against the Holy Spirit is not.

Let me explain. The distinction between blasphemy against Jesus and blasphemy against the Holy Spirit was relevant only prior to Calvary. It has not applied since the resurrection of Jesus Christ and Pentecost, and it is no longer relevant today. That distinction cannot be found in any of the New Testament letters, because Jesus only made that distinction during His earthly ministry. The reason was that Jesus veiled His identity as the eternal Son of God during the thirty-three years he walked among men. So His works and words perplexed people. Some defended Him, and some accused Him of blasphemy. His own brothers and sisters saw Him as the son of Mary and Joseph who had religious delusions about Himself. Others argued, "He is Elijah or one of the old prophets returned to us." Others suggested Jesus was John the Baptist brought back to life. But the Pharisees were most harsh, saying, "He is the devil."

Part of the reason they said such wicked things about Jesus was that He deliberately hid His glory from them. Who would dream that the Lord of glory could come to earth as a baby in a stable in Bethlehem? How could the Messiah hang on a cross between two thieves? Jesus wouldn't let demons announce that he was the Holy One and the Son of God, either. "Keep it to yourselves," he ordered them. He healed some people, then forbade them to tell people who had transformed them.

After thirty years of obscurity, Jesus suffered three years of humiliation. The son of David had nowhere to lay His head. He called himself the Son of Man, but He was a wanderer here on earth. He entered Jerusalem as the prophesied Messiah, but He did so sitting on a little donkey. "Is this the Messiah?" people asked. He made such shadowy application to Himself of Old Testament messianic prophecies that even His own disciples asked, "What is He saying to us? What does He mean?" He talked to them in parables, and they didn't know what they meant. Prior to His resurrection, Jesus prevented people from fully knowing who He was. His divinity was hidden from His baptism right up to the resurrection. For that reason, blasphemies against Him during those years could be forgiven. People who made cruel judgments about Him during His three years of suffering could be forgiven. That is because the Lord Jesus was hiding His identity as the eternal Son of God.

When Jesus comes to Galilee, the veil is lifted for a time. People are given a glimpse of the work of the Holy Spirit in Jesus in His healing, teaching, convicting, resurrecting, saving, and transforming sinners. The glorious person of God the Holy Spirit is revealed when a man blind from birth actually sees, when people are delivered from demons, when people with all kinds of diseases are healed, and when tens of thousands of people come to see and hear Jesus. The Spirit of God is abundantly poured out on Galilee, yet teachers of the law in Jerusalem refuse to entrust themselves to the Lord Jesus, saying, "By the prince of demons this is being done. Beelzebub is at work." They are blaspheming the work of the Spirit of God.

The unforgivable sin is not general antagonism toward Jesus. Many people in Israel heard Him and rejected Him throughout His ministry. The unforgivable sin during the life of Jesus of Nazareth was experiencing the power and presence of God, then attributing that work to the power of Satan. If people were convicted of the sin of that attitude and cried to Jehovah for mercy, they would be forgiven. The same is true of the people who said Christ was an evil blasphemer and sentenced Him to death on a cross. Even those who stood before Him, mocking and taunting Him, would be forgiven if they repented and cast themselves on God's mercy. God would not say, "You have committed the unforgivable sin, so there is no mercy for you!" At Pentecost, many of the people who had cried out for Jesus' execution experienced the love of God. They asked for repentance and were converted.

During Jesus' earthly ministry, you and I would have committed the unpardonable sin if we had taken the locked-in defiant attitude of the Jewish leaders and attributed the works of the Spirit of God through the Lord Jesus to the devil himself. That would have been the unforgivable sin during the years of humiliation of the Son of God.

2. The unforgivable sin after the Resurrection. From Easter morning on, Jesus' conquest of death is confirmed and energized by God the Spirit at Pentecost and preached abroad. In this new era, Christ is preached as the Son of God and as Lord. The apostles boldly preach that Christ is the brightness of God's glory and the express image of His person. From the resurrection on, there is no distinction between blaspheming against the Spirit and blaspheming against Christ. The unforgivable sin exists, but now it can be directed towards the Father, Son, or Holy Spirit. The apostles speak of this sin in Hebrews 6:4–6: "For it is impossible for those who were once enlightened, and have tasted of the heavenly gift, and were made partakers of the Holy Ghost, and have tasted the good word of God, and the powers of the world to come, if they shall fall away, to renew them again unto repentance; seeing they crucify to themselves the Son of God afresh, and put him to an open shame."

This situation is similar to what we have seen in Mark 3. Under the apostles, there has been a wonderful outpouring of the Holy Spirit. Thousands of Jews have tasted the heavenly gift of Jesus Christ. They have shared in the Holy Spirit's convicting work and have seen a foretaste of heaven in God's blessings poured out on the church. Things go well for a while, but then some church members fall away from the faith.

Their falling away is understandable. They are living under enormous pressures. Their families have excommunicated them, and they are lonely. They must also endure persecution from Jews who despise the work of Christ. Then, too, they must long for the old days when they were in Jerusalem and participated in feasts and temple rituals. How different things are now in house fellowships, where they are subject to the stringent Christian ethics. Some cannot measure up and fall away from the faith. They might be saying, "We tried Jesus Christ; it was a big mistake; he was not the Messiah at all but a fake."

In doing so, they crucify the Son of God all over again and subject Him to public disgrace, Hebrews says. In rejecting the Lord Jesus Christ, especially after receiving so many blessings, they are guilty of a sin of eternal dimensions. There can be no forgiveness for those who consider Christ to be a cheat and liar. They cannot know a reconciled Jehovah with such an attitude.

A young woman once told Dr. Ichabod Spencer of New York that she had committed the unpardonable sin. She brooded over her condition for months. Finally Spencer said to her:

> I shall speak very plainly. You will understand every word of it. Some of the things which I shall say may surprise you, but I want you to remember them. All along through the summer I have treated you with the utmost kindness and indulgence. I have always come to you when you have sent for me, and many times when you have not. And it is because I feel kindly towards you still, and wish to do you good, that I shall now say some very plain things which you may not like, but they are true:
>
> First, you say you have committed the unpardonable sin, but you do not believe what you say. You believe no such thing. You know, indeed, that you are a sinner, but you do not believe that you have committed the unpardonable sin. You are not honest, not sincere, when you say so. You do not believe it.
>
> Second, the foolish pride of a wicked heart makes you say that you have committed the unpardonable sin. Influenced by pride, you half strive to believe you have done it. You wish to exalt yourself. You pretend that it is some great and uncommon thing which keeps you from being a Christian. "Ah, it is the unpardonable sin." Pride lies at the bottom of all this.

Third, you have no occasion for this pride. There is nothing very uncommon about you. You are very much like other sinners. It is not likely that you could commit the unpardonable sin, if you should try. I do not think you know enough to do it.

"Why," said she, "isn't there such a sin?"

"Yes," I say, "but you don't know what it is; and you don't know enough to commit it."

Fourth, you are one of the most self-righteous creatures I ever saw. You try to think that you are not so much to blame for your irreligion that you are willing to be a Christian, and would be one, if it were not for this unpardonable sin, which you try in your pride to believe you have committed. You pretend that it is not your present and cherished sin which keeps you in your impenitence. Oh, you are good enough, surely, to repent; you would repent, indeed you would, if it were not for that unpardonable sin which you try in your pride to believe you have committed. You pretend that it is not your present and cherished sin which keeps you in your impenitence. Oh, you are good enough, surely, to repent; you would repent, if it were not for that unpardonable sin. That is your heart; self-righteousness and pride.

Fifth, your wicked heart clings to this idea of the unpardonable sin as an excuse for your continued impenitence, for your living in the indulgence of sin, unbelief, and disobedience to God every day. Your excuse will not stand. You make it insincerely. It is not the unpardonable sin which hinders your being a Christian; but your wickedness of heart, your pride, vanity, and insincerity. I shall never again have anything to say to you about the unpardonable sin. If you have any real and just conviction of sin, you would never name the unpardonable sin.[2]

The unforgivable sin exists, for it is mentioned three times in the gospels. Many Christian are concerned that they may have committed that sin. If you are anxious that you have committed blasphemy against the Spirit, you needn't fear that you have done so, for such blasphemy is always accompanied by complete indifference to losing your soul. In other words, if you are afraid you have committed this sin, we can say with great confidence that you haven't, because your troubled conscience is a sure testimony that you haven't committed it. In our text the

---

2. Ichabod Spencer, *A Pastor's Sketches I* (Vestavia Hills, Ala.: Solid Ground Christian Books, 2001), 227–28.

Lord Jesus doesn't tell the Pharisees from Jerusalem, "You have committed the unforgivable sin." Rather, He tells these religious despisers to take care, because whoever blasphemes against the Holy Spirit will never be forgiven.

Blasphemy against the Holy Spirit is a sin against salvation, the Lord Jesus Christ, the Sermon on the Mount, and Jesus' resurrection from the dead. He offers us salvation, which we have tasted and known. If you read these words and dismiss them as something below contempt, even evil, utterly unholy, beware. The unforgivable sin is willful apostasy. Remember, when the Bible speaks about the unforgivable sin, it is not speaking for the benefit of other people, it is for you and for me. It is a warning to every single Christian. It is not given to me so I may speculate about people I once baptized and have subsequently fallen away. The warning is for me. It exhorts me to live a more holy life, to mortify remaining sin, to walk with the Spirit, and to present my body a living sacrifice to God.

CHAPTER SIX

Asking for the Spirit

And I say unto you, Ask, and it shall be given you; seek, and ye shall find; knock, and it shall be opened unto you. For every one that asketh receiveth; and he that seeketh findeth; and to him that knocketh it shall be opened. If a son shall ask bread of any of you that is a father, will he give him a stone? or if he ask a fish, will he for a fish give him a serpent? Or if he shall ask an egg, will he offer him a scorpion? If ye then, being evil, know how to give good gifts unto your children: how much more shall your heavenly Father give the Holy Spirit to them that ask him?
—Luke 11:9–13

The first three gospels, Matthew, Mark, and Luke, are set in the context of the Old Covenant. Luke, for example, begins with a priest named Zechariah, who is serving in the temple and burning incense. A messenger from God tells the priest that his wife will have a son who "shall be filled with the Holy Ghost, even from his mother's womb" (Luke 1:15). From the time he is young, the child knows he is set aside as a prophet of the Lord. He has the charisma of prophecy, and the Spirit of God is in him. Soon Zechariah is also filled with the Holy Spirit and utters a long prophecy.

Sometime after this, the Spirit of God also comes upon a man named Simeon and tells him to enter the temple to meet with Joseph, Mary, and the baby Jesus. Simeon too is filled with the Spirit and utters prophesies. This is clearly an Old Covenant portrayal of the Spirit anointing gifted men to serve as prophets, priests, or kings for a particular work God gives them to do.

Thirty years pass, and John the Baptist and Jesus begin their public ministries. "The promised one is coming," cries John, "the one the prophets spoke of who is going to pour out the Holy Spirit." Jesus leaves Nazareth and goes to the Jordan River, where the Spirit of God comes upon Him at His baptism. Jesus begins to preach that the kingdom of God has arrived.

This is a critical moment in human history, for it is a time of decision for the people of the Old Testament. The covenant at last is being fulfilled. This time, prophesied with expectancy, apprehension, and longing by the Spirit-filled men of the older dispensation, has finally come; the hour at last is being fulfilled. The Spirit of God is about to be poured out on all flesh, no longer on the Jews alone, and not only upon kings, prophets, and priests for their work but on every believer, even servants and maidservants both old and young. The last days are dawning between the first and second comings of Christ. We too live in those days; for we have tasted the powers of the world to come. We are living in the age of the Spirit because the Lord has already come with redeeming power and might. He has conquered death and removed the guilt of sin. He will be exalted at the last judgment and will baptize the nations far and wide with the Spirit.

The ministry of Christ begins with the declaration that the King has come and His Spirit is about to come upon all believers to an even greater degree than He indwelt every Old Testament believer. Luke's gospel ends with the last words of Jesus, "And, behold, I send the promise of my Father upon you: but tarry ye in the city of Jerusalem, until ye be endued with power from on high" (Luke 24:49). In the opening chapter of Acts, the coming of the Spirit is immediate: "But ye shall be baptized with the Holy Ghost not many days hence" (Acts 1:5).

The gospels are much like the Old Testament prophecies in anticipating the coming of the Spirit. They offer a cluster of teachings about the Spirit at the birth of Christ, in the overshadowing of Mary in Jesus' incarnation, and in the outpouring of the Spirit at Pentecost. The words of our text make the Spirit incredibly accessible to us, for Jesus says, "If ye then, being evil, know how to give good gifts unto your children: how much more shall your heavenly Father give the Holy Spirit to them that ask him?" (Luke 11:13).

THE PROMISE FOR GOD'S CHILDREN

Luke 11 offers a series of great promises that build in earnestness and affection. "I say unto you, Ask, and it shall be given you; seek, and ye shall find; knock, and it shall be opened unto you. For every one that asketh receiveth; and he that seeketh findeth; and to him that knocketh it shall be opened" (vv. 9–10). But these promises are not offered to all people. We cannot put on a billboard outside our church "Ask and It Will Be Given to You," for a person who drives by that sign may think that promise is for him. He may reason, "Ask, and I will receive? Sounds good to me. All right, I'll ask to have that woman. I'll ask for money to take a few days off and fly to Las Vegas. I'll ask to win the lottery this Saturday. I'll win it because God promises that if I ask for something, it will be given to me."

This is not a promiscuous promise. Note how carefully it is presented in our text, which says, "How much more shall your heavenly Father give the Holy Spirit to them that ask him" (v. 13). Jesus says these words to His disciples as part of His discourse on prayer. His followers have asked Him how to pray, and He is teaching them what their heavenly Father will do for His children. If you are a child of God, this promise is for you. If you are a disciple of the Lord Jesus and have received Him as Messiah and Savior, you are given the right to be called a son of God. God is your Father in heaven. This promise is for you, not for those who are unbelievers.

If you spurn Jesus Christ and reject the privilege of adoption into God's family, this promise is not for you. It is only for the sons and daughters of the heavenly Father. It is a promise for His disciples. So multitudes of men and women cannot take comfort from these words. If they ask for something, God is not bound by this promise to give it to them. We must then ask, "Are we truly God's children? Are we disciples of Christ who want to learn what He says about how to pray properly?" There is also a very real possibility that people who pray to God will not receive what they ask for because they are asking amiss; they are asking for things to satisfy their lusts; they are asking while holding sin in their hearts; they are asking God for forgiveness and mercy while they show no mercy to those who have offended them. We are told that in such cases God will not hear us. We have no right to take these great words as assurance that our whims and fancies will be met, because this promise is only for the household of faith who ask for things that are pleasing to their Father.

THE PROMISE IS NOT A CALL TO REPENTANCE

I encourage you to come to worship services and hear the Word of God preached. I urge you to listen intently, seeking to understand and learn and obey what God says. If you are asking God for a closer walk with Him, seeking greater trust in Him, and knocking for entry into the deepest fellowship with Him, keep on doing that. Such longings of asking, seeking, and knocking are indications of saving faith and possessing Christ's salvation. So seek the Lord while He may be found. Seek Him where He may be found: where people gather together in His name and listen to His Word.

Yet I do not believe our text is an evangelistic call to seek Christ. Indeed the New Testament language here is quite the opposite. It does not speak of people seeking Christ; rather, it clearly says that no one seeks God. People do not seek Christ; He seeks us. He seeks us in the testimony of friends, in the preaching of the gospel, in the offer of pardon and forgiveness through Christ, in the prayers of parents, in the Bible and Christian books, in a host of providences that make things of this world less satisfying, and in finding satisfaction in being with other Christians. In all of this, God seeks after us.

I fear that much of what people today refer to as their seeking is actually seeking a better invitation than you might have had so far. Perhaps you want to hear the gospel with more excitement, to feel it more deeply, or to hear it more persuasively so that you won't have to make that painful, lonely, personal decision to entrust yourself to Jesus Christ alone for salvation.

Jesus Christ today is not someone you have to search for as if He were somehow lost in some mysterious place such as a cave in the Himalayas or on a distant island in the South Seas or in some lonely granite cell in Scotland. The Savior is not so far from you. He is near you in the preaching of the Word. You must not sadly shake your head at the difficulty of finding Him. No, He is the one who seeks you. He is so near that even as you read these words, He is seeking you. You do not have to leave the place where you are to seek Him in a garden or by an ocean or on some mountainside. He is seeking you at this very moment. His words to unbelievers are not, "Go and look further into the depths of your own experience and emotions." He says, "I am here; come to me now."

He is seeking you. He is not seeking your seeking or your more intense seeking or deeply emotional seeking or weepy seeking or sighing seeking. He is watching to see if you receive Him as your prophet, priest, and king. He is inviting you to come to Him and to enter the kingdom of God by the door. He is saying the door is right before you. Enter!

ASKING GOD TO FULFILL HIS PROMISES

So then, what should we as Christians ask for? Why should we knock on the gates of heaven? The answer is that we should ask God to fulfill all His promises. As we start to pray, we should first ask whether we have a promise. I don't mean whether we emotionally have a promise that grips us, makes us weep, and deeply touches us. We may have emotional reactions to reading the Word of God and hearing it preached, thanks to the Holy Spirit, but that is not my concern here.

In this great Word that is inspired by God and of which the Savior said, "Thy word is truth," is there a promise? And is that promise ours on the basis that we are children of God? Yes, there is such a promise; indeed, many great and precious promises, and they are all yes and amen in Christ Jesus. These promises are mine, and when I worship God I can pray with confidence that God will fulfill all that He has promised to me and to every Christian.

Such promises are the limits of God's obligations. What He has promised He will give, but no more than that. For example, He has not promised that I will get all A's in my exams or even that I will pass all of my exams. He has not promised that I will be cured of every ailment and disease. He has not promised me riches or marriage or children or a long life. He has not promised us a mighty religious awakening in our own lifetimes. Where there are no promises, God has not bound Himself to us.

But every promise that God has made to us, He will fulfill, such as these: He will work all things together for my good, He will supply all my needs according to His riches in glory in Christ Jesus, nothing will separate me from His love in Christ, I can do all things through Christ who strengthens me, I will learn in whatsoever state I am in to be content, the good work He has begun in me will be complete in the day of Christ. What He has promised He will perform. That is what we are to pray for. Our assurance must be based on such promises. Our heavenly Father is saying to every one of His children, "You may ask Me for the fulfillment of any promise. You may plead for its fulfillment now. You may knock on the door of these promises, and that door will be opened to you."

For every expectation, you must have a promise. You can begin to doubt your God and question His faithfulness only when you discover Him breaking His promises. When He fails my expectations or does not grant my whims, I am not justified in being angry with Him, but when His solemn promises begin to fail, then I may doubt Him.

For example, God made promises about the Holy Spirit. He said through the prophet Joel, "I will pour out my spirit upon all flesh; and your sons and your daughters shall prophesy, your old men shall dream dreams, your young men shall see visions: and also upon the servants and upon the handmaids in those days will I pour out my spirit" (Joel 2:28–29). This promise is for all God's people. It is given to old men and young men, even to male and female servants. God promises to pour out His Spirit in the days of fulfillment when Christ, the Anointed One, comes. So you can go to God and ask Him to pour His Spirit upon you, saying, "Thou hast promised that Thou wilt do this, and I trust Thee to fulfill that for me. I am dead and need the Spirit's life. I am blind and need the Spirit's illumination. I am ignorant and need the Spirit's understanding. Please give to me what Thou hast promised."

Our text offers another promise about the Holy Spirit. The Lord Jesus says, in effect:

> Your little boy is hungry and cries, "Daddy, give me some fish."
>
> "I'll give you something," you snarl at him, throwing him a snake instead.
>
> Your boy asks you for a hard-boiled egg. You drop a scorpion with its stinging tail into his hand.

You object to the scenario, saying, "We wouldn't treat our children that way. We would give them what they ask for: fish and eggs. We would give them good gifts, not evil." Yet you are evil men by nature. You are sons of Adam, and you have gone astray from the womb on. You tell lies. You drink iniquity like water; in your flesh is absolutely no good thing. Yet you say you will give good gifts to your children. How much more then will your heavenly Father give the Holy Spirit to those who ask Him? The Lord is giving us a promise that whoever asks for the Spirit will receive Him.

Our Lord does not tell us here to agonize for Him or be totally yielded to Him so as to win the Holy Spirit. He does not say we must fully surrender to have Him or to be completely dedicated to get Him. He doesn't ask us to renounce all sin or lay everything on the altar for Him or persist in praying that we might have the Spirit. He simply says, *"Ask* for Him!" and the Father will give Him to us. He does not have to be wrested out of the Father's hands. The Spirit is *given;* He is not a gift to be earned or won.

When I paid the miners of Cynheidre on a Friday morning, they did not thank me with tears in their eyes for their pay packets. They picked them up without a word because they had worked hard for them. They had earned their pay. God does not make us work for the Holy Spirit. The Spirit is a gracious, God-sent gift who is received by faith alone.

In Acts 2, we read how the Spirit came upon the church on the day of Pentecost. We are not told that prior to that coming, the church was in agony about earning that gift and meeting all kinds of conditions. There was just one request: that they remain in Jerusalem. The Spirit then came suddenly upon them from heaven. The believers were in one accord in one place, and the Spirit came upon them. He came to Peter, not by works of righteousness that Peter had done. He came to 120 disciples, not because of their holiness and merit and not as a reward for their fasting and praying. He came as a free gift of Christ's infinite grace, just as the prophet Joel had predicted. The Spirit came into believers and upon them in a full measure as they waited for His coming. They appropriated Him and received Him as their own. Let us ask God to fulfill His promise and give us the following:

1. *Power to live for Christ.* The context of our text is the sermon Jesus preached on the most difficult thing a Christian may do: pray. Jesus begins by teaching His disciples the Lord's Prayer, then gives them a simple parable to make prayer come alive, and finally, offers the great promises that God hears us when we ask, sees us when we seek, and opens to us when we knock. We are kind to our children, but our heavenly Father is even kinder to those who ask for His Spirit. The way of the cross is exceedingly long and hard-going. Disciples on this journey must love God with all their hearts and love their neighbors as themselves. They must daily present their bodies as living sacrifices to God. They must be filled with the Spirit. They must take up their crosses, deny themselves, and follow the Lord.

The Christian life is severe, demanding, relentless, and laborious. The burden we bear is heavy enough, but we must also bear the burdens of those weaker than ourselves. The Lord Jesus lays down principle upon principle and precept upon precept for those living in Christ, at church, in the family, and before the watching world and says this is the road to heaven. The disciples who first hear these requirements ask in fear, "Who then can be saved?" Christ responds with our text: "Ask and you shall receive; seek and you shall find; knock and it will be opened to you. Seek the grace to pray as I have taught you, to obey this principle and attend to these standards."

So often we forget that the energy to live the Christian life is given to us by the Holy Spirit. We look at the Christian way of holiness, and we're overwhelmed by our inadequacies. "Lord, I cannot be that kind of Christian," we wail. "I cannot be a preacher. I cannot be a Christian husband. I cannot be a church member." The Savior knew what people were thinking, so He encouraged them with this great promise: Ask, seek, knock, and you'll get what you want. Ask for the Spirit of God to help you. The Christian life is impossibly unattainable. It is the road that stretches before each child of God. It is the only road to glory, and if we're not walking on this road, we will not reach glory. When the Lord teaches us about praying, it is not so we will admire the meditative life; it is so we will live a life of prayer and follow God's way in the power of the Holy Spirit.

What is your first commitment in life—do you hunger and thirst after righteousness? Do you truly believe that for you to live is Christ? How committed are you? What is more important than glorifying God and enjoying Him? Do what you sing: "Take my life and let it be/ Consecrated Lord to Thee." Then ask for grace to follow the way of the cross. Be a proper Christian. Do not be half a Christian and half a follower of the world. Receiving the gift of the Holy Spirit has nothing to do with tongue speaking or being an eloquent preacher. Jesus is not telling you here that you will be healed of an illness or get a promotion at work. This promise is about receiving the energy to walk the holy road that leads to God.

2. More of the Spirit. We can wail that the church is in decline, and we are living in an age of small things. We can have meetings to discuss the crises the church is struggling with, but there is only one remedy for all the problems we encounter as Christians: God the Holy Spirit. That is what Christ is saying to His disciples when He urges them, "Ask God to send God to you." What we Christians need more of is the Spirit. We need His comfort, courage, morale-boosting ministry, energizing, fruitfulness, leading, and perseverance. It is not enough to know that we have wise friends and special inspirational speakers to help us with our problems. The great remedy for all our ills and infirmities is God's gift of the Holy Spirit.

We do not pray for more of the Holy Spirit only for the great awakenings that come through Spirit-sent revival. We need the Holy Spirit for everything we do as Christians. So we pray, "Help me prepare this meal and spend my housekeeping money well. Help me decide what to do in the garden. Guide me as I call the children who are away in college. Help me find the right medication for the kids who have head lice, and instruct me on how to answer our teen's questions about going to the movies." We need the Holy Spirit for every decision we make. Without the Holy Spirit we can do nothing. We will get nowhere in our Christian lives by our own wits.

So often our prayers protest the very nature of the Christian life, which is fraught with disappointments and heartaches. We forget that our usefulness in Christ's service and in the church depends upon our going through the very trials from which our flesh shrinks. Our prayers to be relieved of these trials are thus a protest against our providence. Instead, we must keep going to our Father and ask for help. God is a Father who pities His children. When your children worry you because they do not want to go to school, you wonder if they have had a struggle with a teacher or with other children. They won't tell you what the problem is, but just say they feel sick and want to stay home. You pity them because they are so weak and vulnerable. And you try to help them get through the struggle. Likewise our Heavenly Father pities us in our difficulties. And He sends us His Spirit for our encouragement and survival. He knows what we need.

How marvelous God's love is. He is willing to give grace to us, no matter what, and He makes no mistakes. We know some children act like spoiled brats because they have been given everything they clamor for. God does not make such mistakes. But if we are in the depths and cry out to Him, He will come to our assistance. He will command the Spirit to go into the darkest, dirtiest, hottest, most unfriendly, most hostile, and most remote places in the world to help us. He will go into places where we send sewer workers or SWAT teams or morticians, for the Holy Spirit is willing to operate in the darkest places on earth.

Let us conclude with two fundamental principles. First, you who are Christians must follow the Lord Jesus Christ as His disciples each day. To do this, you need the Holy Spirit and His graces. You must go to God and ask for the grace to live as a follower of the Lamb of God, for God promises that if you seek Him, then you will surely find Him.

Second, you who are not yet Christians must realize that this promise of Jesus Christ is not for you. You may protest, saying, "Is there nothing for me?" There is much for you, for the living God is seeking you. You would not be reading these words if He had not brought them to you. God is seeking you. Isn't that marvelous? At times you may have given up on yourself, and maybe your closest family and friends have come close to giving up on you, but God hasn't given up on you. You are a lost sheep, but the Good Shepherd abandoned all the safe sheep to search for one lost sheep. He will keep looking for you until He finds you. By grace, take Him, in all the glory of His person and in the perfection of all He has done for sinners. Take Him as He offers Himself in the gospel. Enter into the narrow gate. It is open for you.

So, to those who are saved, I say, "Seek!" To those who are not saved, I say, "Take!" However paradoxical it seems, that is the biblical order in the context of Luke 11. Our text tells us the Lord's people are to ask God for the Holy Spirit to help them day by day, and those who are not Christians are to take His freely offered salvation.

CHAPTER SEVEN

Spirit Birthing Spirit

There was a man of the Pharisees, named Nicodemus, a ruler of the Jews: The same came to Jesus by night, and said unto him, Rabbi, we know that thou art a teacher come from God: for no man can do these miracles that thou doest, except God be with him. Jesus answered and said unto him, Verily, verily, I say unto thee, Except a man be born again, he cannot see the kingdom of God. Nicodemus saith unto him, How can a man be born when he is old? can he enter the second time into his mother's womb, and be born? Jesus answered, Verily, verily, I say unto thee, Except a man be born of water and of the Spirit, he cannot enter into the kingdom of God. That which is born of the flesh is flesh; and that which is born of the Spirit is spirit. Marvel not that I said unto thee, Ye must be born again. The wind bloweth where it listeth, and thou hearest the sound thereof, but canst not tell whence it cometh, and whither it goeth: so is every one that is born of the Spirit.

—John 3:1–8

John tells us that Nicodemus came *by night* to the Lord Christ. Was Nicodemus so afraid of his fellow Pharisees discovering his interest in Jesus of Nazareth that he crept through dark streets, hoping he would go unnoticed? Did an evening meeting give him more time for an uninterrupted session with our Lord? Were his rabbinic duties for the day finished so he was finally free to search out Jesus to talk with Him about a new movement?

Did John want us to notice something symbolic about Nicodemus, who was in darkness about who Jesus was and the nature of His message and so approached Jesus in the darkness of his soul? Was this visit to Christ a kind of pilgrimage from darkness to light, which all people must take? Is John saying in this account, "Come out of the darkness of your soul to Jesus, the Light of the World"?

Those are all possible explanations, but we don't know exactly why Nicodemus came by night to Jesus. What is more certain is what we know about the man himself. For example:

1. *Nicodemus was born into the right family,* a son of Abraham, circumcised the eighth day; a member of the covenant people of God to whom belonged the prophets and the promises; yet he is told he must be born again. Josephus, the Jewish historian, says that Nicodemus was a member of one of the most distinguished families in the land. Yet his aristocratic blood did not excuse him from needing a new birth.

2. *He was a Pharisee* with a sterling religious background. He was upright in conduct and one of about six thousand men who were the chief exponents of high moral living. Nicodemus was serious about the law of God and believed it was the revealed Word of God. He also applied the commandments of God to his life daily and urged others to do the same. Yet Jesus told this man that he had to be born again.

3. *He had the best education* the land could offer; he was drilled in Hebrew and Greek writings and could defend the truth against attacks of paganism and Greek philosophy. Yet this Jew with a Greek name was told that he had to be born again.

4. *He was a member of the Sanhedrin,* the highest legislative body in the nation under Caesar. He was a chief authority in Israel for the legislative, administrative, and judicial branches of government and a nationally known politician. Yet this official had to be reborn of water and of the Spirit.

5. *He was a teacher of Israel* (v. 10). Indeed, Jesus speaks of him as *the* teacher of Israel, who is listened to, followed, and admired by many followers. He is like Dr. Lloyd-Jones of today, who is often referred to as '*the* Doctor' because of his eloquence, simplicity, and profundity. That is how we must think of Nicodemus, and yet Israel's teacher is told that he must be born of God if he is to enter the kingdom of heaven. Family privileges, religious commitment, educational attainment, political authority, and teaching skills are not enough to excuse Nicodemus from the need for a radical new beginning wrought by God Himself. In so many ways Nicodemus is

admirable, yet he is a stranger to a supernatural work of God in his life. He is great in the eyes of the people, but he is an unregenerate man.

John 2 ends by saying Jesus "knew what was in man" (John 2:25). This is followed by, "There was a man of the Pharisees, named Nicodemus..." (v. 1). Thus Nicodemus is brought to our attention as a representative of the human race. He is not a common criminal or a street person or the kind of person of whom you would think, "Yes, he definitely needs to be born again." Rather, Nicodemus is a man of many attainments. He is cultured and educated and from one of the best families in the land. Yet Jesus says to this man, "I say unto thee, Except a man be born again, he cannot see the kingdom of God" (v. 3). If a man like Nicodemus needs to be reborn from above, then every other person in the world must be born again.

WHY WE MUST BE BORN AGAIN

Nicodemus starts his conversation with Jesus by saying he believes Jesus is a teacher sent from God who is doing miraculous things. That is quite a compliment, especially from a Pharisee. Yet the Lord Jesus is not wooed by those words. He bluntly says to Nicodemus, "I say unto thee, Except a man be born again, he cannot see the kingdom of God" (v. 3). He repeats that again in verse 5: "Except a man be born of water and of the Spirit, he cannot enter into the kingdom of God." Then—would you believe it?—He says again in verse seven, "Marvel not that I said unto thee, Ye must be born again." Jesus is not making a general statement. He is saying very specifically to Nicodemus that he—*thee*—must be born again.

Christ stresses the importance of these words by saying, "Verily, verily, I say unto thee" (v. 3). That phrase is His famous verbal marker. In the midst of a long sermon, Jesus will insert this phrase in order to summon a listener's thoughts back to what the Teacher from God is saying. Everything Jesus says is true because He says of Himself, "I am the truth," yet in the midst of His daily conversations and observations, He pauses to offer words of outstanding significance that the world would ignore to its peril. He prefaces those words with "Verily, verily, I say unto thee" as if to say, "Prick up your ears and heed these words: *No one can see the kingdom of God unless he is born again.*"

No one, even someone in a primitive society still ignorant of the wheel, can escape the need to be born again. Nor can someone who lives in Manhattan and has the latest technology and is able to purchase anything money can buy escape the need to be born again. Anyone, whether born in the first century or the twenty-first century, must be born again to enter the kingdom of God.

God is sovereign, but natural man cannot see that. God does what He wills in the armies of heaven and here on earth, but many people do not recognize it. They ask, "Where is this mighty king you talk about? We can't see Him." The king came to earth in the flesh and showed His power over creation, the devil, disease, and death, but some people still ask, "Where is this king and His kingdom?" Christ reigns in grace over His own people, helping them to trust in Him and do His will, preserving them from unbelief and despair, sustaining them with every good and perfect gift, meeting all their needs according to His own glorious riches, and helping believers to seek first His kingdom and His righteousness.

Unbelievers say, "We can't see this kingdom." They do not understand the nature of the kingdom of God, this reign of grace over people of all types, languages, races, and ages who confess, "For us to live is Christ." Those who are not born again cannot see the influence of God in the lives of Christians. They cannot enjoy the experience of living under the reign of the king of love. They are strangers to its glory and its blessings.

Nicodemus cannot see it, either. He is quite startled by the strange words *born again*. "Nicodemus saith unto him, How can a man be born when he is old? can he enter the second time into his mother's womb, and be born?" (v. 4). He does not grasp the meaning of Jesus' words. How can anyone be born twice? You cannot rewind your life and live it backwards, getting younger and younger until you are a baby in your mother's womb, then emerge and start life all over again. There is a ratchet on the wheel of time; it moves only one way, each day getting closer to death and a meeting with the living God.

Jesus is not speaking about a physical rebirth here. He says to Nicodemus, "Verily, verily, I say unto thee, Except a man be born of water and of the Spirit, he cannot enter into the kingdom of God" (v. 5). He asks this teacher of Israel why he fails to understand this truth. He says, in effect, "You know the Scriptures, Nicodemus, and you know the two great truths taught there," which are the following:

1. *You must be born of water.* Our souls, hearts, and consciences must be cleansed of their defilement. Only God can do that through the Messiah promised by Isaiah 52 and 53. This Promised One will sprinkle many

nations, Isaiah 52:15 says. He will cleanse Gentiles all over the world of the guilt of their sin. Likewise, the prophet Ezekiel predicts the word of the Lord: "Then will I sprinkle clean water upon you, and ye shall be clean: from all your filthiness, and from all your idols, will I cleanse you. A new heart also will I give you, and a new spirit will I put within you: and I will take away the stony heart out of your flesh, and I will give you an heart of flesh" (Ezek. 36:25–26).

Only God can wash away your sins, Jesus says to Nicodemus. The youngest believer in the world today knows more about this cleansing than Nicodemus with all his religious upbringing. If I should ask a new convert, "What can wash away your sin?" she would say, "Nothing but the blood of Jesus." The Lamb of God takes away the sin of the world. Nicodemus must be born of water, meaning his heart must be cleansed of sin. Sinners who wallow like pigs in mire must be washed before they enter the kingdom of God. That washing prophesied by Ezekiel characterizes the age of the New Covenant being ushered in by Jesus the Messiah. Everyone in the kingdom must be washed of the stain of their sin. They must be born of water.

2. *You must be born of the Spirit.* The Holy Spirit is the agent of this new birth. He has access to our inmost being, which is the control center of our lives. He brings about this spiritual birth because He is the source and agent of change. He regenerates the heart of a person. He goes into us and transforms us from within.

A little girl once picked up a rose bud and tried to open it, first by pulling off the green leaves on the branch that held the bud. Then she peeled off the petals on the bud. She ended up destroying the flower. She cried as she showed her mother the ruined bud. She pointed to other roses in a vase, asking, "Why isn't my rose like them? "They were opened from the inside," her mother said.

Likewise, Jesus challenges Nicodemus, reminding him of what the Lord says in Ezekiel 36:26: "A new heart also will I give you, and a new spirit will I put within you: and I will take away the stony heart out of your flesh, and I will give you an heart of flesh." Nicodemus, a renowned teacher of Old Testament truths, is ignorant of the first principles of the blessings of the new covenant: the washing of the heart, or being born of water; and a heart of flesh, or the birth of a new spirit. Without the work of God the Holy Spirit, you cannot enter the kingdom of God, Jesus says.

Nicodemus had the Scriptures and God's predictions about the Messiah. He understood everything, yet he understood nothing. A fellow I know read George Orwell's *Animal Farm* when he was a boy. He loved the tale of imaginary animals taking over a farm. He missed nothing in the story of the animals, but he totally missed the application of the book, which is a political allegory. So it was with the teaching of Ezekiel about the coming of the Spirit into believers. Not until Pentecost and the pouring out of the Holy Spirit would Nicodemus understand what Joel and Ezekiel and Isaiah and Jesus were talking about.

Our Savior declares the absolute necessity of a new birth. Unless you are born anew, you cannot enter the kingdom of God. You will remain blind to its reality and forever be a stranger to the kingdom. When George Whitefield was asked why he so often preached on the words "ye must be born again," he simply replied, "Because you must be born again!" Without a new birth, you will not go to heaven. Without this new birth, you are destined for hell.

LIMITATIONS OF THE FLESH

The Lord Jesus offers two alternatives to Nicodemus. He says, "That which is born of the flesh is flesh; and that which is born of the Spirit is spirit" (v. 6). Here the word *flesh* stands for sinful fallen human nature. So all that flesh can produce is a sinful fallen human nature. Your parents can give you much, but they cannot give you the divine birth, which is from above. What is begotten by procreation and emerges every time from the womb is a baby with a sinful human nature. "I was shapen in iniquity; and in sin did my mother conceive me," says David (Ps. 51:5). Likewise Job asks, "Who can bring a clean thing out of an unclean? not one" (Job 14:4).

Only the Spirit can give birth to spirit in a man or woman. For, as John 1:13 says, people are not physically born into God's family; rather, they "were born, not of blood, nor of the will of the flesh, nor of the will of man, but of God." The only thing that can transform a person and enable him to please and glorify God is a change wrought by God the Holy Spirit. Without that, all you have is flesh. It may be well-bred and nicely accented flesh; it may be washed and perfumed and well-dressed flesh; it may be well-educated and scholarly flesh; it may be religious and ethical flesh; it may be politically important flesh or eloquent and authoritative

flesh, but in the end it is only flesh. Nicodemus may have the best attributes, but he is still born of the flesh. That means the following things are
true of him as well as all people of the flesh, including me and you:

1. *His mind is hostile to God and cannot please God.* In his letter to the Romans,
Paul says, "Because the carnal mind is enmity against God: for it is not
subject to the law of God, neither indeed can be. So then they that are in
the flesh cannot please God" (Rom. 8:7–8). Like Jesus, Paul teaches that
the sinful nature can be educated, well-bred, eloquent, powerful in society, and influential in religion, as Nicodemus was, but nothing done "in
the flesh" can please God. The sinful mind is hostile to Christ. It cries out,
"Crucify Him! Crucify Him!" It declares, "Who is the Lord that I should
obey His voice?" It says, "We have no king but Caesar." The mind of the
flesh is a clenched fist raised against God.

2. *He cannot come to the King.* In John 6:44, Jesus says, "No man can come to
me, except the Father which hath sent me draw him." The first step of the
journey to Jesus is moving away from any confidence you have in yourself, with the awareness of your guilt and shame and poverty. You have
to go to Jesus to find salvation. But the Savior says no one comes to Him
while in the flesh. People are helpless to make such a life-transforming
change, which deplores the proud thoughts they have and turns their
back on everything they are. They are helpless to go to Jesus Christ to beg,
"Wash me Savior, or I die." No person can make the journey from the flesh
to Christ unless the Spirit of God first works a great change in his heart
and unless the Father who sent the Son draws the sinner to Christ.

3. *He can produce only the works of the flesh.* Paul writes in Galatians 5:19–21,
"Now the works of the flesh are manifest, which are these; adultery, fornication, uncleanness, lasciviousness, idolatry, witchcraft, hatred, variance,
emulations, wrath, strife, seditions, heresies, envyings, murders, drunk-
enness, revellings, and such like: of the which I tell you before, as I
have also told you in time past, that they which do such things shall
not inherit the kingdom of God" (Gal. 5:19–21). The influence of earlier
grace in Israel, a wise upbringing in a believing family, knowledge of
the Scriptures, and the restraints of society may together clamp down
on the wilder expression of the flesh, but these fleshly desires lurk as
seeds in the hearts of all people. And the flesh may bring those seeds to

flower as it did one day in the life of the shepherd who wrote Psalm 23. After he became king and was walking one day on the roof of his palace, David saw a beautiful woman taking a bath. The evil actions of the sinful nature then sprang up in David's heart, causing all kinds of discord, including adultery, deception, and murder. This view of the natural man is so pessimistic. His only hope is a birth from above.

HOW THE SPIRIT CHANGES US

The Bible at times uses images to describe regeneration. It uses the image of taking away a heart of stone and replacing it with a heart of flesh. It uses the image of making a new creation of what was dead in sin. It uses the image of resurrection by the power that raised Christ from the dead. All of these images tell us that we who once were dead in trespasses and sins may be made alive by God the Holy Spirit through the redeeming work of Jesus Christ.

In John 3 Jesus uses the image of being begotten or born of the Spirit. No one can be certain which is the exact expression, but whatever it is, both phrases mean one thing: we are wholly dependent upon the Spirit for the incredible transformation that takes place in the new birth. We also learn the following:

1. *The new birth is a sovereign work of the Spirit.* The Lord says in verse 8, "The wind bloweth where it listeth, and thou hearest the sound thereof, but canst not tell whence it cometh, and whither it goeth: so is every one that is born of the Spirit." The Hebrew word for spirit is *ruah,* which is also the word for the blowing wind or the breath of God. On the day of Pentecost, the Holy Spirit comes upon believers as a rushing mighty wind.

If you own a wind farm on a Welsh mountain, you want the wind to blow steadily, not too strong and not too weak, so that every day it generates an electric current. You may want to sell that electricity to a power company, but you have no power over the wind. You may rise early and cry to the wind like the prophets of Baal cried to their god. You might shout, "East wind blow at thirty miles per hour!" You can look at the weathercock and see where the wind is blowing and can guess its speed or read its velocity on a wind gauge, but you have no power over the wind. Jesus says, "So is every one that is born of the Spirit" (v. 8).

Everyone who sees the kingdom of God is born through a sovereign work of God. The Lord does not put that work in anyone else's hands. It is His divine prerogative and no one else shares in that work. God does not give an evangelist a Spirit switch to push as He calls people to salvation. The work of the new birth is not a human work.

Consider the words of James 1:18: "Of his own will begat he us with the word of truth." The choice of giving birth to believers is God's, James says. To enter the kingdom of God, we are wholly dependent upon an action of the Holy Spirit. This birth is compared to the physical birth by which we entered the world. We were not begotten by our parents because we decided to be born. We were not a clamoring voice in the mind of one of our parents, saying, "I want life. I want to be a girl five feet, eight inches tall, with blond hair, blue eyes, a high I.Q., musical talents, and a good sense of humor." Our parents conceived us and bore us totally without our consent. So too the Holy Spirit wills our new birth. The wind blows with certainty and efficacy where it wills. The wind is not at our beck and call, and neither is the regenerating power of the Spirit.

You might ask, "So if the Spirit moves, I shall be saved; and if He does not move I will not be saved. So should I do nothing and wait for Him"? No, that is fatalism. It is like what a fisherman says at the beginning of the day: "If I am to go out and catch fish, then today the wind must blow." That is true, but then if the fisherman does nothing, even refuses to let out the sails on his boat, he will certainly catch no fish. God's wind must blow, yes, but the fisherman must put up the sails to catch fish.

Likewise, you must listen to the preaching of God's Word, then turn the sermon into a prayer, crying to God, "Create in me a clean heart, O God." Men and women are born *of the Spirit*, verse 8 tells us, but verse 16 goes on to say that whoever believes in Him will not perish but have eternal life. You must believe on the Lord Jesus Christ. Whether you feel anything or not, you must cry to Him for help to entrust yourself to Him. For as it says in Acts 16:31, "Believe on the Lord Jesus Christ, and thou *shalt* be saved!"

For example, a baby in the womb is diagnosed with spina bifida. The doctor tells the mother a prenatal operation may help the baby. She responds, "No, I don't want surgery. If my baby is going to get better, he will get better without the operation." That is fatalism. Someone who believes in the sovereignty of God will arrange for the operation but throughout the surgery will pray mightily to God to help the baby through the extraordinary skill of the surgeon.

Likewise, Ezekiel saw a valley full of dry bones. When he was asked if they could live, the prophet called upon God. "You prophesy to them," the Lord responded. So Ezekiel spoke to the bones, and they came together and lived. Prophesy and cry out to the God who can make dead bones live. New birth is a sovereign work of the Spirit.

2. The new birth is an effective work of the Spirit. "Look at the wind," we say as trees toss and sway or flags on the promenade flutter or clothes on the wash line strain at their pegs. But what you see is not the wind; it is the effect of the wind. The sound of a howling wind is not the wind, either. It is only evidence of a strong wind.

So if you are born of the wind of the Spirit, we will not see the Spirit, but we should hear His presence in your speech if He is in you, and we should see Him in your daily living if He is working in you. In his first letter, John lists the evidences of the Spirit's activities. He says, first, "Ye know that every one that doeth righteousness is born of him" (1 John 2:29). So a man who is a father, husband, workman, neighbor, and church member will do what is right in all he does by the strength of the indwelling Spirit.

The second evidence of the Spirit, according to 1 John 3:9 is this: "Whosoever is born of God doth not commit sin; for his seed remaineth in him: and he cannot sin, because he is born of God." The Holy Spirit is holy, so the fruit He produces is holy fruit. He makes His people fruitful in a sinful, hostile world that entices them to abandon the Lord. God keeps those who are born of Him from the world's allurements, for 1 John 5:4 says, "For whatsoever is born of God overcometh the world."

Third, John reminds us of the vertical and divine dimensions of the life of the Spirit. It is good to do right and not continue in sin, but that is not good enough for the children of God. As 1 John 4:7 says, "Every one that loveth is born of God, and knoweth God." He adds in 1 John 5:1: "Whosoever believeth that Jesus is the Christ is born of God." Someone may say, "I truly believe that Jesus of Nazareth is the Messiah." We may then respond, saying, "You have been born of God." The birth by the Spirit is extremely effective in changing those who once were dominated by the flesh.

3. *The new birth is a mysterious work of the Spirit.* The people of the British Isles still speak of the great wind that blew on October 15, 1987. That wind blew on my birthday, so I remember it well. The wind blew at 106 knots in Norfolk and 83 knots at the London Weather Centre. The temperature rose almost ten degrees centigrade in twenty minutes, which happens only once in two hundred years. Hundreds of thousands of trees were blown down, and thousands of homes lost their roofs.

I would be foolish to believe that my upcoming birthday will bring another mighty wind from heaven, because I know that God is utterly sovereign in sending a hurricane. However, I do ask that God will send the mighty wind of His Spirit on our land as he did when Spurgeon preached in London in the 1850s and 1860s or when, a century earlier, Whitefield and Wesley preached across England and Wales.

I do not know why God favored the land with a Great Awakening in the eighteenth and nineteenth centuries, but not since. I don't know why one sister in a family is regenerated and another not, even though both have experienced the same godly influences at home and at church. What a mystery regeneration is! It is a mystery in its recipients and in how the Spirit operates within us. As the hymn writer D. M. Whittle so beautifully writes:

> I know not how the Spirit moves,
> Convincing men of sin,
> Revealing Jesus through the Word,
> Creating faith him Him.

Some people receive only a tiny part of truth, yet God is pleased to use that to save them, while others must have truth filling their mouths and coming out of their ears before they are regenerated. Some, such as Peter, are difficult to gauge as to an exact time when the Spirit of God gave them a birth from heaven. Or was Peter born from above when Jesus said to him, "Come follow me" and the fisherman followed? Was it when Peter said at Caesarea Philippi, "You are the Christ, the Son of the living God"?

We know that Saul of Tarsus was reborn on the Damascus Road when he was confronted by Jesus. Some of you know the day you were born again, while others of you are not sure even of the year, but all of you who are true children of God may say today, "I know whom I have believed, and am persuaded that he is able to keep that which I have committed unto him against that day" (2 Tim. 1:12). That is enough. You know you cannot go to heaven without a new birth. You know you cannot claim the new birth without a life of holiness and love for God. That is enough.

We are not to trouble ourselves that we did not have a crisis experience or that our conviction of sin came in the years *following* our conversion rather than preceding it. We must instead dwell on the great words of John 3:16: "For God so loved the world, that he gave his only begotten Son, that whosoever believeth in him should not perish, but have everlasting life." You must entrust yourself just as you are to the Lord Jesus. When you do that, you may be assured that the Spirit of God will be at work in you, giving you a new birth and making everything new.

CHAPTER EIGHT

The Father Sends the Counselor

*And I will pray the Father, and he shall give you another Comforter, that
he may abide with you for ever; even the Spirit of truth; whom the world
cannot receive, because it seeth him not, neither knoweth him: but ye
know him; for he dwelleth with you, and shall be in you.*

—John 14:16–17

Twelve young disciples had been summoned from their businesses as
fishermen and tax collectors. They had left their families and homes to
travel with the itinerant rabbi Jesus. They had experienced years of breathtaking miracles, mind-blowing teaching, and faithful provision; a good
measure, pressed down, shaken together, and running over had been
poured into their laps. What a trip these wandering preachers had taken!

But now the Master of those disciples has begun to confirm the hints
He gave them earlier that it is time for Him to leave them. What on earth
was He thinking? He had so disrupted their lives that they'd never be the
same again. They couldn't go back to what they had been doing prior to
following the young rabbi, yet they couldn't go forward without Him,
either. What would happen to them?

They would be on a train without a driver. Yet how could they dis-
embark from that train? They had been dreaming that the promised
kingdom would be restored to Israel and they would participate in King
Jesus' reign, yet now there was little evidence of that new kingdom. How
could they build a kingdom without the king?

The disciples were in shock. They feared they wouldn't be able to
cope without Jesus. They had always needed Him, but then Jesus gave
the most wonderful sermon they had ever heard, describing the future
and telling them not to be troubled but to keep trusting in Him because
of a new provision He has made for them.

JESUS' PROMISE OF A COMFORTER

Jesus eases their fears by saying, "And I will pray the Father, and he shall give you another Comforter, that he may abide with you for ever; even the Spirit of truth" (v. 16). The Holy Spirit, who gives birth from above, does not fly away after doing His supernatural work of regeneration. He does not abandon believers to their own wits but promises to remain with them forever.

Jesus assures the disciples that they will have unlimited access to the Holy Spirit of truth. He stops halfway through His sermon to assure the disciples, "It is expedient for you that I go away: for if I go not away, the Comforter will not come unto you" (John 16:7). Did this ease their fears, or were they still disappointed? Did they, like so many of us today, view the Holy Spirit as the faceless person of the Godhead?

When we think of God the Father, our hearts are drawn in love to Him, and when we think of our Savior Jesus, we love Him for laying down his life for us. But the Holy Spirit is rather difficult to relate to. Let me test you by asking what you would rather have today: the physical presence of the Lord Jesus speaking to you and answering your questions and giving you advice, or God the Holy Spirit in you for strength and enlightenment, leading you to purity?

THE TRINITY IN US

The Spirit is God, the Son is God, and the Father is God, and these three are one God. When Christ ascends to heaven, all three persons of the Godhead will dwell in the disciples. It is difficult to think of the Trinity in us. Yet this is clearly spelled out in the great sermon of John 14. In verse 18, Jesus assures His disciples that, having taken them away from their families and homes, He will not leave them parentless. He says, "I will not leave you comfortless: I will come to you." This will be evident in His return from the dead in resurrection power, when He will live as their Savior in the power of an endless life. It will also be true in His second coming in the clouds and in great glory at the end of the age. At that time and for evermore He will be seen as the "everlasting Father" of His people (Isa. 9:6). But before that time of glory, it will also be true of the twelve disciples as they seek to fulfill their chief end in a life of glorifying God and enjoying Him forever.

The Lord Christ will never leave them—or us—for He promises, "Lo, I am with you alway, even unto the end of the world" (Matt. 28:20). This wonderful friend sticks closer to us than our own brothers or sisters, who may live miles away and see us once a year at the most, though they are bone of our bone and flesh of our flesh, but Jesus will never leave us. What a friend He is for us always!

AT HOME WITH GOD

Then Jesus adds another mind-blowing promise to those who love and obey His teaching: "My Father will love him, and we will come unto him, and make our abode with him" (v. 23). We will not be homeless orphans but will go to a home created by God.

Let me give an example. A couple you love makes the long journey to your home every few years and stays with you a couple of days. It is the high spot of the year, for your time with them is happy and blessed. You are sad when they must go back home. Now multiply that experience by infinity. Think of God, the creator of the universe, author of all the good and perfect gifts you have received. Think of this king of love coming to see you along with His blessed Son, your savior. Both Father and Son will make their happy home with you. You will never feel crowded or exhausted by their presence. You will never think, "Will they never leave us?"

Hans Christian Andersen greatly admired Charles Dickens. Dickens once invited Andersen to stay with him in London. So Andersen came to Gad's Hill in the summer of 1857. He stayed and stayed and stayed. Andersen and Dickens did not have much in common, so by the second month Dickens was dropping unsubtle hints that it was time for Andersen to move on. But Andersen stayed. After Andersen finally did leave, Dickens walked into his bedroom and wrote on the mirror, "Hans Andersen slept in this room for five weeks—which seemed to the family ages!" Dickens's kindhearted daughter Kate described Hans as "a bony bore who stayed on and on."

No Christian feels like that when the living God comes to stay. Our fears are rather the very reverse—that the God of love won't stay but might leave us. The Trinity is the most perfect guest. We cannot imagine life without Father, Son, and Holy Spirit, for they soothe our sorrows, heal our wounds, and drive away our fears. They make life complete. The

Father, the Son, and the Holy Spirit make their home with the youngest Christian and the oldest believer.

If you ask a woman what she does, she may answer rather shyly, "I am just a homemaker." But her husband and her children feel supremely loved because she makes the family what it is. The whole family depends on her. She is the hub of the home; they'd be loose spokes without her. They are blessed because she is the homemaker. So it is with the Christian; life is good because the Holy Spirit has made our hearts a dwelling place for God!

AN INDWELLING PROMISED BY SCRIPTURE

This promise of Jesus is another example of what was promised and fulfilled in Scripture. In the Old Testament, Ezekiel prophesied that the Lord would purify and cleanse His people and put a new spirit within them. That promise was fulfilled in the New Testament with the coming of Christ and the new birth of His disciples.

Again, in the Old Testament, King Solomon asks somewhat tentatively at the dedication of the temple, "But will God indeed dwell on the earth? behold, the heaven and heaven of heavens cannot contain thee; how much less this house that I have builded?" (1 Kings 8:27). In the Upper Room Discourse of John 18, Jesus quiets the fear of Solomon and others by saying that yes, God will truly dwell on earth, first, in the incarnation of the Son of God, and then when Father, Son, and Holy Spirit dwell on earth in the lives of God's people. God anticipates this time with delight, saying, "My tabernacle also shall be with them: yea, I will be their God, and they shall be my people" (Ezek. 37:27).

Later, in Zechariah 2:10, God promises, "Sing and rejoice, O daughter of Zion: for, lo, I come, and I will dwell in the midst of thee." That promise is fulfilled when Christ comes to earth as a baby, for John 1:14 says, "The Word was made flesh, and dwelt among us." Everything that Christ accomplished in His saving work makes it possible for believing sinners to become the residence of a holy God. God writes His holy name on the shining brass plate outside the front door of our lives in marks of indelible grace: "The Dwelling Place of the Holy God, Father and Son and Holy Spirit." Do you realize that you are God's residence?

Think of how that theme is continued in the New Testament. Paul writes in 2 Corinthians 6:16, "For ye are the temple of the living God;

as God hath said, I will dwell in them, and walk in them; and I will be their God, and they shall be my people." Paul also prays that the Father "would grant you, according to the riches of his glory, to be strengthened with might by his Spirit in the inner man; that Christ may dwell in your hearts by faith" (Eph. 3:16–17).

These promises are the blessings of the new covenant; they are part and parcel of eternal life. They are the great mark of evangelical faith. If the essence of Roman Catholicism is to focus on the church, its priesthood, and its ceremonies, and the essence of modernism is to center on man and his good works in society, then the essence of evangelicalism is to center on God's dwelling in the lives of His people. The Lord makes His home in each Christian. In saying this we are not deifying ourselves or pronouncing ourselves to be gods but saying that, through Christ, this extraordinary gracious humbling of God is the privilege of all who believe in Jesus. The Son of God humbled Himself in the virgin's womb, and that same Lord humbles Himself by dwelling in us.

AN INDWELLING THAT PROMPTS HOLINESS

How can you hook up with a prostitute if God is indwelling you, Paul asks the Corinthian church. How can any of you profane the holy place of God? What you watch with your eyes, or make with your hands, or where you go with your feet is as a person indwelt by the Maker of the rolling spheres, the loving Savior, and the Spirit of holiness.

But let us not speak of God's presence in our hearts as a threat but in terms of privilege. Let us respond as Sinclair Ferguson once did in reminiscing about the first sermon he heard about the Lord indwelling us. He said he went home from that meeting with his feet hardly touching the pavement.

Let us discuss what Jesus specifically meant in saying the Holy Spirit would come to His disciples as another counselor.

1. He would send another counselor. Don Carson stresses the word *another* in Jesus' statement by saying,

> In English we have but one word for *another*; in Greek there are two common words, and often they are distinguishable in meaning. For

instance, in Galatians 1:6–7 Paul expresses astonishment that the Galatian believers could so quickly abandon the one who called them into the grace of Christ and turn to *"another* gospel: which is not *another."* The first *another* really means a different gospel, while the second means a gospel of the same kind. That is why the NIV translates this passage as "turning to a different gospel, which is really no gospel at all."

In John 14:16, the word for *another* in "another Paraclete" is the same word as the second *another* in Galatians 1:6–7. So Jesus is promising not a *different* Paraclete but a Paraclete who is *essentially the same kind* as Jesus is.[1]

So the Spirit is another counselor who would be all that Jesus was to the disciples.

2. He would send a counselor. The Greek word for "counselor" in Jesus' promise is *paracletos,* which has been transliterated as the familiar word *paraclete,* which means a person who is called alongside another person. The word *paracletos* outside of the New Testament refers to a legal adviser or counselor who stands beside you as your advocate. If you were in legal trouble, you might ask a good friend, "Will you speak up for me as my counselor, plead my cause in court, and tell the truth about me?" The Holy Spirit was Jesus' most intimate friend. No one could speak the truth about Jesus like the Spirit. The Spirit had been with Christ from all eternity, and then was with Him throughout His life on earth, strengthening and keeping Him.

Likewise, Christ offers the Holy Spirit as advocate to every Christian. He brings out one exhibit after another, one example after another, one memory or saying after another to show you the truth and beauty and grace of the Lord Jesus Christ. The Spirit shows you the loveliness of the Lord Jesus, His holiness and tenderness. He shows you that Christ is a lamb without spot or blemish. He speaks to the heart of every Christian, persuading us that Jesus is worthy of our constant love and service.

The Counselor also supports us when we tell sinners that their lives are wrong in the sight of God. He is like a prosecuting attorney who exposes the sins of the world. The Comforter also helps us overcome our personal limitations by helping us to speak up for the Lord. He is an

---

1. Donald A. Carson, *Jesus and His Friends* (Carlisle: Paternoster, 1995), 49.

enormous source of strength and comfort to us as we work for Christ. He helps us understand who Jesus is and what He has done.

If we put together all the descriptions of the Spirit's work, we can rightly call Him the Vicar of Christ. The word *vicar* means substitute, and Jesus promises His disciples that the Spirit will be the substitute for the physical presence of the Lord Jesus Christ. Jesus will be leaving His disciples and in His glorified body will not return to the world until the last day. In the meantime He and the Father send onto the field of conflict the glorious and magnificent Substitute to do the work of the Son of God. The Spirit comes alongside us as no mere imitation of the Lord Jesus, for the Spirit is equal in power and glory to Christ.

The Spirit will continue the instructing, enlightening, and sanctifying work of Christ. He will come into this world to teach and counsel the disciples and guide them into all truth (John 16:13). He will bear witness to the world that the gospel message is true (John 15:26–27). He will convict the world of its sin as Jesus did (John 16:8–11). So the Godhead makes His grace and love known to us by the Spirit. He does this, not just in Galilee or Jerusalem, but all over the world. Think of His work in the eighteenth century in Wales, in England, throughout Scotland, and in New England. On identical days the Spirit was turning sinners from darkness to light in two continents.

The man Christ Jesus preached the Sermon on the Mount on one mountain, at one time; He could not be anywhere else. He spoke in one Upper Room on a single evening prior to His crucifixion, but today the Spirit of Jesus Christ does the work of Jesus on a thousand mountains and in ten thousand rooms, all at the same time. The Spirit knows no physical limitations in duplicating the work of Jesus. Thus Jesus could say to the disciples that they would do greater works than He. For all they would do would be through the Spirit, the Vicar of Christ.

3. *He would send the Spirit of truth.* In John 14:6, Jesus says, "I am...the truth." In the next chapter, Jesus refers to the Spirit as the Spirit of truth. He says, "But when the Comforter is come, whom I will send unto you from the Father, even the Spirit of truth, which proceedeth from the Father, he shall testify of me" (John 15:26).

To become believers in Jesus Christ, some people have to overcome the thought that the gospel is a fairy tale dreamed up by a group of fanatics, who, over a period of a hundred years, embellished the simple tale

of a martyred healer. The enemy of their souls tells them that Jesus' followers blew the whole tragic story out of all proportion to what actually
happened. In other words, what we have in the gospels and letters is
really an elaborate hoax and a tissue of lies. Yet consider the Jewish background of the writers of the New Testament. These men felt the authority
of the ninth commandment, which forbad giving false testimony and
bearing false witness. It would be blasphemous for them to deceive others, especially about holy Jehovah. How could religious men construct
such a fraud?

There is no evidence for such a deception. Not one believer broke
ranks to say, "You are being duped by rogues." Instead, what we see in
the New Testament are men and women who within thirty years after
the resurrection, long before tall tales could be elaborated, carefully
researched and wrote an extraordinarily uniform testimony of Jesus
Christ, saying, "This is who He was; this is what He said; this is what He
claimed; this is what He did, and we were eyewitnesses of these things.
We will lay down our lives for its truthfulness." Many of Jesus' followers
did die for the truth. They were led by apostles indwelt by the Spirit of
truth that came into them from God Himself. By the Spirit's energy and
insights they testified about Christ in a way that far outlasted them.

In John 16:12–13, Jesus also refers to the Spirit of truth, saying, "I have
yet many things to say unto you, but ye cannot bear them now. Howbeit
when he, the Spirit of truth, is come, he will guide you into all truth: for
he shall not speak of himself; but whatsoever he shall hear, that shall
he speak: and he will shew you things to come." This Spirit is obsessed
with truth. He is not interested in pious exaggerations, for deceit and lies
grieve Him.

Jesus Christ does not need the falsehoods of men. He guides the
apostles away from any thought of believing that they can win followers to the cause of Christ by lacing their gospels with a few lies. He is
not the conniving or crafty Spirit; He is the Spirit of truth. The world
may excuse a little white lie, but of the Spirit, Jesus says, "Whatsoever
he shall hear, that shall he speak: and he will shew you things to come"
(16:13). Jesus spoke exclusively the words that the Father gave Him, and
the Holy Spirit likewise speaks only what He hears from the Father and
Son. He would tell the disciples "things to come." He knew all about the
mysteries of Jesus' departure from this world and would relate those
mysteries to the disciples.

Without Jesus' physical presence, the disciples would not be rudderless or lacking in purpose. They would not drift away from each other or break up because of mutual incriminations. Jesus' ascension was not the end of Jesus' work; it was just the beginning. Jesus never leaves His people in the lurch, without provision, without a guide, without a sovereign protector, or without an explanation of the crucifixion of the Son of God. No. He promises, "I will see you again" (16:22). The Spirit who comes to us is the successor of Jesus, sent by the Father as the Vicar of Christ. He is with us now as closely and lovingly as Jesus was with the disciples during the days of His flesh. They could go running to Jesus and blurt out their questions and troubles. So too we may go to the Comforter, the Spirit of truth, today, saying, "Help me, Spirit of God." Our cries are not in vain, for the gospel church is the fellowship of the Spirit.

AN INDWELLING MARKED BY TRUTH

In John 14:17, Jesus assures His disciples that they already know the Spirit, "for he dwelleth with you, and shall be in you." Though the disciples already know the Spirit, He had not yet been poured out on them in His fullness and glory like He would be at the time of Pentecost. The disciples knew about the Spirit from the teachings of the Old Testament revealing that He was active in creation and was the one who anointed Israel's kings and inspired her prophets.

John and Peter and others had also experienced the comfort and power of the Holy Spirit as they preached and cast out demons, were put on trial in synagogues, counseled people, and preached to crowds. They had already experienced the enabling gifts of the Spirit, though they were not yet aware that the Spirit was helping them. All the insights and moral convictions they had developed since following Jesus of Nazareth had come to them through the Spirit. They knew the Spirit, for He was living in them, but He had not yet made Himself evident to them in His fullness and glory as the Spirit of Christ. They would not see that until the Lord Jesus was raised from the dead, was exalted at God's right hand, and poured forth His Spirit on the church (John 7:39).

Jesus uses two prepositions when telling His disciples about the Spirit. He says the Spirit will be *with* them and *in* them. It is not exactly clear that *with* them refers to the presence of the Spirit in the church, and *in* them refers to the Spirit's presence in them as individuals. However, it is clear that *with them* suggests an association, personal sharing, or special kind of fellowship, while *in them* suggests true indwelling. Let us look more closely at this distinction.

1. *The Spirit is with us.* As believers, the Spirit is with us, even when we fail to feel His presence. He is with us when we judge ourselves in a gospel church to be as cold as ice. He is with us because Jesus says, "He will be with you." The Spirit is with us as much as Christ is with us. So as Christians we are an association of the Spirit, a movement of the Spirit, a body of the Spirit, a community of the Spirit, and a society of the Spirit. The Spirit is with all of us, and all of us desperately need Him, for the presence of the Spirit is never an option in our midst. We need the Spirit, and we need one another. We cannot grow as Christians in isolation, so if we try to do so, we will develop into distorted and handicapped believers. We only rightly grow as members of one another and under the influence of fellow believers whom we have come to love with a fervent pure love. We thus share each others' burdens as we share the life of the Spirit and the ministries the Spirit gives to us.

The Spirit is *with* us as we, the church, face the future, climb mountains, and cross rivers. He is with us as we battle temptations and are built up in the likeness of Christ. We grow with the Spirit's corporate inspiration, morale-building ministry, guidance, and keeping power. We do not do this on our own. We move forward, conscious that the Spirit is with us all.

2. *The Spirit is in us.* We are individually and personally in need of the Spirit. We feel this need especially when we are alone; when no other Christian is close by, when the rest of our family and school or workplace are led by another spirit, or when we live far from a place of worship. In all times and places we yearn for the Spirit's presence within us, giving us new life, sanctifying us, and helping us to cope with loss, heartache, and ignorance. The Counselor makes the presence of God immediate, bearing witness with our spirits that "we go not forth alone against the foe," as one hymnist expresses it.

Pause and think of this: the Spirit is the transcendent, infinite God, but this immeasurable, immense Spirit chooses to live within us, yet is never reduced to such narrow confines. The Spirit fills the heavens and the earth; there is no place without God's Spirit. From the bottom of the deepest sea to the remotest edge of the cosmos, the universe is confronted by the Spirit of God. Yet, marvel of marvels, the Spirit chooses to live within us, to make us His home as the seal of our personal adoption into the family of God. He energizes, enlightens, and makes us holy as He convicts, comforts, and works faith and trust in us. He cleanses, assures, leads, assists, intercedes, transforms, and endows each individual believer with His gifts.

So the Spirit is *in* us, and He is also *with* us. He must be *both*. If we think of Him only *in* us, we will slide into thinking of Him as if He belonged to us and is someone we can virtually control as our own personal spirit. That increases the danger of failing to distinguish between God the Holy Spirit and our own spirit, hunches, desires, hopes, and wills. We may choose to identify such promptings as the leading of the Holy Spirit. But if someone too often makes the claim, "The Spirit told me this, or led me there, or stopped me from doing that," we might suspect mysticism, which is a defamation of the Spirit. We need more than the Spirit in us; we need Him also in His ministry *with* all other Christian men and women. By one Spirit we are all baptized into one body. So we must be accountable to fellow Christians as they bravely reject our feelings, rebuking us if necessary, teasing us, bringing us down to earth, or saying sweetly, "Hang on a minute; I don't think the Spirit is saying those things to me." We cannot protest, saying, "He's in me and I know what He wants us to do, so it has to be done this way," because the Spirit is with them too.

Likewise, if you think the Spirit is exclusively *with* you, you will lose out on appreciating the wonderful pity of the almighty God who comes to us, takes up residence in our lives, and is the inner witness of truth and power. If you think of the Spirit as being only *with* us, that may lead to denominationalism, and even cultism. Jim Jones's followers all took poison and killed themselves because they thought only of the corporate *with-ness* of the Spirit. They said, "He is with us, so we will all die together." What horror! No, the Spirit must be *in* us individually as well as *with* all of us. That balanced insight delivers us from ecclesiastical tyranny and cult leadership.

AN INDWELLING REJECTED BY THE WORLD

The Lord says in our text, "The Spirit of truth; whom the world cannot receive, because it seeth him not, neither knoweth him" (14:17). Jesus told Nicodemus that he could not see the kingdom of God unless he was born of water and the Spirit. To see God's Spirit, God's kingdom, and God's gospel, Nicodemus had to die to the world and be regenerated in the spirit, or born again. In the New Testament, *world* usually refers to a moral and spiritual entity rather than a geographical and spatial entity. *World* thus stands for loveless, defiant, selfish, and fallen humanity in a sewer of infidelity and a habitation of cruelty. The world promotes greed and is the source of torture, pornography, knife attacks, and unfaithfulness. Yet God loves this world and sent His Son to die for it. He also sent His Spirit to regenerate and redeem and indwell this world.

The world refuses to accept the work of the Spirit as He strives, convicts, illuminates, and draws sinners to Him. Grace is irresistible and effectual only to those who were chosen to be God's elect. The world does not accept the saving work of God the Spirit in its midst. It says, "We cannot see Him! We do not know this Spirit you are talking about. We understand your eloquence and oratory and persistence in speaking to us. We even find some of what you say attractive. But seeing and knowing the Spirit of God? That is your imagination. It is unacceptable to us."

So Jesus warns us that the world cannot accept Him because it neither sees Him nor knows Him. So we should not be surprised that unbelief is the background for our ministries. The world does not have the power to see and know Christ, so it does not have the power to accept Him. What a closed circle of wretchedness the world lives in!

I, too, must see Christ to receive Him. Like the world, I am blind to the work of the Spirit. Oh wretched man, who can deliver me? God can do what the world cannot do. In love, God gives His Son. In love He gives us His Spirit. Forgiveness is accomplished by the Son, and life and grace are applied by the Spirit. The Spirit comes and I can see Christ. The Spirit comes and I can receive Christ. By grace, I am delivered from the bondage of blindness and helplessness and brought into the liberty of the children of God.

So what must I do? Just wait? No. I must cry mightily to God, asking for His Spirit. Out of the awareness of my helplessness will come the true prayer of longing for deliverance from the world.

AN INDWELLING GIVEN BY FATHER TO SON

Jesus says to His disciples in verse 16, "I will pray the Father, and he shall give you another Comforter, that he may abide with you for ever." He, in effect, says to God the Father, "Here are My apostles, eyewitnesses of My glory. Give them the Spirit of truth. They will be writing gospels and letters and eyewitness accounts, including a revelation from heaven. Every Christian for the next two thousand years will depend on what they write to know what to believe and what to reject. Lead them into all truth."

You see what Jesus is asking the Father to give them. Ten verses later, Jesus asks His Father to "teach you all things, and bring all things to your remembrance, whatsoever I have said unto you" (v. 26). Jesus asks that not even a membrane will separate the words that the apostles write from the words that the Spirit says. What Paul writes, the Spirit says; what the Spirit says, the apostles write. That will be so because Jesus has asked His Father that it might be so. The most reliable advocate for Jesus is the Spirit, the Counselor, the Spirit of truth.

Jesus then asks His Father to send the Spirit of truth to select sinners in the world to convict them of all the follies and falsehoods they have believed throughout their lives. He asks for them to come from ignorance to the truth. So He asks the Spirit to urge them to read the Bible and to help them understand it. He asks the Spirit to bring them to a church where the Bible is taught. "Illuminate their understanding," Jesus says to the Spirit. "Give them inner knowledge and assurance that I am the truth."

Finally, Jesus prays for a preacher who will be so fired up by the truth that he will preach Christ in the power and inspiration of the Holy Spirit, when the Spirit is sent down from heaven in Jerusalem at Pentecost. Under that preaching and the preaching of other Spirit-led preachers, people all over the world may come to love and serve Christ by the power of His Spirit.

CHAPTER NINE

The Spirit Convicts the World of Its Guilt

Nevertheless I tell you the truth; it is expedient for you that I go away:
for if I go not away, the Comforter will not come unto you; but if I depart,
I will send him unto you. And when he is come, he will reprove the world
of sin, and of righteousness, and of judgment: of sin, because they believe
not on me; of righteousness, because I go to my Father, and ye see me no
more; of judgment, because the prince of this world is judged.
—John 16:7–11

Jesus' words to His disciples in John 16:7–11 are critical for us to understand how the Holy Spirit works in the world. In former verses, Jesus
promised to send His Spirit to His disciples to lead them into truth and
to magnify Christ by taking the things of Christ and glorifying them.
By the grace of the Spirit, believers may also participate in this work, but
now we ask, specifically what does the Spirit do in the world and how are
we to work alongside Him?

No doubt the Spirit continues to do what He did in the Old Testament
in gifting individuals of all faiths and ideologies with intelligence and
creative skills. All people are made in the image and likeness of God, and
to each the Spirit displays His goodness. Our God also works through the
powers that be and so restrains lawbreakers while supporting lawkeep-
ers. We also know the Spirit gives to people everywhere enlightenment,
a taste of the heavenly gift—a share in Himself and a taste for the Word
of God—and the powers of the coming age (Heb. 6:4–6). This work of the
Holy Spirit continues in all who are touched, however remotely, by the
gospel of Jesus Christ. However, the main activity of the Holy Ghost in
the world, as our text says, is to convict the world of guilt regarding sin,
righteousness, and judgment.

GOD'S INTEREST IN THE WORLD

The gospel of John often draws our attention to God's interest in the world. We read in John 3:16, one of the best-known texts in Scripture, that God the Father so loved the world that he gave His only begotten Son so that whoever believes in Him should not perish but have everlasting life. God did not send His Son into the world to condemn the world but that the world through Him might be saved. So God the Father is vitally interested in the world.

Likewise the gospel of John draws our attention to the activity of Christ in the world. The witness of John the Baptist was to announce the arrival of Christ, saying, "Behold the Lamb of God, which taketh away the sin of the world" (John 1:29). In the first epistle of John we also read that Jesus Christ is the propitiation, not only for our sin but for the sin of the whole world. Thus both Father and Son are interested in what Scripture calls "'the world."

Now John 16:8 draws our attention to the activity of God the Holy Spirit, saying, "When he is come, he will reprove the world of sin, and of righteousness, and of judgment." Jesus is telling His disciples that the day is soon coming when the Holy Spirit will move beyond the geographical confines of Israel to work among people all over the world. The wall of partition that strictly forbad any Gentile from access to God in the temple will be broken down by the saving work of Christ. At Pentecost, the Holy Spirit of God will move out of Jerusalem to Samaria and Judea and to the uttermost parts of the world. Wherever He goes, the Spirit will convict the world of guilt regarding sin and righteousness and judgment.

Convicting people of sin is the primary work of the Holy Spirit in the world, for if He did not do this, the world would remain unconvicted of sin. The mark of the Holy Spirit at work in a congregation is not how many people worship at a church or the length of its meetings or the number of programs it offers. Rather, what counts most is a congregation's conviction of its unworthiness.

Jesus begins the Sermon on the Mount by saying, "Blessed are the poor in spirit: for theirs is the kingdom of heaven. Blessed are they that mourn: for they shall be comforted" (Matt. 5:3–4). He is speaking here, too, of the convicting work of the Spirit. The Holy Spirit will use sin, righteousness, and judgment to convict the world, for the highest interest of Christ's kingdom is to deliver sinners from their guilt and lostness. James Montgomery Boice says John 16:8 is "the greatest statement of the Spirit's work of conviction and regeneration in the entire Bible and a ground of real encouragement to us, as it undoubtedly was to the apostles."[1]

WHY CONVICTION OF SIN IS NECESSARY

How important are sin and righteousness and judgment to you? To what extent are these matters central to your thinking? If these truths are not central in your thoughts, you are not thinking God's thoughts, and if you are not thinking God's thoughts, ungodliness has taken possession of your minds and interests. Let each preacher ask how much sin, righteousness, and judgment occupy his sermons, thoughts, and practice. How much are preachers concerned about convicting men and women of the sin of unbelief?

Apart from this work of the Holy Spirit, fallen human beings will never come to terms with the truth of their state before Almighty God. What else will make a proud, self-sufficient man turn around to acknowledge his own guilt and shame, confessing that his only hope of mercy and eternal life is through the saving work of his Lord Jesus Christ? That is our desire for every person we meet. Yet our failures in evangelism convince us that only when the Holy Spirit is at work in a person will that person respond to the Word of God. Only with the Spirit's help will a person face up to sin, righteousness, and judgment. Only when convicted by the Spirit will he cease being a mere member of the world and enter into the kingdom of God. True evangelism is a sovereign, divine work that only the Holy Spirit can accomplish.

The Son of God tells His disciples in the upper room that when the Holy Spirit comes, He will convict sinners. You will know the Holy Spirit is present when you see people being convicted of sin. This activity of the Spirit is in accord with His work as a counselor of the law. In a court of law, a man is on trial. A prosecutor has the duty of convicting a criminal of wrongdoing. He brings forward evidence to prove the man guilty. He brings the truth to light, showing precisely what this man has been doing.

Likewise, the Holy Spirit acts as a counselor of the law in convicting the world of sin. He brings a sentence of condemnation upon the world so that people's carelessness and indifference give way under the evidentiary weight of guilt. His concern is not to stroke the affections of moral

---

1. James Montgomery Boice, *The Gospel of John* (Grand Rapids: Baker Books), 4:289.

and righteous people to make them feel good about themselves, but to deal with guilty men and women, convicting them of their sin, righteousness, and judgment. This is the first necessary step in their spiritual life, for only the sick will ask for a physician.

WHAT SIN IS

If you ask a worldly person what sin is, he might say it is murder, stealing, incest, or some other wrongs that are reported day after day in the news. Certainly such foul deeds are sin, but as long as a person knows he is not guilty of such activity he may never consider himself to be a sinner. Many people invariably think of sin in terms of horrid outward manifestations. God, however, has a far more rigorous standard. The Holy Spirit convicts men and women that sin also includes the following:

1. *Sin is missing the target.* Every person should aim at conformity to the law of God. Think of an experienced archer teaching a novice how to fire an arrow at a bull's-eye. The target God places before us is to love Him with all our heart, soul, mind, and strength, and to love our neighbors as ourselves. Scripture says every human being has missed the target. Everyone in the world has sinned and fallen short, not only of the law of God, but also of the glory of God. That's the standard. We haven't just missed the bull's-eye; our lives haven't even reached the target.

2. *Sin is trespassing the boundary.* Certain frontier posts mark the boundary of the kingdom of God. The first post says we are to have no gods except the true and living God. The second says we are not to make and serve idols. The third says that we are not to take God's name in vain. The fourth is that we are to remember the Sabbath and keep it holy. The fifth is that we are to honor our father and mother. The sixth is that we are not to do violence to anyone. The seventh forbids sexual sin. The eighth tells us to respect the private property of others and not to take what belongs to others. The ninth condemns lying, while the tenth tells us not to long for anything that belongs to our neighbor.

God has deeply planted those boundary markers, and no one may remove them. We are to live our lives within the space enclosed by these markers. Those who wander outside of these markers will be prosecuted by the Lord. Yet each of us wanders outside of these boundary markers quite deliberately day after day. Sometimes we crash through the barriers of God's laws into forbidden areas. Sometimes we slip back and forth across the lines. But whether or not we are caught, we are transgressing God's laws, and transgressing is sin.

3. *Sin is defiant unrighteousness.* Sin is disobedience. The great voice of our Creator that sounded in a time of early grace and was written in the Bible still echoes in every heart, saying, "My will is that husbands love their wives, wives obey their husbands, young people heed their parents, preachers preach these truths, and neighbors love one another." These are the Creator's orders for creatures who live and move and have their being in Him. Yet humans constantly respond in defiance to this Creation order: "No! We will not have this Lord rule over us."

4. *Sin is rebellious lawlessness.* Men and women are not meant to live on their own in this world. They were not created to say, "Well, this is what I think of God, and obeying Him is not the way I choose to have a good life." Such people are a law unto themselves, and the way they choose to live ends in chaos. We are meant not to live for ourselves but to serve God, finding our chief delight in loving Him with all our hearts.

THE HOLY SPIRIT CONVICTS US OF SIN

The Holy Spirit teaches sinners what sin is. His work is to convict them that they are sinners. He convinces me that my life has missed its target, my life has transgressed the boundary lines of God, my life has disobeyed the voice of God, and my life is lawless.

When God the Holy Spirit comes to a person and begins to work grace in him, his superficial assessment of standing righteous in God's sight vanishes. He sees that his problem is not with outward notorious sins because he is convicted by the Holy Spirit that sin is something inward. He is driven right down into the depths of his being until he sighs, "Lo, there too I find my sin." He sees the effects of sin, not just in his words and actions, but in his thoughts and ambitions, his desire and emotions, his aspirations and affections. Jesus says it is not what goes into the body through eating unclean foods that makes a person unclean but what comes out of man's heart that leads to greedy, cruel, lustful, destructive acts. The heart of the problem is the human heart. The problem is not that human actions have missed their target; it is that the human heart is rebelling against its Creator. When the Holy Spirit convicts a sinner of that, it is a most glorious lesson.

Some of the Ten Commandments are found in other religious codes. But the tenth commandment, "Thou shalt not covet," is peculiar to Scripture. The tenth commandment condemns yearning for something or someone belonging to somebody else. The Word of God does not look simply at what we say or what we do; it goes right down to the wellsprings of human behavior and condemns our aching itch for what belongs to another. It says covetousness is sin.

Coveting might never lead to sinful words or sinful behavior, but the sinful desire for what cannot be ours as well as the envy we feel toward the possessions of others is sin. It may never register itself by a flicker of disapproval on our face, yet the desire itself is sin. Sin is not just action or word; it is also wrongful thinking or desire that is entertained in our hearts. We are too inclined to think that as long as we can keep the lid on sin, we do not sin. But the New Testament says that the very desire to sin is sin because sin is something inward.

Think of what Jesus says about the sixth commandment, "Thou shalt not kill." He tells His disciples that the commandment doesn't simply mean that they should not assault a person physically and violently. It does not just refer to muggings and assaults on a wife and children. It does not just condemn manslaughter or suicide bombings or abortion or euthanasia. While all of those actions are sin, the sixth commandment also forbids hatred, anger, and spite. We may keep the cover on a well of contempt, yet that does not excuse the core of contempt that burns within us. The constraints of respectability, the desire for a good image, and outward obedience to the law may prevent us from an outburst of violent words and deeds. Yet Christ says merely hating someone is a sin.

Jesus does the same thing with the law condemning adultery. The commandment does not just condemn the act of adultery, but also the unlawful desires of lust and sinful longing. Lust may not express itself in actions or word, yet savoring and receiving such attitudes in our hearts is sin. Sin is not simply a matter of words and actions; it is also what lies in the depths of our hearts.

All of us are guilty of such sin. You see that depravity particularly clearly in children. They may lack the physical strength to express their sin in actions, but their constant cries for attention and complaints reveal their depravity. Their heart constantly craves, "More, more, and more," when they quickly discard the new toys they received at Christmas and long for the gifts a brother or cousin has received. A heart that is angry, hateful, discontented, and dissatisfied is the chief problem of every person. Think of the frequent complaints, the demands for attention, and the petty quarrels of elderly people in a nursing home. Even old people must be convicted of sin by the Holy Spirit and confess those sins before God.

In particular, the Holy Spirit has to convict men and women of the sin of rejecting Christ. The blameless life of Jesus, His superb teaching, His extraordinary miracles of healing, His rule over winds and waves, and even His raising people from the dead are so powerful, yet so many people of the world respond, "We're not persuaded that this all happened. We don't see that Jesus was God. I wish it were possible to be certain about this." Christ is the supreme manifestation of God, the brightness of God's glory, and the express image of His person. Yet people who met Him in person said, "This man is a sinner." They rejected Him and His claims. Their attitude was as abhorrent as a husband who after twenty years of marriage turns against his wife, saying she has never loved him. That is wicked unbelief.

THE HOLY SPIRIT CONVICTS US OF RIGHTEOUSNESS

People do not truly know what righteousness is unless the Holy Spirit convicts them of it. A man I know had been a student at the university where he was persuasively witnessed to by Christian students. One day he went back to his room under deep conviction and cried out to God, saying, "O Lord, make me a righteous man." The Holy Spirit made him conscious of righteousness for the first time in his life.

The Old Testament tells us often about the pervasive hostility of His people to righteousness. God sent a procession of righteous men to speak to the Jews, including Noah, Abraham, Moses, Elijah, and Jeremiah. Did people put these prophets on a pedestal crying, "All our lives we've been looking for men of integrity, and now, at last we have found them"?

No. The Bible tells us God's people despised these men, considering them extremists, fanatics, and troublemakers. We are told in Hebrews 11 that righteous men and women were tortured. Some faced jeers and flogging, while others were chained and put in prison. They were stoned, sawn in two, and put to death by the sword. They went about in sheepskins and goatskins. They were destitute, persecuted, and ill-treated. They wandered in deserts, mountains, caves, and holes in the ground (Heb. 11:35–38). The world was not worthy of these prophets, yet the world did not appreciate righteous men. It might have felt sorry for them and pitied them, but it also might have killed them.

When the Son of God came into this world, people treated Him exactly as they had treated the prophets before Him. Though He was the most righteous man the world has ever seen, the world refused to accept that truth. Some said Jesus was Beelzebub, and others that He had a demon. Some said that according to God's laws, Jesus should be declared guilty of blasphemy and sentenced to death.

John Murray once talked about two preachers in Scotland. One said in his afternoon sermon that if virtue should come down from heaven, the whole world would bow down to it. In the evening, the other preacher said that virtue *had* come down from heaven, and the world crucified Him. That is the world's judgment of Christ's righteousness.

How different was God the Father's view of His Son. He said after Jesus' baptism: "This is my beloved Son and in him I am well pleased." Twice God spoke from heaven to affirm His acclamation of Jesus as the righteous man. And though men found Jesus guilty and put Him to death, God raised Him from the dead after three days. The world said Christ was unrighteous, but God exalted Him to His right hand and endued Him with power. God gave Him a name above every name. The world may have crucified Christ, but God exalted Him. The world declared Him unrighteous, but God called Him "the righteous one." The world denied the holy and just one, but God raised Him from the dead. God vindicated Jesus in His resurrection as a complete reversal of the world's judgment.

The Holy Spirit's task is to change the verdict of the world and convict people of Jesus' righteousness. God raised Jesus from the dead. The tomb was empty; the body was not there. The grave clothes were there, but the stone was rolled away and the body gone. Who took Jesus' body? His followers came to the tomb to embalm Jesus' body and sweeten it before the rot of death set in. His enemies put an armed guard at the grave to prevent anyone from stealing Jesus' body, but the corpse disappeared from the sealed tomb.

After His resurrection, Jesus appeared for forty days in all kinds of places to individuals and crowds of men and women. First, He revealed

Himself to the women in the garden, then to the twelve disciples in the upper room; then on the road to Emmaus to two disciples, and then to Peter. He revealed Himself to the disciples at the Sea of Galilee as they were fishing and prepared them bread and fish to eat. He appeared to five hundred people who had gathered to see Him. Then He said good-bye to His disciples as He rose into the air and lifted His arms in blessing until a cloud hid Him from their sight. They were not to expect to see Him again. Instead, they were to go on doing the work He had given them to exalt Him as the glorious Savior by the power of the Holy Spirit.

Jesus rose on the third day to live in the power of an endless life. He who once died now lives forever. That was the testimony of the disciples from the day of Pentecost on. God loved His righteous Son and exalted Him by raising Him from the dead. This was incarnate righteousness. The life of Jesus Christ is the only truly righteous life this world has ever seen, and the proof of it is that Jesus has gone to the Father.

After Peter and John healed the crippled man at the temple, Peter said to the people who were watching, "But ye denied the Holy One and the Just, and desired a murderer to be granted unto you; and killed the Prince of life, whom God hath raised from the dead; whereof we are witnesses" (Acts 3:14–15). The Holy Spirit gives that conviction to His people. Jesus is now with the Father in glory. All the preaching in Acts from Pentecost on centers on the glorious exaltation of the Lord Jesus. He is the righteous one.

THE HOLY SPIRIT CONVICTS THE WORLD OF JUDGMENT

After Jesus' death and resurrection, the Holy Spirit set out to reverse the evaluation that all fallen creatures had made of Christ. The first judgment that He turned around was people's view of themselves as decent people. The Holy Spirit comes and writes on favored hearts that they are sinners under condemnation because they have rejected Christ, who is the Son of God.

The second judgment is the world's evaluation of Christ as poor, defeated, and dead. The Holy Spirit reverses that judgment by convincing people that Jesus' dust is not buried somewhere under the Syrian sky. He has risen from the dead. Jesus is more powerful than death. He is the righteous one who is now hidden from the eyes of people because He has been exalted to the right hand of God in heaven.

Third, the Holy Spirit reveals Satan's slander about Christ. The deceitfulness of the Prince of Darkness put Jesus Christ on the cross. The crucifixion of Jesus Christ was the arch crime of human history, perpetuated by the enemies of truth. The Holy Spirit accomplishes the reversal of this crime by revealing to the world that Satan is the one who was actually condemned by Jesus' death. Yes, men condemned Jesus; both the highest court of the Jews as well as the representatives of Caesar judged Christ worthy of death, but God, the mighty judge of all, became the praise of Jesus, for in Christ's death God was reconciling the world to Himself. God actually delivered our Lord to Jews and Gentiles for crucifixion, for Christ's death was ordained by the determinate counsel and foreknowledge of God. The crucifixion of the Son of God, the greatest sin this world has ever known, was perpetrated by forces that hate the truth. But when this happened, God opened wide the lid on hell, and out came all the hosts of hell to rejoice that the Holy One had been crucified.

The most important event in the history of the universe was the judgment of the cross. Jesus was crucified outside the city walls of Jerusalem on a spot where a degree of latitude crosses a degree of longitude, in calendar history, under the noses of the representative of Rome and witnessed by the Jewish chief priests, yet all of them were utterly oblivious to what was truly happening. True, a dying thief was given grace to realize who was being crucified. But most others did not see that the Prince of this World did not emerge from the crucifixion as a triumphant victor but as a condemned and defeated one.

The Son of God took everything the devil could fling at Him, yet all during His time on the cross Jesus displayed superior power and grace. The devil with all his cronies thought he was making a public spectacle of Jesus on Calvary, but the very reverse happened. In His suffering and death, Jesus was disarming the devil's principalities and rulers. He was making "a shew of them openly, triumphing over them in it" (Col. 2:15).

The demonic powers saw themselves as a mighty army that had subdued the Gentile world. They reigned over a kingdom of darkness in which men worshiped idols of gold and stone and wood shaped as men or four-footed beasts. People everywhere were bowing before the sun and moon and stars. They were offering human sacrifices to their handmade deities.

On the cross Christ drew the forces of evil out of the darkness to Himself; He sucked them out of the caverns of the pit and made them turn all their weapons upon Him. What a disarming that was! The world had never seen such a victory and never would again. For Christ then proceeded to crush the serpent's head by rising alive and triumphant from the dead. No devil or death could contain Him. What's more, Christ then commissioned His little band of warriors to go forth into the world—the devil's former territory—and spread the reign of grace by preaching deliverance through the cross.

You might compare such a triumph to David's defeat of the giant Goliath or Gideon's handpicked men of three hundred who defeated the whole army of Midian. For twelve men were sent into all the nations of the world to conquer them by preaching the gospel of Christ. They were totally up to their task because King Jesus gave them these orders; "Be determined not to make known anything in your messages except Me, especially that I was crucified. Tell the gospel of the cross to the world, for then the One who is in you will be greater than the world."

These disciples had no long-range policies. They were not in a command room, looking at a giant map of the world to target countries and peoples. They founded no bishoprics, no Vatican, no universities. They built no prayer towers. They did not promise people money or property. They merely told people about Jesus Christ's life and teaching and royal victory on Calvary. We have no clear idea where most of the apostles went, but we do know they preached Christ with holy confidence, for they had been freed by the truth and were armed with the weapon of Christ crucified. What is more, the Holy Spirit enabled them to turn the world upside down with their preaching.

Soon light was shining everywhere in what had been a kingdom of darkness. No longer was the world the devil's sole sphere of influence, for people were now translated from that kingdom into the kingdom of God. The Holy Spirit thus convicts the world of the judgment of Satan and persuades men and women of the great victory of Jesus Christ. That conviction comes to life in the hearts and minds of all who come to Him.

The work Christ did on the cross is the crucial turning point in the history of redemption. It is the pivotal mark of the defeat of the prince of this world and the beginning of the plundering of the kingdom of darkness by the servants of Jesus. Yet there is an immense urgency to continue this battle against evil. So wake up to any false judgment you've made about Christ, because that is the devil's own judgment of Jesus. Know that the devil's lies have been exposed. The devil has been defeated and moves around today, dragging his chains. Whenever Satan oversteps the mark or gets too close to a new believer, King Jesus yanks the chains to rein Satan in.

Do not lose heart. Consider what Don Carson says: "I would quit all forms of Christian ministry immediately if I were not convinced that the Lord Jesus is building his church; that the Father has given over a people to his Son; and that the blessed Holy Spirit is working in the world to convict it of its sin, of righteousness and judgment."[2]

If the work of the Spirit is to bring the world to conviction of sin, let us be coworkers with the Spirit. Let us abandon every ploy to make people think they are safe, every device of the professing church, whether by sumptuous ritual or psychological manipulation or enhancing the feel-good factor of religiosity, to tell people they are Christians. We should have no interest whatsoever in making people religious. People's religions are their worst crimes. Rather, our intent should be to do what the Holy Spirit does by His power and under His blessing, which is to bring people to a conviction of sin and righteousness and judgment.

Of course we must do that tenderly. We do not yell at people but are faithful to the fellowship of the Spirit in bringing the Spirit's verdict to bear on their lives. Those lives are utterly wrong about sin and righteousness and judgment. As Scripture says, there is none righteous, no not one; all have sinned and come short of the glory of God. That is what we must tell people so they may, under the conviction of the Holy Spirit, become ready for redemption in Christ alone. Our responsibility by the cross of Christ and the power of the Spirit is to plant conviction in the hearts of people of their lostness and Christ's loveliness, which can be theirs for eternity.

---

2. Carson, *Jesus and His Friends*, 145.

CHAPTER TEN

Preparing for Pentecost

Then the same day at evening, being the first day of the week, when the doors were shut where the disciples were assembled for fear of the Jews, came Jesus and stood in the midst, and saith unto them, Peace be unto you. And when he had so said, he shewed unto them his hands and his side. Then were the disciples glad, when they saw the LORD. Then said Jesus to them again, Peace be unto you: as my Father hath sent me, even so send I you. And when he had said this, he breathed on them, and saith unto them, Receive ye the Holy Ghost: whose soever sins ye remit, they are remitted unto them; and whose soever sins ye retain, they are retained.
—John 20:19–23

Pentecost, as recorded in Acts 2, is the climax of the Holy Spirit's ministry in the Bible. All the teaching on the Holy Spirit prior to this prepares us for Pentecost, and everything that follows is made possible because of Pentecost. This event is as significant as the incarnation, crucifixion, and resurrection of God the Son. Let us now look at the gospel of John to see how it leads up to the day of Pentecost.

In John 20:19–23, the risen Jesus appears to His disciples. God the Father has vindicated and given a name above every name to the one whom people have judged to be a criminal worthy of crucifixion. He has risen from the dead. And now on the first day of the week, Jesus appears to His disciples, saying, "Peace be with you!" He tells them that as God the Father has sent His Son to the world, He is now sending His disciples. Then He breathes on His disciples, saying, "Receive ye the Holy Ghost: whose soever sins ye remit, they are remitted unto them; and whose soever sins ye retain, they are retained" (John 20:22–23).

Jesus of Nazareth stands before us as the conqueror of the grave. He has proved to be more powerful than death and is now in the upper room, as He promised, to baptize every believer with the Holy Spirit. Three years earlier, John the Baptist baptized Jesus, after which the Holy Spirit descended on Him as a dove. And the night before His crucifixion, Jesus told the disciples that He would soon give them the Holy Paraclete.

Now the resurrected Christ is about to send His disciples into the world, just as the Father sent His Son into the world thirty-three years earlier. Jesus' work of humiliation is over, but the work of His disciples is just beginning. They are to about confront an indifferent and hostile world with the gospel of forgiveness.

PREPARING FOR PENTECOST

The Lord Jesus does something He has never done before. After speaking, He blows air from His lungs upon His disciples. In that act He visibly and audibly demonstrates His authority to give them the Holy Spirit. He also shows them the provision He will make for them to do what He commands.

But what exactly is going on here? Is this a pre-Pentecost Pentecost? Certainly the apostles are spiritually strengthened every time they meet the risen Christ. They are encouraged by this confirmation that Jesus Christ has risen from the dead. Each time they meet the risen Christ, the disciples understand more about Him, His victory over the grave, and the meaning of His death, for the risen Christ continues to answer their questions and minister to them.

You see the contrast between the disciples who meet with the risen Christ and those, such as Thomas, who miss the event. The disciples say to Thomas, "We have seen the LORD" (v. 25), but since he has missed the occasion, Thomas is full of doubts. So Christ's appearance and His breathing upon His disciples is a wonderfully strengthening event. Yet we cannot say that this breathing out regenerated the disciples. That cannot possibly be what Jesus is doing here, for a number of reasons.

1. Not all of the disciples were present. The risen Jesus has met with individuals or small groups of disciples, such as Cleopas and his companion on the road to Emmaus, Mary Magdalene in the garden, and His half-brother James. On some occasions, He has met with some of His disciples while others were absent. So it wouldn't be suitable at this time for Jesus to give the regenerating Spirit to some of the disciples and not to others.

He does impose some order on their coming and going by telling them not to break up and go off in all directions but to stick together in Jerusalem, where they are to wait for the Spirit. So it is significant that the account of the day of Pentecost begins by saying all the disciples were together in one place. No one was off somewhere else. Thus no one fails to receive the Holy Spirit when He is poured out on Pentecost.

2. These disciples were already regenerated. This divine breathing could not be regeneration because Jesus has already told His disciples that they have been made clean (John 13:10). In other words, they have already been washed and cleansed from the guilt and defilement of sin. All except Judas have experienced the internal purifying work of the Holy Spirit. Jesus does not need to give them the Holy Spirit again for them to receive life from heaven. They already have that life because they have been given inward illumination to confess Jesus as Christ, Son of the living God; they have already confessed Him before men by preaching and healing in His name.

3. Jesus is preparing the disciples for ministry. In breathing upon His disciples, Jesus is confirming His words "As my Father hath sent me, even so send I you" (v. 21). This group of young and relatively inexperienced men will be sent into a hostile world, but how can they possibly stand before thousands of people and preach to them? In light of that seeming impossibility, verse 22 tells us: "And when he had said this, he breathed on them, and saith unto them, Receive ye the Holy Ghost."

In other words, Jesus is assuring His disciples that He will prepare them for ministry. He will give them the Spirit so they may serve Him by making known the good news of Jesus. They need His help for the work that lies ahead. They will so need Him that they will daily cry out, "Breathe on me breath of God, fill me with life anew."

The disciples are about to go to all parts of the world to assure people everywhere that if they entrust themselves to the Lord Jesus Christ, their sins will be forgiven. Every day they will say this with the wonder of hearing it themselves for the first time. Their words must never grow stale, so they will daily need the Lord Jesus' breath upon them. He must provide them with the personal spiritual resources of discernment, energy, and authority to preach so that they might evangelize and disciple others.

4. *The Holy Spirit will come after Jesus' ascension.* The God-man Jesus cannot give His Spirit to the disciples until after He has ascended from earth to heaven, is welcomed by the Father, and is enthroned at God's right hand. That is God's order. Pentecost will happen in less than forty days.

So the upper room was not the place and a small group of disciples were not the people to whom the Savior King would reveal His glory. It was the place for a striking sign of that imminent event, but not for the reality. Jesus first had to ascend to heaven and be seated in the midst of the throne. There the God-man would pour the Spirit forth in a manner that would give Christ much glory in the world. Christ's breathing the Spirit upon the disciples in the upper room was only a sign of what was yet to come. He must ascend before sending the Spirit upon His disciples. Jesus makes that clear in John 7:39, saying, "For the Holy Ghost was not yet given; because that Jesus was not yet glorified."

This breathing on the disciples is a visual sign of prophecy, just as some of the acts of Jeremiah the prophet were visual confirmation of his words. At one time Jeremiah warned Jerusalem that she would be destroyed. God then told the prophet to give a sign to confirm that prophecy. Jeremiah was to take his linen belt and bury it, then later to recover it. By that time, the linen belt would be utterly ruined. So the word of judgment on Jerusalem was confirmed by a linen belt that was ruined, much like the nation of Judah and the city of Jerusalem would be ruined.

In the upper room Jesus blew His breath upon His disciples, thereby giving them a sign that He would surely give them His Spirit to prepare them for the work that lay before them. That is the bridge from the end of the gospel of John to Pentecost. We now come to Acts 2.

THE SPIRIT'S OUTPOURING AT PENTECOST

Pentecost is celebrated by the Jews fifty days after Passover, which is the day on which Jesus was crucified. For forty days, the risen Jesus met with His disciples, then ascended to heaven. Before rising to heaven, Jesus told His disciples to wait in Jerusalem, promising, "Ye shall be baptized with the Holy Ghost not many days hence" (Acts 1:5). Why did God make the disciples wait so long? The sovereign God often tests our obedience by making us wait. But mere sovereignty is not the reason why God made the church wait for ten more days in Jerusalem. Let me suggest some other reasons for the delay.

1. The ascended Christ needed to be glorified in heaven. A person who had never before been seen in heaven was now ruling over it. The body of a glorified man, a God-man, was now seated on the throne in the center of heaven to dominate heaven and earth. Before that time, God was surrounded by angels (all spirits), the spirits of just men made perfect, the redeemed people of God waiting for the day of resurrection, and men such as Enoch and Elijah who did not die before passing from earth to heaven. But now in the midst of the throne was a man who was also God the Son.

Of course, as the eternal Son of God, Jesus had been in the midst of the throne from all eternity. Then, for thirty-three years His divine nature was joined to a human nature in the womb of Mary, not temporarily but forever. This God-man was a real man with wounds still gaping wide, yet He was now being glorified, and all that His Father could do to make Him radiate with the divine beauties of heaven would be done. So the Father says to the Son, "Sit at my right hand right until the end of this age—until I will make your enemies your footstool" (see Psalm 2).

It was right and becoming that ten days passed before Jesus' Spirit was poured out upon His disciples, for the Father wanted time to express His profound delight in the return of His Son to glory. He wanted time for Jesus' blessed enthronement at the heart of heaven and for Father, Son, and Spirit to rejoice at being united once more.

God would not be rushed. A thousand years is as a day to God, but God did not make the church wait for a thousand years before giving Jesus the right to send forth the promised Holy Spirit at Pentecost. The three members of the Godhead took ten days to experience the joy of inter-Trinitarian fellowship. It was a time of joy that Christ had anticipated and had sustained Him in His humiliation. In ten days of delight, the Father showed all of heaven's love to the Son, and Jesus displayed His love as God-man to the Father and the Holy Spirit. All of heaven welcomed the Son of God back from humiliation, suffering, and death on a cross.

2. The Spirit would be poured out on Pentecost. The Feast of Pentecost was a Jewish holiday. It was one of three feasts on which the faithful were summoned to go on pilgrimage to Jerusalem. Josephus, the Jewish historian who lived at this time, tells us the city of Jerusalem, with a normal population of 150,000 people, often swelled to more than a million people during Pentecost. The suburbs were also crammed with people. So were the hills surrounding Jerusalem, on which people were camped.

Great crowds of people came together during the Feast of Pentecost. Far more people were in the city than had ever heard the Lord Jesus speak. Is it any wonder, then, that Christ chose this time to send forth the Holy Spirit? "You will do greater things than I did," He said to His disciples, partly meaning that they would speak to more people at Pentecost in Jerusalem and all over the world than Christ Himself had done.

But something else was significant about the Feast of Pentecost, which Jews referred to as the Feast of Weeks (seven weeks since Passover), or the Feast of Harvest, which was when believers offered the first fruits of harvest to God. At this harvest celebration, the Spirit of God would be poured out, in effect saying, "See here, in a single day, three thousand people will be gathered into God's garner. They will be the first fruits of a glorious new harvest that will be gathered from all over the world. These first fruits are a sign of the time when the whole earth will be filled with the glory of the Lord." The Holy Spirit's work at Pentecost is one of many harvests that will occur in the thousands of years to come.

Harvests in the Bible are always joyful days, and Pentecost, which followed the sober feast of Passover, was also a time of happiness. Indeed, God commanded His people to rejoice at this time, saying, "And thou shalt keep the feast of weeks unto the LORD thy God.... Thou shalt rejoice before the LORD thy God" (Deut. 16:10–11). People gave each other presents at this feast. Gifts were given to children, servants, the fatherless, and widows. Pentecost was a day to look forward to.

What joyful day on the Jewish calendar could be more appropriate than Pentecost for the outpouring of God's Spirit? God, who had given His Son to mankind, now gave His Spirit to all classes of people, whether old or young, manservants or womanservants, Jew or Gentile believers. This great gift was received with holy joy because possessing it meant everlasting life, salvation from death, and proof of obtaining heaven itself, for it is the down payment on being with God forever. So the Holy Spirit was poured out on Pentecost.

3. The Spirit of God was poured out on the new Sabbath. The Spirit of God was poured out at 9:00 a.m., the day after the old Sabbath. The old Sabbath, celebrated on the seventh day of the week, was the sign of the old covenant, but the Spirit came down on the church on the first day of the week as a sign of the new covenant. What the Old Testament believers longed for had now come. The day of Pentecost had arrived.

Scripture does not dwell on the outpouring of the Spirit on the Lord's Day, but I think it is encouraging to consider that gospel churches not only celebrate a weekly Easter to commemorate the resurrection of our Savior but also to celebrate Pentecost, which was the day the Spirit of God was poured out on God's people, who then became the fellowship of the Spirit. When we meet together for worship on Sunday, we are saying, "By myself I could not cope with the next six days without the Holy Spirit's help to live a Christ-honoring life. Pour out your Spirit on me again, dear Lord." We remember that on the first day of the week Christ filled the people of God with the Spirit, so on the first day of the week we also ask Him to fill us so that we may serve others in the power of the Holy Spirit.

THE COMINGS OF THE HOLY SPIRIT AND OF CHRIST

There are many parallels between the advent of God the Son and the advent of God the Holy Spirit. They include the following:

1. Both were accompanied by miraculous signs. Both God the Son and God the Holy Spirit came from heaven, and both events were accompanied by mighty signs. When the Son was born in Bethlehem, the archangel appeared in the heavens and spoke to shepherds announcing the Messiah's birth. Luke 2:9–10 tells us, "And, lo, the angel of the Lord came upon them, and the glory of the Lord shone round about them: and they were sore afraid. And the angel said unto them, Fear not: for, behold, I bring you good tidings of great joy, which shall be to all people." The starry skies around the stable were filled with millions of angels. Likewise, the arrival of the Holy Spirit was accompanied by supernatural signs, such as the sound of a mighty rushing wind, cloven tongues of fire appearing on the heads of the disciples, and their sudden ability to speak in foreign languages so they could tell people all over the world about the mighty works of God.

2. Both events were anticipated. These two comings were not unexpected events. The coming of the Messiah was predicted by psalmists and prophets, who said this Mighty One would bruise Satan's head and be bruised for our sins. The prophets Joel and Ezekiel predicted the outpouring of the Holy Spirit. Then, too, heralds such as John the Baptist spoke of the imminent arrival of the Son of God, and Jesus Himself spoke of the arrival of the Spirit "not many days hence."

3. The timing of both was perfect. Scripture tells us that when the fullness of time had come, God sent forth His Son. Likewise, when the day of Pentecost had fully come, God sent forth His Spirit. Miraculous signs from heaven accompanied both of these events. A new, vibrant star hung over the place where the young child Jesus lived with His parents, and a rushing mighty wind filled the house where the Spirit was poured out.

4. They both came to benefit believers. The Son of God came to the earth as the Incarnate One when the eternal Word became flesh. Likewise, the Spirit of God came to earth to become incarnate in the redeemed people of God; He took up His abode in people, while the Son of God lived among people.

5. Their arrival threatened unbelievers. The arrival of both God the Son and God the Holy Spirit caused great anxiety and perplexity in the unbelieving world. When Christ was born in Bethlehem, King Herod and all Jerusalem were troubled. Likewise, when the Holy Spirit came to Jerusalem, Scripture tells us, "a multitude came together, and were confounded" (Acts 2:6). When Christ came to the world, He was rejected and unappreciated. So also the Spirit's arrival was met with disbelief. People could not accept Him as the third member of the Godhead because they neither saw Him or knew Him (John 14:17).

6. Their roles were much alike. The Son honors the Father in all the Son does. Likewise, the Spirit glorifies Christ in all the Spirit does. The Father says to people about His Son, "Listen to Him." And the Son says to men about the Spirit, "He that hath an ear, let him hear what the Spirit saith unto the churches" (Rev. 2:7). "Listen to the Son," says the Father. "Listen to the Spirit," says the Son.

So there are many similarities in the arrivals of both God the Son and Spirit in the world. Surely this is to be expected because both are equal in power and glory as divine persons of the Godhead.

WHAT THE SPIRIT DID AT PENTECOST

Let us look more deeply at the arrival of the Spirit at Pentecost. Why did this extraordinary event happen? What did God intend to accomplish by sending the Holy Spirit upon believers at Pentecost? I suggest three main reasons for this coming:

1. *The Spirit testified of the glorious exaltation of Christ.* Pentecost was a seal of God's delight in His holy Son. It was proof of God's pleasure in everything that Jesus of Nazareth accomplished. It was a declaration to the world that God had accepted the finished work of Christ; redemption had been accomplished, and now its cosmic application had begun. It was proof that Jesus Christ had received from His Father the authority to bestow the Holy Spirit on the church.

Prior to this, the name of Jesus of Nazareth was cursed in Jerusalem. He was despised, rejected of men, and crucified. Jews and Romans stood together to condemn Him. Even His disciples forsook Him and fled from Him. His family had no understanding of who He was and what He was doing.

God did not send angels to restore Christ's reputation. He did not tell Peter to speak up and say a good word about Jesus. God Himself came to earth to do that. The Holy Spirit came to Jerusalem, where the religious leaders of the Jews had murdered God's Son. There He cut people to their hearts for what they had done. He so convicted them that they cried out in agony, "Men and brethren, what shall we do?" They were facing the God whose Son they had nailed to a cross. But in His infinite mercy, God saved three thousand Jerusalem sinners. That is how God vindicated His Son's name. Sinners fell before this Son, confessing Him as their Savior and Lord. At Pentecost, God the Spirit bore witness to the glorious exaltation of our Lord.

2. *The Spirit took Christ's place.* The Holy Spirit was the Paraclete Christ promised to send to His disciples. The Spirit had come to earth, just as Christ said, but the Spirit would not stay with the disciples for three years and then leave them. He would stay with and in them forever. Christ had ascended to heaven, but God had sent the Holy Spirit as His substitute. God had taken His Son to glory and had sent in His place the Spirit, who alone is equal to Him in power and majesty. When the man Jesus was on earth, He was confined to one place at one time. If He was

in Bethany, He could not be in Jerusalem. If He was on the Sea of Galilee, he could not be in the temple. The Holy Spirit has no such restrictions and so can be equally everywhere with each believer and at the heart of every gospel congregation.

Jesus once said, "I am come to send fire on the earth; and what will I, if it be already kindled? But I have a baptism to be baptized with; and how am I straitened till it be accomplished!" (Luke 12:49–50). The book of Acts tells us how the gospel spread through the world like a fire, leaping from one place to another. Throughout His life, our Lord gathered together a people for Himself. He prepared them so that when the risen Christ opened Scripture to travelers on the road to Emmaus, their hearts burst into flame. Everything was ready for fire to fall from heaven, where it was fanned by the wind and spread over all the earth. Jesus longed for that fire to fall so that His work of preparation could be fulfilled and be completed. On Pentecost, the Holy Spirit enflamed and blew upon the disciples to spread the gospel throughout the earth. No longer was Jesus distressed, for He was now sending forth His Spirit on Jerusalem and to the ends of the earth.

3. *The Spirit empowered Christ's servants.* The risen Christ commanded His disciples to stay in Jerusalem until they were clothed with power from on high (Luke 24:49). The Holy Spirit did that at Pentecost. He blessed the disciples with every spiritual blessing in Christ Jesus. They received the fruit of the Spirit to live like Christ. They received Him in a measure that was sufficient for any possible difficulty they would encounter. No problem, suffering, temptation, or challenge would be too great for them, for the Spirit had transformed and equipped them for every circumstance. God endued them with all glory and every privilege.

In moments of trial, they could not blame the Lord for their failures. They could not say He had failed to give them adequate resources, for He had given them the Holy Spirit. They were filled with that Spirit and blessed with every spiritual blessing in the heavenly places. Jesus once said to them, "Take no heed of what you shall speak." In other words, they should not torment themselves with anxious thoughts if they were thrown out of synagogues or were summoned to appear before magistrates who threatened their lives. Jesus said, "The Spirit will fill you again and again." And He did.

Was their experience true only of these handpicked disciples of Christ, not of ordinary, struggling Christians like us? Acts 2:4 tells us, "They were *all* filled with the Holy Ghost." This blessing pertained to the whole company of believers.

Was this group of people who gathered together on the day of Pentecost in one place simply a religious group of kindred spirits who belonged to the Christian church? No, they were the *entire* Christian church, who had gathered together to celebrate Pentecost and to await the coming of Christ's Spirit. This group of about 120 people were the seed from which the Christian church would grow. When our Lord poured out His Spirit on Pentecost, every person in this group received Christ's Spirit. As a consequence of Pentecost, every believer from that time forth would receive the gift of the Holy Spirit. That is the privilege of every Christian.

If you have not received the Spirit of Christ, you are not a true believer, for the Spirit came to bear witness to the exaltation of Christ, to take Christ's place, and to empower every one of Christ's servants.

CHAPTER ELEVEN

What Happened at Pentecost

And when the day of Pentecost was fully come, they were all with one accord in one place. And suddenly there came a sound from heaven as of a rushing mighty wind, and it filled all the house where they were sitting. And there appeared unto them cloven tongues like as of fire, and it sat upon each of them. And they were all filled with the Holy Ghost, and began to speak with other tongues, as the Spirit gave them utterance.
—Acts 2:1–4

People in Jerusalem on the day of Pentecost witnessed three supernatural events: the howling of a mighty wind, tongues of fire on the heads of disciples, and the sudden ability of the disciples to speak in many languages. Neither the exaltation of our Lord nor the actual coming of the Holy Spirit nor the preaching of Peter was as stunning as these miraculous events. The signs were not like peals of thunder giving a momentary shock to listeners, but were events that gripped their attention. Any one of these signs would have gotten attention, but the three of them together so stunned people that they asked in astonishment, "What meaneth this?" (v. 12).

It is quite legitimate to believe that the disciples were gathered in one of the porches of the temple at this time. It would have been a natural place for pilgrims to meet, since a house in Jerusalem would not have been large enough to contain 120 people. The "whole house" mentioned in verse 2 was likely the house of God, or the temple, in which many thousands of people pressed together to hear Peter explain the meaning of these miraculous signs.

The Spirit's arrival is majestic and public. There is no longer any need for secrecy about the Messiah. It would have been unthinkable for God the Holy Spirit to be sent by the risen Lord Jesus for the first time without humbling an entire community by the fearful reality of God. We usually define a mighty work of God as powerful preaching that results in the conviction of sin, the conversion of many people, and the fear of God falling upon unbelievers. The three signs in Acts 2 all testify to this. Wind and fire are dangerous phenomena, while speaking in multiple languages gives power. The howling of wind, flames of fire, and the sudden ability to speak in multiple languages said to the world, "Something divine, dynamic, and perilous has come upon people today. You are living in the supernatural world of the living God."

So let us consider the meaning of the signs, then the meaning of the event.

THE MEANING OF THE SIGNS

1. The howling wind. We recently watched a film of Hurricane Katrina hitting New Orleans. We saw people blown off their feet, trucks blown off the road, and roofs lifted off houses. Likewise, the sound of a violent wind blew against the believers gathered in Jerusalem. The wind was not from the north, the desert, or from the sea; it was from Jesus. The same person who had breathed on the disciples in the upper room was now blowing His Spirit from heaven upon His people.

Acts 2:2 tells us, "And suddenly there came a sound from heaven as of a rushing mighty wind, and it filled all the house where they were sitting." Scripture's first reference to the Spirit of God says this Spirit hovered over the waters that covered the whole world (Gen. 1:2). In that chaotic darkness, the Spirit was in control. Now that same Spirit appears in dark Jerusalem, which contained the house of God and whose citizens had crucified the Messiah.

Genesis 2 tells us that God formed man of the dust of the earth, then breathed into his nostrils the breath of life. Man then became a living creature. So, the God in control of creation, who gave life to our first parents, now breathes from heaven upon His people at Pentecost, giving them new life and power. As the body of Adam was given life by the breath of God, so the body of Christ, the church, is given new life by the breath of God.

You can experience a very powerful wind without hearing it, but at Pentecost the wind was howling! It blew against people who came running to the group of disciples with the dust of Herod's temple, lifting men's long flowing robes. It was neither a draft nor a breeze; it was a force-ten wind. People had never encountered a gale like this.

Normally a mighty wind disrupts and destroys, but this wind brought order. Many years before, the prophet Ezekiel watched a wind from heaven blow through a valley of dry bones. Before the coming of the wind, the bones of that valley were like an old box full of Legos, but after the wind from heaven blew, all the pieces were put together, clothed with sinews, covered with flesh, and became living people. That is what the wind of God can do. The living Lord who once addressed Job in a great wind (Job 38:1), was in the temple on Pentecost.

Wind is sovereign. We cannot command it to come on a hot day and cool our faces. It blows where it pleases. So this wind came suddenly, in God's time. There is nothing you can do to get God to send a wind from heaven. There is no formula, no regimen of activities, or rigorous self-denials that will bring gales from heaven. No, Scripture says the Lord will suddenly come to His temple. The heavenly nuptials celebrating the return of the Son to the bosom of Father and Spirit have ended. The Son has been enthroned and given all authority in heaven and earth. At that moment when the day of Pentecost has fully come, God the Son says to His Spirit, "Now go to the temple in Jerusalem." And the Spirit who cannot be manipulated by men, obeys.

2. Tongues of fire. The fire also came from heaven. Like the other signs, this fire did not come from the depths of people's subconsciousness. It did not come like an electric shock as they all held hands and prayed. The wind and fire and tongues came from beyond themselves. The believers had not stayed in Jerusalem pleading for a heavenly wind because they didn't know that a wind was coming. They didn't ask for fire because they didn't know a fire would rest on them, and they didn't beseech God for the gift of tongues. They were simply told to wait for Christ's Spirit. The signs of the Spirit came to them as pure sovereign grace. They were gifts.

So we are told that people saw "cloven tongues like as of fire, and it sat upon each of them" (v. 3). They looked at one another and saw 120 flickering flames of fire spreading from one to another and then resting on each one. They were not all standing together as if in the midst of a furnace, but individual cleft flames were resting on each person. Normally fire consumes and destroys, but this fire did not do that. Think of the three young men in Babylon who were cast into the burning fiery furnace, yet were not burned. They walked in the midst of those flames with the Son of God. Better yet, think of Moses seeing a bush in the desert that burned with fire but was not consumed. In this fire, God came to Moses, charging him to lead His people out of bondage in Egypt to the Promised Land.

Pentecost was the beginning of a new redemption; it was cosmic deliverance from the slavery of sin as well as stifling legalism in Israel. It offers a gospel that will save thousands of men and women and bring them into the glorious liberty of the people of God. So the church is given the life of God. The cloven tongues of fire say, "Do not be lukewarm, but be burning and shining lights for the Lord as John the Baptist was." The fire says, "The flames resting on you are shaped like a tongue so that you will speak up brightly for Jesus."

Fire is a suitable symbol of God because God is life. God has no need of some external life-support system to keep Him going. He never needs to check His fuel gauge or carry a reserve tank or refuel because His supplies are running out. Heaven's reservoir of gifts and graces are inexhaustible. Everyone else depends on other resources, but God is complete. In Him is life.

Fire is also a symbol of God's purity. God is a consuming fire. So Scripture warns us that it is a fearful thing to fall into the hands of the living God. When John the Baptist tells people that Jesus is coming, he warns that though John baptizes with water, Jesus will baptize with the Holy Spirit and with fire. If you are baptized by Christ, He won't simply rearrange the rooms of your heart, give them a lick of paint, or reposition some furniture. No, fire from heaven is coming to purify and purge us.

In *The Lion, the Witch and the Wardrobe* in the Chronicles of Narnia series, the children who come to Narnia ask whether Aslan the lion is safe. The response is, "Safe? No, he is not safe, but he is good." Holiness is dangerous, for it puts sinners in the hands of an angry God. As Malachi 3:2 says, "But who may abide the day of his coming? and who shall stand when he appeareth? for he is like a refiner's fire." Yet this holy flame is now resting on the people of God in the temple and they are safe. The heavenly baptism with the Spirit and fire does not destroy anything good in a believer, for Philippians 4:8 tells us, "Whatsoever things are true, whatsoever things are honest, whatsoever things are just, whatsoever things are pure, whatsoever things are lovely, whatsoever things are of good report," it will not be destroyed if you come to Jesus. You must bring everything to Him. He will then purify you of all your inner idols and the sin that so easily besets you. He will burn up the chaff with unquenchable fire.

When fire rests on the disciples, they are not consumed. It is because the fire of destruction for our sins has been taken away by Jesus. He has entered the lake of fire of all our trashy deeds and words. The wrath that our sins deserve consumed our Savior as He hung on the cross in our place. The holy Judge has borne the fires of condemnation and so exhausted them that the heavenly fire of the Spirit can now rest on us and we are safe. Every believer in Christ need not fear the wrath of a sin-hating God in the place of woe, for as Joseph Swain says:

> That wrath would have kindled a hell
> Of never-abating despair
> In millions of creatures, which fell
> On Jesus, and spent itself there.

So fire was another sign of God coming upon His people. It was another divine credential that these people were God's authorized spokesmen. The baptism of the Holy Spirit was a baptism of fire. The God who answers by fire is God. The Sadducees managed the Jerusalem temple for a couple of centuries, yet they never saw fire fall from heaven. They were too concerned about collecting temple taxes and cutting special deals with money-changers and selling animals for sacrifices. They turned the house of God into a robbers' den. They were as far from God as the prophets of Baal. No fire fell when they cried to their god. But the living Lord who sent fire on the sacrifice of his servant Elijah also sent fire on His servants in Jerusalem. Jesus Christ brought fire to earth. Thus the tongue of fire must be the perennial symbol of the Christian faith.

3. *The gift of languages.* We are told that disciples in Jerusalem "began to speak with other tongues, as the Spirit gave them utterance" (v. 4). The crowd of people who observed this miracle were so shaken that they cried out to one another, "And how hear we every man in our own tongue, wherein we were born?" (v. 8).

The disciples were not speaking some sort of ecstatic speech, or gibberish. Rather, the people who had traveled to Jerusalem from countries all over the Mediterranean basin discovered that they could understand what many of these disciples were saying as they gave thanks and glory to God. "They are speaking in my language," they said to fellow pilgrims. "Yes, and in mine too," said another.

The disciples were from the country area of Galilee. They weren't international businessmen, so they didn't speak the Greek of commerce. They could speak some Greek; Peter later wrote a couple of letters in very good Greek. But they didn't know the common language. Yet here they were, now praising and preaching in the minority languages of Parthia, Media, Elam, Cappadocia, Libya, and Crete. Fifteen language groups are mentioned in this chapter, from distant Iran to places west of Rome. Every language heard on the streets of Jerusalem at that time was spoken in the name of Jesus by the servants of God at Pentecost. The mighty works of the Lord were spoken in all the known languages of the world.

The wind from heaven was a sign. The cloven tongues of fire were a wonder. Speaking in languages they did not know before was a mighty work. There were all kinds of barriers in the ancient world, such as race, language, slavery, poverty, and discrimination against unwanted babies and women. The Holy Spirit came to break down those walls. Henceforth all who possessed the Spirit would be one in Christ Jesus.

In Genesis 11, God brought judgment upon the builders of the tower of Babel who thought they could reach God by erecting this tower. They thought they could destroy the difference between Creator and creature. But God judged their arrogance by taking away their common language. Suddenly, no person could understand another. They looked at one another in fear and consternation because they could not make themselves understood. They could not understand what others were saying. So building on the tower ceased.

Likewise, the spread of Greek and Latin failed to bring unity to the divided world at the time Christ was born into the world. Roman law did not do it. Neither did roads and better communication. But now, by the work of the Spirit, people of all languages could sing together from the same score. They would be united into one body by one Spirit with one hope of their calling, with one Lord, one faith, one baptism, one God and Father of them all. The gift of languages now transcended any differences in language that had formerly kept people apart. It allowed them to say, "Our brotherhood is not going to be through Greek or Latin or anything men say or do, or anything that Caesar does. It will be through the miraculous work of God in our lives." Roman would say to Jew, "My brother." Mede would say to Elamite, "My brother." Instead of the bricks of Babel would be a new temple of living stones in Jerusalem.

This gift of languages in the temple in Jerusalem was also a sign of judgment on Jewish unbelief. When Paul deals with the gift of speaking in languages in 1 Corinthians 14:21–22, he cites the prophecy of Isaiah 28:11–12: "With men of other tongues and other lips will I speak unto this people; and yet for all that will they not hear me." Isaiah was referring to the time the Babylonians commanded people in walled-up Jerusalem to open their gates and surrender. Yet the city refused.

Likewise, when the Jewish Pharisees and Sadducees rejected the Messiah and killed Him, their command to execute Him was spoken in Latin or Greek through the lips of Pilate, a foreigner. God now spoke to the unbelieving Jews of Jerusalem on the day of Pentecost through various languages. This was a sign to unbelieving Jews of judgment that would come upon them and their temple. The Roman army would tear the temple to the ground, stone by stone. Only the Wailing Wall would be left standing. The gift of languages was a sign of condemnation on those who refused to speak the language of faith in the Son of God, particularly on Jews to whom God had spoken clearly and at length, but who still rejected the Christ. Now Gentiles in abundance would honor Jesus Christ as Lord, singing His praises in their own languages.

The gift of languages was also a sign of the church's vocation as a proclaiming church. The gift of languages was not given to lighten the burden of the missionary who needed to become fluent in the language of the people to whom God sent him. This mainly Jewish group of 120 people, from the very beginning of receiving Christ's Spirit, knew that henceforth they had to become familiar with speaking in many languages about Jehovah and His Son, Jesus of Nazareth. Jesus had told them to wait in Jerusalem until they were endued with power (Acts 1:4, 8). But what was this power for? To dominate the world, build a global empire centered in Jerusalem, and have scores of people follow their orders? No, it was given so *they* could spread the message of the Messiah to the utmost corners of the earth.

The Spirit of God comes so that everyone in the world may understand the greatness of Christ and His relevance to every nation, for the Spirit wants the glory of Christ to be made known among the nations. He wants His disciples to bear witness from Jerusalem, to Judea and Samaria, and to the uttermost ends of the earth. That is what this gift is saying. So in Acts 2: 9–11, Luke gives an exhaustive list of the people who were in the temple: "Parthians, and Medes, and Elamites, and the dwellers in Mesopotamia, and in Judaea, and Cappadocia, in Pontus, and Asia, Phrygia, and Pamphylia, in Egypt, and in the parts of Libya about Cyrene, and strangers of Rome, Jews and proselytes, Cretes and Arabians."

Acts 2 prepares us for the ongoing story of the spread of the church. No longer would God favor one nation above all. The middle wall of partition in the temple would no longer separate Gentile converts from Jews. That barrier was destroyed by Jesus Christ when He, as the Lamb of God, took away the sins of the world. Now Jews and Gentiles, young and old, men and women may run past the harsh warning signs that were attached to the old wall of the temple, threatening death to those who trespassed. People of every nation were now invited to enter the holiest part of the temple. They could run through the torn veil into the very presence of God and cry, "Abba, Father!"

So the gift of languages prepares us for the book of Acts, the letters of the New Testament to Christians living in Rome, Greece, and Asia; for the gospels written in Greek, a Gentile language; and for the spread of the gospel to the ends of the earth.

THE POWER OF PENTECOST

Pentecost profoundly shook not only the 120 believers who gathered in Jerusalem to await the coming of Christ's Spirit; it would also shake the world. Here are some of the reasons why Pentecost is so meaningful:

1. It means the Spirit of God will be poured out on all flesh. Pentecost ushers in the era in which the Spirit will be poured out on anyone who believes in Christ. The apostle Peter says in Acts 2:16–17: "But this is that which was spoken by the prophet Joel...I will pour out of my Spirit upon all flesh." The Spirit will be poured out on all people who repent and believe in Christ. From this moment on, people of God will be found everywhere in the world.

Consider China, where the church is growing fastest today. About sixty years ago Chairman Mao and the Gang of Four tried to stamp out all vestiges of traditional Chinese religion, including Christianity. They thought they had succeeded, but the church went underground and began to multiply. In the 1980s, the ban was lifted, and Westerners began to enter China. What they saw was astonishing. Not only had the church survived; it had thrived. From a small beginning, and through decades of terrible persecution, the church had multiplied. No one knows how many Christians there are in China today: perhaps a hundred million. But the church in China has multiplied faster than any other nation in the history of the church. In China believers are equipped with what the New Testament Christians had: godly living, prayer, and knowledge of the gospel. Those are the means that the Spirit of God uses to grow the church.

2. *The Spirit of God will free the world from darkness and shame.* The Old Testament offered hints and promises of God freeing the world from sin, but the main responsibility of the nation of Israel was to keep the seed of faith alive. One evil king followed another, as did one false prophet after another. The ten northern tribes were absorbed into other nations. The two southern tribes were carried off into exile in Babylon for seventy years. How could the seed of faith survive in such a long, dark, cold winter of unbelief?

On the day of Pentecost, the seeds of faith in Israel began to grow. Very quickly a great tree rose into the air. It was so large that the birds of the air nested in its branches. Likewise, for centuries yeast was stored away in Israel, but at Pentecost yeast was mixed with flour to rise and grow throughout the world.

The stream of grace in Israel was a little trickle that had been damned up for centuries, but at Pentecost it overflowed from Jerusalem to Judea and Samaria and throughout the earth. The light of the Messiah was hidden under a bushel for centuries, but at Pentecost the bushel was removed and the beams of light shone out and filled the world.

3. *The Spirit of God is henceforth spiritual.* Prohibitions about cooking a kid in its mother's milk, the need to go to Jerusalem three times a year for feasts, and the need for circumcision were all finished when the Spirit came at Pentecost. The Mosaic economy was over. People no longer needed to be treated like children; they no longer needed to obey prohibitions against clean or unclean food. Now they have the kingdom of God within them; its laws are written on their hearts; they have an inward desire to do God's will. As the old church fathers said, wherever the Spirit of God works, there is the church of God.

This time also marks a transition from the old covenant to the new. The law was given to Israel from Mount Sinai. Not long after that, the children of Israel asked for a golden calf. The people danced around the calf, crying, "These are your gods, O Israel." The people were running wild, but the Levites went to Moses. He told them to strap swords to their sides and go through the camp killing their brothers, friends, and neighbors. About three thousand people were put to death that day. That was an old covenant situation, which is utterly alien to new covenant practice today.

But at Pentecost the weapons of the church's warfare changed. Peter did not cry out for vengeance for the murder of the Lord Jesus. There would be no more jihads or holy wars in the dispensation of the Spirit. Our breastplate is one of righteousness, and our shield is faith. Peter used the sword of the Spirit, which is the Word of God, and as he wielded this sword, it cut three thousand people to the heart. Whenever the church of God has abandoned the Word to bring in the inquisition, the stake, and other weapons of torture, it is abandoned by the Spirit of God.

4. *The Spirit of God now works more powerfully than before.* I have no doubt that the Spirit of God was active in Old Testament times, for He was regenerating and sanctifying the minds of the remnant in Israel. How else would Shadrach, Meshach, and Abednego have chosen to be burned to death in a furnace rather than bow before an idol? The Spirit of God empowered them.

Yet the promise to people in Old Testament days was that in the last days all the people of God would receive God's Spirit, not just kings, prophets, and priests who were spiritually gifted during the old dispensation. From Pentecost on, even servants, male and female, would be filled with the Spirit. The church would be a fellowship of saints, which Christ would present as a holy church without spot or wrinkle.

Some time ago, three Christian men in Turkey were murdered by five young Muslims because they sent Bibles all over Turkey. Was that a tragedy? No, it wasn't a tragedy. Let me tell you about a tragedy. There are religious men and women in Wales who spend their evenings year after year watching television. There are people who take early retirement and leave the churches that they've attended for years. They were the backbone of their churches for years, but now they sit in the sunshine of the Costa del Sol in Spain, excusing themselves by saying, "We go to a weekly Bible study." That is a tragedy. Some Christians are more enthusiastic about cultural matters than the gospel of Jesus Christ. That, too, is a tragedy.

At Pentecost, God equipped His church with such energy that it would be His witness to all the nations, and sinners would begin to walk the way that leads to life. In light of Pentecost, then, let me ask you four questions that I once read in a sermon by Steve Cole:

- *Is my focus on God's glory in all things?* Did I ask myself that question even once last week? Did I determine how I would resist temptation and seek to grow in knowledge, and to ask for help in speaking to others?

- *Is my passion that nations will glorify God through the gospel?* If my heart does not long that lost people will be saved, can I claim that my heart is in tune with the Lord? He wept over Jerusalem sinners.

- *Is my daily life dependent on the Holy Spirit?* Am I walking in step with the Spirit each day? Would I miss Him if He withdrew from me during the past week? Am I leaning on Him for self-control, courage, wisdom, and purity of power to obey God?

- *Am I waiting for Him to open a door for me to speak to others?* What actions and words of mine will help men and women without Christ to seek the Savior? The power of the Spirit is not given to make me feel happy, but to make me a holier person so that my life may count for Christ. That should be the meaning of Pentecost for you and me.[1]

1. Steven J. Cole, "The Meaning of Pentecost: Acts 2:1–13," preached on October 8, 2000. www.fcfonline.org/content/1/sermons/100800m.pdf.

CHAPTER TWELVE

The Preaching of Pentecost

And they were all amazed, and were in doubt, saying one to another, What meaneth this? Others mocking said, These men are full of new wine. But Peter, standing up with the eleven, lifted up his voice, and said unto them, Ye men of Judaea, and all ye that dwell at Jerusalem, be this known unto you, and hearken to my words: for these are not drunken, as ye suppose, seeing it is but the third hour of the day. But this is that which was spoken by the prophet Joel.... —Acts 2:12–16

To understand Pentecost we must turn to Peter, the authorized, inspired interpreter and witness of what happened. Peter explains to the crowd surrounding the disciples at Pentecost what has happened to them. He begins by saying, "Hearken to my words" (v. 14). If people truly listen, they will understand how and why the Spirit of God has come, but if they do not listen to an apostle full of the Spirit of God, neither will they listen to someone who rose from the dead.

THE CHURCH UNDER ATTACK
Immediately after the Spirit of God came upon the church, the believers were attacked. Crowds in the temple heard the disciples speaking in languages they had not known before and tried to find some ordinary explanation for this extraordinary miracle. They said, "They've been drinking. These disciples have been on a binge and are drunk."

The devil always attacks the church, He is either scathing or subtle in his attacks, but he never ignores the church. Some Christians say they never defend themselves from attack. I agree that if our own names and reputations are under fire, we should respond as the Lord Jesus teaches when He says, "Love your enemies, do good to them which hate you, bless them that curse you, and pray for them which despitefully use you" (Luke 6:27–28). But when the Lord Himself is attacked, we are called to speak up for Him and not be ashamed of being identified with His cause. When truth is being trashed, we are to defend the gospel.

The New Testament is full of examples of how our Lord and His apostles responded to attacks. For example, when Jesus was accused of casting out demons by the power of Beelzebub, He responded by saying that if Satan gave power to Jesus, who opposed Satan in every way, he would be supporting an attack upon himself. That would be crazy since a house divided against itself cannot stand. But if the Pharisees claimed to cast out demons in God's name, as Jesus did, then the devils themselves would be their judges.

The church has a right to be heard, but if it serves Beelzebub, it forfeits the right to be heard. If its leaders are drunk, they have no right to be heard. If its leaders are immoral, they have no right to be heard. If the church regularly sides against ordinary people and supports the aristocracy, it loses its right to be heard. If the church is choked with ceremonies, committees, summit conferences, pronouncements, and interviews, it alienates itself from the masses and loses the right to be heard.

PETER'S DEFENSE OF THE CHURCH

The early church was a humble group of people who were overwhelmed with what they had heard and seen of the Lord Jesus during His three-year ministry. Now they became beneficiaries of the Holy Spirit. And Peter, as their authorized spokesman, defended their actions, saying, "For these are not drunken, as ye suppose, seeing it is but the third hour of the day. But this is that which was spoken by the prophet Joel; and it shall come to pass in the last days, saith God, I will pour out of my Spirit upon all flesh" (vv. 15–17).

Jerusalem had to make one of two choices about what happened at Pentecost. The first choice was humanistic and natural: these men have been drinking, and their babbling in strange tongues is the result of inebriation. The second choice was that God had poured out His Spirit on these men, gifting them with the ability to speak in foreign languages. Everyone had to decide what the explanation was for such phenomena: alcohol or the fulfillment of the prophet Joel's words.

Perhaps you, too, have a difficult choice to make. Maybe you are unwilling to slander these fine men by saying they were drunk by 9 o'clock on a Sunday morning. They did not look like the drunks you've seen in the past. However, you're not yet willing to acknowledge that God the Holy Spirit, the third person of the Godhead, had come upon these men and filled them. Is there some nicer way between these two extremes?

I cannot be neutral; I listen to what Peter said and am totally persuaded. He quotes from Joel the prophet, who predicted that such an event would occur. "This is that," Peter declared. God promised to pour out His Spirit upon the church of the Messiah. The people of Jerusalem are now on the spot in redemptive history. They are eyewitnesses of a divine event. God is keeping His word by fulfilling His prophecies. Students of Scripture knew that what Joel prophesied would happen one day, and that it would be marked by three characteristics. Peter now challenged these people, saying, "I want to prove to you, searchers of the word, that those aspects of Joel's prophecy have been fulfilled today." It is being fulfilled in the following ways:

1. *Pentecost is a day of extraordinary events.* Joel wrote that Jehovah God said about the day of Pentecost: "And I will shew wonders in heaven above, and signs in the earth beneath; blood, and fire, and vapour of smoke: the sun shall be turned into darkness, and the moon into blood, before the great and notable day of the Lord come" (vv. 19–20).

That prophecy was fulfilled on Good Friday. The sun gave way to darkness at noon on the day Jesus died. The birds stopped singing. The sun's disappearance was not a mere eclipse, for it lasted too long. The moon was present in the middle of the day, like a great drop of blood in the sky. Day turned to night when Jesus of Nazareth, whom the Jews condemned and executed, died on the cross.

Along with those wonders in heaven, cataclysmic events took place on the earth. A great earthquake shattered rocks and broke open graves. People were raised from the dead. People in Jerusalem saw these risen people walking around. So there were signs on the earth and wonders in the heaven when Christ was taken down from the cross and buried in a tomb. His body was guarded by soldiers who stood around a smoky fire as the air grew cold and dark.

That was the ghastly background of Calvary, when three men were crucified on crosses, with Jesus of Nazareth in the middle. That's all people talked about afterwards, for deep in their souls they recognized they had a part in killing Jesus.

These wonders in the heavens and signs on the earth did not just happen at Calvary. For the past three years, people in Galilee, Judah, and Jerusalem had been overwhelmed by miraculous signs and wonders. When Jesus was born in Bethlehem, a brilliant star appeared in the sky. Wise men from the East followed that star from Babylon to Bethlehem, where the young child Jesus and His parents were living.

When Jesus was baptized by John the Baptist in the River Jordan, people heard the voice of God speaking from heaven, saying, "This is my beloved Son in whom I am well pleased." Miraculous events continued to occur throughout Jesus' life. He and His disciples were on the Sea of Galilee when a violent storm threatened to sink the boat they were in. But Jesus spoke a few words, and the winds and waves calmed down. His disciples were so amazed that they cried out, "What manner of man is this that even the winds and the waves obey Him?"

Jesus of Nazareth also performed miracles. He went to a wedding in Cana of Galilee. When the wine ran out, He turned the contents of huge water pots into wine. Later, He fed five thousand people by multiplying five loaves and two fishes. He delivered many people from demons and healed hundreds of people from blindness, lameness, leprosy, and all kinds of diseases.

So many people were healed by this rabbi that His reputation spread all over Israel. He even raised some people from death. Jairus's daughter is one example. After she died, Jesus came to her, took her hand, and said to her, "Maid, arise" (Luke 8:54). She sat up and returned to life.

A widow from Nain was mourning the loss of her son in a burial procession when Jesus took pity on her and raised the boy to life. He also raised Lazarus, brother of His friends Mary and Martha. Lazarus had been buried in a sepulcher three days when Jesus ordered the man to come out of the grave. Lazarus came out of the cave with burial cloths still clinging to him.

What sort of man could raise people from the dead? The prophet Joel predicted that prior to the great day when the Lord would pour out His Spirit on all kinds of people, there would be wonders and signs in heaven and on earth. Hadn't this been happening three years prior to Pentecost? Then, on Pentecost, the wind howled like a hurricane in Jerusalem. Tongues of fire burned on the heads of men who followed Jesus, and many of them suddenly spoke in foreign languages to proclaim the greatness of God. This day of extraordinary events was the culmination of wonders in heaven above and signs on the earth below.

2. *Pentecost was Christ's day of glory.* The day on which the sun turned to darkness and the moon to blood was the great and glorious day of the Lord Jesus Christ, Peter said to the crowd of people gathered in Jerusalem on Pentecost. Haven't they listened to Jesus' parables? Haven't they heard Jesus tell about the prodigal son, who was welcomed back by Father God into the family after the boy behaved so reprehensibly toward Him? If there was hope for this son, there is also hope for Jerusalem, who killed the prophets that God sent her, Peter said. So listen, Jerusalem, you killers of the prophets and of God's Son, Jesus, there is hope for you!

Haven't you heard about Jesus' parable of the farmer, who planted some grain on rocky soil, some on sandy soil, and some on fertile soil? Doesn't that story explain why some of you listen to Jesus for a while but then quickly give up? You are the stony ground on which the Word is planted. You are enthusiastic about the gospel in the beginning, but then stray from it because you are more interested in materialism than in God.

Again, haven't you listened to the Sermon on the Mount? Haven't its truths spread like wildfire through the land? Don't people still talk about it? Jesus offered this extraordinary teaching with such authority. No other person spoke like Him. No one quotes what the rabbis say in the synagogues, for the teaching of Jesus is on everyone's lips. What He said is on the tongues of the men who sit at the city gates, on the lips of women who draw water at the well, and even in the mouths of children who repeat His words and stories. This was the great and glorious day of the Lord.

Yet you crucified Him. The Sanhedrin and chief priests bribed men to say Jesus was a blasphemer. They handed Him to the Romans and pressured Pilate to crucify this righteous man. Jesus offered life and health and hope to thousands of people. He did so much to glorify God, yet you yelled, "Crucify him! Crucify him!" You hated the Lord and nailed Him to a cross. Think of it! You murdered the loveliest and most blameless one. But do you know that He prayed for those who crucified Him? That was so typical of Him. He loved those who tortured and killed Him, praying to His Father to forgive them because they didn't know what they were doing. Who could such a man be?

His death was no accident. Jesus was not just another failed prophet. He was delivered up to death, the prophet Isaiah says, by God's set purpose and foreknowledge (v. 23). "Yet it pleased the LORD to bruise him; he hath put him to grief," Isaiah says (Isa. 53:10). God was in all of that suffering and death, summoning His Son to act as He did to redeem us from our sins.

Scripture says there can be no remission of sins without the shedding of blood. Yet the blood of bulls, sheep, goats, or pigeons cannot possibly atone for our wickedness. God required the sacrifice of animals and birds in the days prior to the Messiah as teaching aids pointing forward to the Messiah who would come one day and bruise Satan's head. When Jesus' forerunner, John the Baptist, came, he said of Christ, "Behold the Lamb of God who takes away the sin of the world." God sent His own Son to the cross. His enemies merely did what was essential for redemption to be accomplished. Good Friday was the Lord's doing as much as Easter Sunday was, for Christ is Lord of the cross and the empty tomb.

You might ask for proof that Jesus is the Lord. Peter's response to that question is: "Whom God hath raised up, having loosed the pains of death: because it was not possible that he should be holden of it" (v. 24). A corpse that lies in a coffin for three days, then suddenly opens its eyes, gets up, and walks out of the tomb is proof enough. Jesus did that. He raised himself on the third day, Scripture says. The significance of the resurrection is that it didn't take place in the realm of theology or ideas or philosophy, but in space and time, here on this earth. Peter himself saw the risen Savior, whom he had denied three times. He listened humbly as the Master asked him three times, "Do you love me, Peter? Then feed my sheep."

This happened fifty days before Peter preached at Pentecost. The preacher of the Sermon on the Mount was officially dead; He was taken down from the cross and buried in a tomb, which was sealed and guarded. But God raised Him from the dead (v. 24), Scripture says. That simple sentence explains what happened to the body of Jesus. The mighty creator and sustainer of the universe who had raised the widow's son in the time of Elisha, who had given Job the confidence to cry, "I know that my Redeemer liveth," who had raised Jairus's daughter and the son of the widow of Nain and Lazarus also raised Himself.

It was unthinkable that death should keep its grip on the Lord of glory. Death itself finally met its conqueror, the omnipotent God, with whom nothing is impossible. Peter says, "This Jesus hath God raised up, whereof we all are witnesses" (v. 32).

If just one person said, "I saw a ghost," you'd have every right to be cynical or believe there was another explanation for Jesus' post-death appearance, but Peter says he was not the only one to see the resurrected Jesus. A dozen people saw Him on more than one occasion, and five hundred on another. When have five hundred people together seen a ghost? Peter and the other disciples testified that they spent almost six weeks with Christ after His resurrection. "We were there on the first day of the week when we went to the grave," Peter says. "The stone was rolled away. The grave clothes were there but Jesus wasn't. The men who were guarding the tomb were sleeping like men in a coma."

Jesus made more appearances. He met with a woman in the garden, all the apostles in the upper room, Peter, and two friends who were traveling to Emmaus. Jesus wasn't a ghost; He ate and drank with the disciples in the upper room and by the lake. "We gathered to meet with Him, and He spent hours talking to us," Peter says. "We saw Him on the hill of ascension, where He blessed us, then rose to heaven. Now He is exalted to the right hand of God. He has received from the Father the promised Holy Spirit and has poured out what you now see and hear (v. 33). This is the Lord's great and glorious day."

The people gathered at Pentecost should have been ready for Jesus' day of glory because King David predicted it when he said, "I foresaw the Lord always before my face, for he is on my right hand, that I should not be moved: therefore did my heart rejoice, and my tongue was glad; moreover also my flesh shall rest in hope: because thou wilt not leave my soul in hell, neither wilt thou suffer thine Holy One to see corruption. Thou hast made known to me the ways of life; thou shalt make me full of joy with thy countenance" (vv. 25–28). David called the Christ *Lord* and *Jehovah*.

In addition, when David said God would not abandon him in the grave, he was not speaking of himself because King David eventually died and was buried. We know where his grave is, and we can visit it. David was speaking of another king who would not decay in the grave but rise to walk the paths of life. That is exactly what happened with Christ. "We have seen Him and talked to Him and touched Him," Peter says. "Each one of us here at Pentecost who has been praising God in

Gentile languages has spent time with the ascended Christ during the last fifty days. We can no more doubt that He is alive than that we are alive."

You might say, "Show us this risen Jesus and we will believe." Do you know who you are talking about? Can we summon a whale from the Irish Sea to shuffle up a slipway to us? Can we make a wild eagle fly down from heaven to us? Bring the Son of God here? The one David called "My Lord" is the Messiah. This Jesus who rose from the dead is now seated at the right hand of God. God has made this Jesus, whom you crucified, both Lord and Christ (v. 36).

Jesus will not leave that throne until the end of the age when He comes to judge the living and the dead. We must all appear before His throne at that time. That is the day of the Lord, but now we are speaking about Pentecost, a day that is great and glorious because it is a day of grace.

A DAY OF SALVATION

The prophet Joel said about this great day, "Whosoever shall call on the name of the Lord shall be saved" (v. 21). Just think of what people do to save themselves from boredom: they read, go to concerts, travel, find a hobby, and listen to the radio. Think of what people do to save themselves from loneliness: they marry or join clubs to mix with people of similar interests. Think of everything people do to save themselves from unhappiness: they drink or smoke or watch TV. Everyone does something to save himself from despair.

What do people do to save themselves from guilt? Don't you feel guilty about the people you've hurt? No one hasn't hurt *someone*. How do you cope with that? You may confess your wrongdoing; apologize to the one you've harmed, even try to make restitution. God will help you do that, but what happens to the guilt of having done that deed? What will save you from the dark thoughts about your weaknesses and tendencies to hurt others?

The people who shouted, "Crucify him!" got what they asked for. Jesus was wholly innocent. He had not hurt anyone but rather helped thousands of people, yet the Jews hated Him and wanted Him dead. He was not merely the best of men, harmless and loving; He was the Son of God. He was the Word made flesh; the brightness of God's glory and the express image of His person. If you want to know what God is like, look at Jesus. Some of you imagine God to be an old man, but a better picture of God is a man who kneels on the floor with a bowl of water and a towel, then washes the street filth off the feet of His followers. That is what Creator God is like.

"You hated Him and wanted him dead," Peter said. "What can save you from the guilt of doing that?" Peter then urged the murderers of Jesus, "Call on the name of the Lord." This Lord has a name above every name. He is Jehovah Jesus. Call on that name, Peter said. How fascinating that Peter did not say, "God is calling on you, so please say yes." Rather, he said, "You must call on God's name, no one else's. Appeal directly to the Lord and He will save you from your sin."

That is what happened on the day of Pentecost: the sound of a mighty wind, cloven tongues of fire resting upon each disciple, and the disciples' sudden ability to speak in various languages so that people from around the world could understand them. Some people accused the disciples of being drunk, but Peter defended them, saying this day of extraordinary events was prophesied long ago. It is the great and glorious day of the Lord Jesus. It is the day of salvation.

When the sermon is over, you walk home to your wife and children. You tell them what you saw that day in Jerusalem, and they are miffed that they missed it. You say, "I saw Jerusalem TV recording the whole incident, and soon it will be on the evening news. Let's watch it. By the way, who do you think was right? Were these men really drunk, or is Jesus really the Messiah? I vote for Peter."

"Well, I think they were drunk," says your wife. So you call the kids and you turn on the TV. "Now kids," you say, "your mom and I have been discussing these strange things going on in Jerusalem. I think one thing caused it, but your mother thinks another. Let's watch the news." After the report, you ask the kids their opinion on what happened. You vote again, then go to bed.

Is that how Pentecost ended in Jerusalem? Did people vote on who had the better case? Did some people say, "What Peter said makes sense to me," and others, "They're all a bunch of fanatics"?

No. Peter did not encourage anyone to think the Christians were on trial. Peter began with Joel's prophesy, then went on to David's psalm, showing how Christ fulfilled all that Joel and David predicted about this long-promised day. Then Peter said, "Ye have taken, and by wicked hands have crucified and slain" (v. 23). You have killed the only begotten Son of God. You ended the life of Jehovah Jesus. God has made this Jesus, whom you crucified, both Lord and Christ (v. 36). You murdered Him, but He is now at the right hand of God. He is waiting for you; you will see Him, for He is your judge.

Peter was saying, "You think you're in the jury box, passing judgment on what's happened here today. But you are in the sinner's box, and the judge of all the earth has passed sentence on you. God has found you guilty of putting His Son to death."

Nobody left Jerusalem that day thinking they had merely listened to an interesting speech. For Peter ended his sermon by saying, "Repent, and be baptized every one of you in the name of Jesus Christ for the remission of sins" (v. 38). Peter pleaded with his listeners to call on the name of the Lord to repent for what they had done. He begged them to recognize that their sins needed forgiveness in Jesus' name. He warned them of the folly of ignoring what they had seen and heard on Pentecost. He pleaded with them to be saved.

That sermon transformed three thousand people. It cut them to the heart (v. 37). They were convinced that every single word Peter spoke was true, and they had to do something about it. They knew they were guilty of crucifying Christ, the promised Messiah, and were now headed for a personal encounter with Him. They knew they had earned the wrath of the Lamb. What could they do? How could they be forgiven?

Peter didn't let his listeners go with a fascinating story or anecdote. He didn't share his personal testimony with them, either. He didn't say, "Let me tell you what it is like to be filled with the Spirit." God gave Peter the sword of the Spirit, which is the Word of God, so he took that sword and plunged it into the hearts of his listeners. Three thousand people were convicted that day that they weren't ready to meet God. "Repent and be baptized," Peter said to them. "Save yourselves from this untoward [corrupt] generation" (v. 40). And they did.

Go now with those words ringing in your ears. Do not forget them until you have done what they say.

CHAPTER THIRTEEN

Did You Receive the Holy Spirit?

And it came to pass, that, while Apollos was at Corinth, Paul having passed through the upper coasts came to Ephesus: and finding certain disciples, he said unto them, Have ye received the Holy Ghost since ye believed? And they said unto him, We have not so much as heard whether there be any Holy Ghost. And he said unto them, Unto what then were ye baptized? And they said, Unto John's baptism. Then said Paul, John verily baptized with the baptism of repentance, saying unto the people, that they should believe on him which should come after him, that is, on Christ Jesus. When they heard this, they were baptized in the name of the Lord Jesus. And when Paul had laid his hands upon them, the Holy Ghost came on them; and they spake with tongues, and prophesied. And all the men were about twelve.

—Acts 19:1–7

The apostle Paul had walked the long road from Corinth to Ephesus. He now looked for the small group of Christians in the city. He soon discovered they had a limited knowledge of God. For example, they had never heard of the third member of the Godhead, the Holy Spirit. Perhaps these men had visited Jerusalem, where they heard about John the Baptist and his mighty preaching in the wilderness near the Jordan River. They went to hear him, and, along with thousands of others, repented of their sins and were baptized. Or perhaps one of John's disciples came to Ephesus and began preaching about the need to repent and be baptized, and about twelve people responded to that message and were baptized.

However they came to Christ, these believers now met with Paul, and one of the first questions he asked is if they had received the Holy Spirit when they believed. They said no; they were not at all aware of the Spirit.

They are disciples of John, they say, but they know nothing about the Holy Spirit or His outpouring at Pentecost.

A LIMITED BAPTISM

How could these people become Christians without receiving the Holy Spirit? We are told plainly that these people were *disciples*. Whenever that word is used in the book of Acts, it always refers to Christians. These people believed John the Baptist, who said the Messiah would soon come and baptize believers with the Holy Spirit. He showed Jesus of Nazareth to them, saying He was the Lamb of God who would take away the sins of the world.

The Ephesians believed this, but from that point their knowledge fizzled out. They did not know that the Holy Spirit had been poured out on the church in Jerusalem on Pentecost. They did not know that, from that time on, every Christian had the Holy Spirit, or we might say that the Holy Spirit had every Christian.

The Bible clearly says that the Christian life begins with new birth in the Spirit. John 3:8 says that we are "born of the Spirit." Now if any man have not the Spirit of Christ, he is none of his," Paul says in Romans 8:9. He also says to the troubled church in Corinth, "Now we have received, not the spirit of the world, but the spirit which is of God" (1 Cor. 2:12). He adds, "We have all received him, all of you and me as well, the Spirit who is from God." He also tells the Galatians that God's promise to Abraham is now fulfilled, "that we might receive the promise of the Spirit through faith" (Gal. 3:14).

The means by which we receive the Spirit is faith in Christ. We do not receive the Spirit by works, such as agonizing over our sin or good works or fasting, but by faith in the Savior. At Pentecost Peter's great message was, "Repent, and be baptized every one of you in the name of Jesus Christ for the remission of sins, and ye shall receive the gift of the Holy Ghost" (Acts 2:38). Turning from sin by faith in Jesus Christ is the means by which we receive the Holy Spirit.

The disciples at Ephesus did not progress in understanding after they were baptized by John, unlike Simon Peter and Andrew, who were also disciples of John but later became disciples of Jesus and were baptized by the Holy Spirit on Pentecost. John's baptism was a preliminary baptism; it was an outward sign of the inner change of a repentant heart. The Spirit of God was at work in John's preaching and baptizing, but people could experience the work of the Spirit without knowing anything about the person of the Holy Spirit. That was so of the twelve men at Ephesus. They repented of their sins and were baptized. They regularly met with other like-minded disciples to worship God. But there were black holes in their theological vision. They had an imperfect grasp of the Christian faith.

These twelve men received the baptism of John too late. The baptism of John prepared them for the coming of Christ and for His work, but after our Lord finished His work, ascended to heaven, and poured out His Spirit at Pentecost, the only valid and authorized baptism became the baptism of the Spirit in Jesus' name.

So these twelve men in Ephesus said to Paul, "We have not so much as heard whether there be any Holy Ghost." They knew nothing whatsoever about Pentecost. This does not mean they were total strangers to the operations of the Spirit. They were like Old Testament believers, who were acquainted with the ministry of the Spirit in creation, in inspiring the prophets, and in preparing kings and priests for their work. They knew how Jeremiah and Daniel and Joel spoke of a time when the Spirit would come in the days of the Messiah. They knew that King David prayed that God would not take His Spirit from him. They knew this was part of their own experience of becoming real disciples of the Lord, and they knew it from the teaching of the Old Testament. But now Paul challenged them by asking if the indwelling, sanctifying, and empowering work of the Spirit, which every other Christian in the world received at Pentecost, also belonged to them.

These twelve men, who showed the marks of being true disciples through the Holy Spirit, were missing out on the indwelling of the Spirit in all His fullness, just as Old Testament believers missed out on His fullness. In many ways, the twelve in Ephesus were like Abraham, Moses, David, and other heroes listed in Hebrews 11. They lived by faith in the Lord and were saved by grace, but they did not have the power and influence of the Spirit at the level of even the youngest believer today. In the Old Testament, the Spirit worked sporadically through some favored individuals, prophets, priests, or kings, but after the Lord Christ poured out His Spirit at Pentecost, the Spirit began working in old and young people, manservants and maidservants, and on everyone baptized by one Spirit into one body throughout the world. But that was not true of the believers of Ephesus. They were like the Japanese soldier who lost touch with his superiors. Only when he was captured did the lone soldier learn that the war was over. Likewise, Paul rescued these twelve men in distant Ephesus from an incomplete faith and educated them in the ways of the Holy Spirit.

Ephesus was on the eastern coast of Turkey, hundreds of miles away from Israel. At the time of Christ, the inhabitants of this Gentile nation belonged to the kingdom of darkness. The Son of God came into the darkness of the world to redeem it through His suffering, death, and resurrection. Believers who were transformed by the Holy Spirit were now spreading the good news of Christ throughout the world. So as Paul brought the New Testament gospel to Ephesus, he began to find out what was missing in their faith.

THE MISSING GIFTS

The believers in Ephesus lacked the important gifts and operations of the Spirit. They knew something about the indwelling of the Spirit, though perhaps not in those terms. They had experienced faith, repentance, discipleship, and fellowship, but they lacked the following three graces:

1. *The full assurance of faith granted by the Spirit.* The Spirit had not yet borne witness with the spirits of these believers that they were children of God. If you traveled eastward from Ephesus to Jerusalem and talked to any Christian there, you would not find many disciples who lacked assurance of his interest in the Savior's blood. Few believers in the church in Jerusalem lived in uncertainty about their spiritual privileges or relationship with the Lord. Yet the twelve believers from Ephesus had no assurance that a finished work of reconciliation had been done for them by the Messiah; they had John's baptism and no more.

2. *The Spirit-given power to testify.* Years had gone by since Pentecost, yet the church in Ephesus had only increased in size to twelve men. Then one man full of the Spirit of God, the apostle Paul, arrived and began working with the believers. The consequence of this Spirit-led ministry, according to Acts 19:10, 20, was that "all they which dwelt in Asia heard the word of the Lord Jesus," and "so mightily grew the word of God and prevailed." That is what the fullness of the Spirit did for these believers through Paul.

Think of what happened before the Spirit's outpouring at Pentecost. Peter was asked by a servant girl if he knew Christ, and the disciple angrily denied ever knowing that wretched fellow. All the apostles made sure the door was locked after entering a room because they were afraid of who might burst in and arrest them. Even on the hill of ascension forty days after the resurrection, some of the disciples lacked the courage to witness or to preach. However, when the Holy Spirit overwhelmed them at Pentecost, they were no longer ashamed of the gospel of Jesus Christ and fearlessly preached it to all the enemies of Jesus in Jerusalem.

3. The gift of understanding and speaking in foreign languages. This great gift of the Spirit given to believers at Pentecost was necessary to spread the gospel to the uttermost parts of the earth. The miraculous gift was also needed by believers in the mighty city of Ephesus. So Paul placed his hands upon the believers, and the Holy Spirit came upon them. And those converts who are Gentile converts who lived eight hundred miles away from Jerusalem, received the same miraculous gift of tongues that had been given to believers in Jerusalem.

Now the gospel could go out from Ephesus into the surrounding area. Acts 19 tells how Paul brought the gospel to people all over Ephesus and the surrounding province of Asia. Acts 20 tells how the gospel went further, into Macedonia and into Greece, and how Paul planned to go further into Syria. The gospel went forth into the entire world by the power of the Holy Spirit. The sign of that power for believers in Ephesus and Jerusalem was the same: the gift of speaking and understanding Gentile languages.

HAVE YOU RECEIVED THE HOLY SPIRIT?

My concern, like Paul's, is whether you received the Holy Spirit when you believed. You say, "Yes, by the grace of Christ I did." That is the only answer a Christian can give if what the Bible says is true. By the Holy Spirit, you have become a partaker of the divine nature. You have unlimited access to God the Holy Ghost, who indwells you and affects every part of your being. You are complete in Him, but why then do you lack the important gifts and graces of the Holy Spirit? Why is the fruit of the Spirit just as small and undeveloped as it was when you first believed? Why aren't you more like Christ if the Spirit of Christ indwells you? What about other gifts, such as the following:

1. The gift of discernment. Why isn't the gift of discernment more evident in you? This gift would give you a moral and theological dimension that is created and sustained by the Spirit of God but is constantly nurtured by you. Do you have the gift of discernment, which is evident in your being wise, fair, open-minded, and long-term in your thinking, not being hypercritical, but also not being gullible and naive? Are you mature enough in this gift to assess a preacher who is interviewing for a position at your church? Can you wisely judge a visiting preacher to be a suitable man to occupy this gospel pulpit?

The gift of discernment is in short supply among evangelical Christians today. Consider some of the terrible errors of judgment made by men you once greatly esteemed but who have since veered off the way of truth and picked up strange teachings. Such misjudgments can also be made by congregations that once seemed to be centers of orthodoxy. The preacher they called has become like Samson, who pulled an entire temple down on himself, destroying everyone in it. Where is the discernment in such congregations? How many people in a congregation say they received the Holy Spirit when they believed? Did their minister receive the Holy Spirit when he believed?

2. The gift of illumination. There is an old saying that if something is new, it is not true; and if it is true, it is not new. Why do believers swallow such notions? What happened to the Holy Spirit's gift of illumination? Why do new movements arise and get accepted by so many Christians today?

For example, one group suggested a new perspective on the teaching of Paul on justification by faith. Orthodox leaders, seminaries, and publishing houses began embracing the thinking as if it came from God above. What happened to the Spirit's gift of illumination? We think of the collapse of Christianity in Europe a century ago, which can be ascribed to the Spirit's withdrawal from pulpits that stopped offering sound, biblical preaching. But the Spirit also withdrew from the pew and took illumination away from the church's elders and deacons.

How many people in those congregations received the Holy Spirit when they believed? If they say they did, where did their understanding of God go? Where did the basics of faith go? Why wasn't truth preached to the people? Why were truths in the Bible ignored? Who are we to ignore what God says? Where is the gift of illumination? Did believers in the church today receive the Holy Spirit when they believed?

3. *The gifts of evangelism.* I am convinced that we have tended to restrict the work of the Holy Spirit to the new birth, while ignoring other aspects of His work that are utterly indispensable to the church today. They are the workings that only the Spirit can give and which the church greatly needs. They are gifts for Christian service, especially of evangelism.

The Holy Spirit indwells the church so that we may reach out to the whole world with the gospel. We pay lip service to this calling, but we also ignore it, don't we? I believe evangelism no longer has the highest priority in our lives. Do we think often of the great day of judgment, on which all people—including us—will be gathered before the throne of the Lord, who will judge all people, granting bliss to those who have loved and served Christ, and pronouncing fearful judgment on the rest? Why doesn't the day of judgment affect us more? Did you receive the Holy Spirit when you believed?

In the book of Acts, we read about the dynamic self-sacrifice and tireless service of believers in the early church. How different they were from believers in the church today! In the days of the apostles, rioting and anger were often the responses to the preaching of the gospel. But the church also experienced great growth and a rich life of faith. Compare that with the life of the professing church today. It is weaker and less powerful in its preaching, but even more disastrous is our tolerance for an anemic and weak pulpit as well as ineffective evangelism. How many of us are pleading with God to visit us with the gift of evangelism? How often do we bring our deficiencies to the Lord, pleading for forgiveness?

4. *The gift of assurance.* When I ask if you received the Holy Spirit when you believed, I expect a better response than, "I *hope* that God has begun a good work in me." Why are you so uncertain? Why are so many people in the church somber and unsure about their faith? Where is their assurance of pardon? Where is the comfort that the Spirit offers when we find our all in all in Jesus Christ? Where is our power and boldness to witness for Christ in a Christ-hating world? It is good for believers to be concerned about their souls and the things of God, but the witness of God's Spirit with our spirits is that we *are* children of God, and the love of God is shed abroad in our hearts.

There is a so-called breakthrough work of the Spirit in individuals and the church. Does your congregation need such a spiritual breakthrough so that it will reach more people for Christ? Do many Christians need renewal in their spiritual life, which at present seems to be stagnating? Do you suspect defensiveness when you hear questions like this and begin to feel resentful? Are you concerned when people justify old patterns of religious life which have produced so few results?

We are often comfortable with our spiritual routines and don't want them to be upset. But did you receive God the Holy Spirit when you believed? Are you so satisfied with your spiritual growth that you long for nothing better? Do you think the unchanging spiritual life of many is better than those who speak with assurance, "My beloved is mine and I am His"? Do you feel suspicious about those who speak with assurance of faith? Do you suspect they might be victims of pride and self-deception? Do you imagine yourself to be wrapped in a mantle of humility while others cover themselves with superficiality and delusion? Is that the reason you give for thinking you have received the Holy Spirit when you believed?

5. *The gift of growth.* "Blessed are the poor in spirit," Jesus says. By God's grace we have faced up to our sin and have gone to God, asking Him for forgiveness, mercy, and new life. Jesus has lived and died so that we might have life. We have no other foundation but that. We see our remaining sins and weaknesses and say, "How could I possibly get to heaven without the righteousness and blood of Jesus Christ, God's Son?"

Having gone in my poverty to Christ, I am rich in Christ. I am full and complete. I need nothing more. That is my gospel testimony. "I am the chief of sinners," I say, but I don't stop there, for I go on to say that Jesus Christ is also my wisdom, my righteousness, my sanctification, and my redemption. The Son of God is mine in all the glory of His person and in the perfection of His finished work for me. That is the testimony of the poor man who believes in Jesus Christ. He can and must say this because the Word of God demands that he confess it. His testimony to the world is not that he is a dreadful man, limping and staggering through life, but that Jesus Christ is a great Savior.

I plead with you to get beyond the first principles of salvation. Do not restrict the work of the Holy Spirit to what is absolutely necessary to get to heaven. The Bible demands more, the church demands more, and the age we live in demands more. Do not think that as long as you are converted, your sins are forgiven, and you go to church on Sundays with a believing heart that you have enough. The new birth and conversion are not the sum of the Christian life; they are just the beginning. You are also promised a growing relationship with the Lord and a growing relationship with the Lord's people.

The Holy Spirit equips you for communion with God and the service of God's people. He begins with the Spirit's gift of the new birth and saving faith in Christ, then empowers you to be a blessing to others. We are first the object in which the Holy Spirit dwells, regenerating and illuminating us. Then we become the object through which the Holy Spirit works to benefit our neighbors.

Is the Spirit working through you to touch others? Did you receive the Holy Spirit when you believed? The Spirit works *in* us to save us, and He also works *through* us to benefit others. You cannot separate those blessings. If they are separated, your spiritual life will languish and stop growing.

Take no comfort in your low level of spiritual progress, reasoning that in His sovereignty, the Spirit distributes His gifts and graces as he sees fit. Never use God's sovereignty to make excuses for your own disobedience. You have not, not because God refuses it, but because you don't ask. Do we find anywhere in the Bible that the Holy Spirit would rather see God's people starve than feast? Where does Scripture say that the Spirit is pleased when believers in Christ get just a taste of their only comfort in life and death? Is it to God's glory and honor that we keep groping in the dark, limping as we go? Are we not told instead to rejoice in the Lord always? Is it not His delight for us to rejoice in Him?

KEEP GROWING

Paul looked at the twelve believers in Ephesus, who were such fine disciples but in many ways were such babies in the faith, and he asked them if they had received the Holy Spirit when they believed. He then put his hands upon them and baptized them in the Holy Spirit, and they became complete Christians. They went on to become the founding members of a mighty congregation.

But that is not the end of the story. Some years later, Paul wrote to the mature believers at the Ephesian church that he wanted them to keep growing so they might experience more of the Spirit's work in their midst. He prayed that the Lord would strengthen them by His Spirit, "that Christ may dwell in your hearts by faith; that ye, being rooted and grounded in love, may be able to comprehend with all saints what is the breadth, and length, and depth, and height; and to know the love of Christ, which passeth knowledge, that ye might be filled with all the fulness of God" (Eph. 3:17–19).

That must also be our longing: that our growth in the Spirit will never end. If we received the Holy Spirit when we believed, our constant, earnest prayer must be that we will be filled to the measure of all the fullness of God.

There are two ways we can answer the question about whether we received the Holy Spirit when we believed. The first is to read the gracious promises God makes to believers and take those promises to heart. For example, God says that if we love our fellow church members in Christ, that proves we have the Holy Spirit. If we love the Bible, we have the Holy Spirit because the Bible is the Spirit's inspired book. Again, if we love holiness, we have the Spirit because He is the Spirit of holiness. No person could love the things of God without receiving the Holy Spirit. We refer to this way of arguing as a "practical syllogism," which is a way of reasoning. This is the practical syllogism:

- God says those who have received the Holy Spirit love fellow Christians.

- I love Christians; therefore,

- I must have the Holy Spirit.

We look for evidences that can only be created by the Holy Spirit, such as love of the Lord's Day, hate of sinning, and love of the Savior, and we conclude that those attitudes can only be created in our lives by the Holy Spirit. So I must therefore have the Spirit!

But there is another kind of assurance than this kind of logic. Sometimes the light of assurance surprises a Christian while he sings, or when he is listening to a sermon, or when he prays. This experience is a direct witness to our own spirits that we are God's children. It can be a heaven-on-earth experience, which is, in the words of the Westminster Confession, "an infallible assurance." This kind of assurance can make a martyr strong to face the flames the night before he is taken to the stake and sustain him while he burns. Latimer thus could say to Ridley, as they were chained to their stakes and the wood was set on fire, "When I live in a settled and steadfast assurance about the state of my soul, methinks I am as bold as a lion."

That kind of assurance made Martin Luther stand firm in Worms during the inquisition of the papacy. It made the early Calvinistic Methodists in Wales stand firm when people threw stones and filth at them as they preached in market squares. They had confidence in God; they knew with assurance that they received the Holy Spirit when they believed.

Today, more than ever, we need to ask God for a greater measure of the assurance that we have the Spirit of God. We need more of the holy boldness we receive when the Holy Spirit bears witness with our spirits that we are children of God.

CHAPTER FOURTEEN

The Spirit Buries Our Misdeeds and Intercedes for Us

For to be carnally minded is death; but to be spiritually minded is life and peace.

—Romans 8:6

Romans 8 is probably the greatest chapter in this epistle. Along with Ephesians 1, these two chapters are some of the most majestic pieces in the New Testament. Romans 8 is particularly important for us because of its observations on the person and work of the Holy Spirit. Let us focus on three themes in this chapter: the Holy Spirit leads us, buries our misdeeds, and intercedes for us.

THE HOLY SPIRIT LEADS US

Romans 8:14 says, "For as many as are led by the Spirit of God, they are the sons of God." According to B. B. Warfield, that verse is the "classical passage in the New Testament on the great subject of the leading of the Holy Spirit."[1]

Imagine that you are a North American settler crossing the continent on a wagon train through deserts, facing hostile Indians and outlaws. The role of the experienced wagon master is indispensable for leading you to your appointed destination.

Or imagine that you are a new recruit, entering battle along with a long line of advancing troops. How important it is for you to be confident that the army commander knows where to deploy you and what you must do.

---

1. B. B. Warfield, *The Person and Work of the Holy Spirit* (Merrick, N.Y.: Calvary Press, 1997), 31.

Again, imagine that you are climbing a mountain and a thick mist falls; how crucial it is for you to have a guide who knows that peak like the back of his hand. We all need leaders. The evangelical church may be weak today because of its lack of leaders. The countries of Europe may also lack strong leaders, for who can name the presidents or prime ministers of those countries today? Where are the inspirational political leaders in your country? Who will you follow?

If you are a young person about to begin the great journey of life, how will you live? What values will you have? What will you do with your gifts and energy? Who will guide you? What if you fall in with people who lead you astray? Do you know a leader who will rightly guide you through life and death? If so who is that person?

I am not that leader, nor should you put your trust in other human leaders. Paul speaks about a favored people, who are privileged to be led by the Spirit of God. Jesus was led by the Spirit into the wilderness. Now Paul tells the Galatians, "But if ye be led of the Spirit, ye are not under the law" (Gal. 5:18).

In Matthew 21 the word *led* specifically refers to animals, but generally it describes people who are being led. In the parable of the good Samaritan, the Samaritan *led* the wounded traveler to the inn (Luke 10:34), and the blind man of Jericho is *led* to Jesus (Luke 18:40). Jesus is *led* to Caiaphas (John 18:28); Stephen is *led* to the council (Acts 6:12); Christians are arrested and *led* to Jerusalem (Acts 9:2); and Simon Peter is *led* by his brother Peter to Jesus (John 1:42). The Holy Spirit leads like that; He is very personal and has a controlling influence over the people of God. These chosen ones have been delivered from the leadings of sin, which had been telling them to ignore God, the Bible, and church and had given them morbid thoughts of death and eternity.

Submission to that cruel master is now behind them. They are no longer doing what sin told them to do; they are being led by the Spirit, and they are willfully and joyfully following Him. They have been given new life, the power of a new affection, and pure desires to walk as the Spirit directs them. They go through life not where *they* would but where *He* would have them go. They don't do what *they* wish, but what *He* determines. The leading of this Spirit may be viewed in the following ways.

1. This Spirit originates from heaven. The Spirit comes from the omnipotent Creator, the sovereign Lord, and this Spirit *is* the mighty God. The third person of the Godhead is at work in believers, overcoming their inclination to continue sinning, making them restless about their poor efforts by recalling their memories of past falls, and giving them a longing for the time when these battles will be over. So this leading is a divine and supernatural work of the third person of the Godhead. The whole journey of the Christian life is a divine and supernatural occasion. We were once led by self, which put a ring through our noses and took us wherever it wanted, but now, praise God, we are led by the Spirit of God.

2. This leading is not experienced only by super-Christians. There is nothing spooky in being led by the Spirit, for it is the privilege of every believer without exception. It is what differentiates us from unbelievers. We may properly modify the inspired words by saying, "If a person does not have the Spirit of Christ, he—and he alone—is not led by the Spirit." A Christian who says that he is led by the Spirit is not boasting. Rather he is exhibiting humility in asserting, "I am an unworthy and unstable person so I must be led by the Spirit. It is a sheer necessity." As William H. Parker (1845–1929) says in his hymn,

> Holy Spirit! help us daily by Thy might,
> What is wrong to conquer and to choose the right.[2]

3. The Spirit leads us not to enable us to escape the difficulties, dangers, trials, or sufferings of this life, but specifically to conquer sin. Romans 1 begins by explaining the sheer rottenness of sin, then goes on to describe the great deliverance that Jesus Christ obtains for His people. The Spirit's work is to bring new life to us and clean us from the inside, making us holy people. The leading of the Spirit is another phrase for the tough Latin-based word *sanctification*. So we are being led into Christlike living and constantly restored to Christlike living when we fall and repent. That cannot be the privilege of a few hyper-Christians who have had a second blessing. It is the blessing that every Christian experiences.

4. This leading of the Spirit is a continuous work. This leading affects a believer's entire person: his mind, his imagination, his affections, his soul, and his body. The Spirit has made up His mind that everyone whom God has sent Him will be freed from sin. They will be led into holiness

---

2. William H. Parker, "Holy Spirit! Hear Us," stanza 3.

during the years of their earthly pilgrimage, so the Spirit of God will be at work in every part of them that needs to be delivered from sin. When we talk about being "led by the Spirit," we are not speaking of special and extraordinary promptings, insights, deliverances, hunches, and feelings. We are talking about how the Spirit helps us break sinful habits and guides us down the path of good works and service.

When we consider other people to be better than ourselves, we are being led by the Spirit. When we bear the burden of the weak, we are being led by the Spirit. When a husband loves his wife as Christ loves the church, he is being led by the Spirit. When a wife respects her husband, she is being led by the Spirit. When we are ready to give an answer to anyone who asks us the reason for our hope, we are being led by the Spirit. When we present out bodies as a living sacrifice to God, we are being led by the Spirit. When we clothe ourselves in the armor of God, we are being led by the Spirit. That is how He leads us.

5. The Spirit does not teach us to let go so the Spirit does the work for us. Paul captures the tension of the Christian life in Philippians 2.12–13 in saying, "Work out your own salvation with fear and trembling. For it is God which worketh in you both to will and to do of his good pleasure." You must work out what it means to be a Christian in your heart and mind, in the home, in the workplace, with your neighbors, and with members of the congregation—wherever God puts you. You apply yourself to seriously working out what it means to please God as a saved person in every activity of life. If that responsibility crushes you, never forget that God the Spirit is working in you. He supplies you with power, motivating and encouraging you each day. That is how we are to understand the leading of the Spirit.

The Holy Spirit is not a kind of autopilot who carries us along as if we were in a trance. The Spirit is certainly leading us, but we must constantly also follow Him step by step, often fighting to plant our feet as we slowly advance. Part of our pilgrimage leads us through trials and temptations in places such as Vanity Fair, the Slough of Despond, and Doubting Castle, but we move away from Enchanted Ground and through the Valley of the Shadow, even to the river of death, as the Spirit leads us. We do not bypass conflict or do nothing, expecting the Spirit to do everything. We do everything, working out our salvation with fear and trembling. The Spirit does everything, too; He works in us by leading us each step of the way. His impulses and our impulses concur; so do His desires and our desires, His hatreds and our hatreds. We are active agents under the Spirit's active leading.

6. The Spirit leads us according to the teaching of the Bible. However difficult the way, however strenuous the effort, and however mysterious are the trials and sufferings we pass through, we make progress because the Spirit is leading us all the way. We are not going down the road of life in our own power but in the power of the one who leads us to the appointed goal, the throne of God. Let us substitute the word *Spirit* for *My Savior* in the following verse;

> All the way the Spirit leads me,
> Cheers each winding path I tread;
> Gives me grace for every trial,
> Feeds me with the living bread.
> Though my weary steps may falter,
> And my soul athirst may be,
> Gushing from the rock before me,
> Lo! A spring of joy I see;
> Gushing from the rock before me,
> Lo! A spring of joy I see.[3]

What a consolation it is to know that we have been led by the Spirit of God to this very moment. Even when we find ourselves falling into sin, let us not despair as Christians because the indwelling Holy Spirit is far greater than all our sin. We would despair if we simply gave way to sin after sin, but we do not. We meet mercy after mercy while experiencing the energy to move forward in our journey. The Spirit of grace produces conflict in the believer against sin, and He also spurs the believer to continue the fight. The victory is sure; the Spirit is within us, and we cannot fail. He will lead us home.

THE HOLY SPIRIT BURIES OUR MISDEEDS

The Bible says the Christian is delivered from the dominion of sin by the Holy Spirit. The Spirit is the Christian's new master and king. Sin is no longer his lord; the believer has been freed from sin's insistent commands

---

3. Fanny Crosby, "All the Way My Savior Leads Me," stanza 2.

to satisfy its lusts. Every true Christian is now able to defy sin and do what is righteous. But that does not make him sinless. On this side of heaven the virus of sin and its misdeeds will ever trouble us; they will make their presence known even on our deathbeds. What are we to do with the remaining sin that does not control us but yet is still within us?

We must keep looking to the Lord Jesus Christ, who is the source of our victory over sin, and constantly trust in Him. Paul tells us we must constantly put to death the misdeeds of the body, that is, to mortify the sin that remains within us. We are to weaken, starve, and murder anything evil that rises up within us and urges us to defy God and His law. We are to continue this work with the energy and under the direction of the Spirit of God. Regeneration is vain without the work of the Spirit. So is sanctification. We will never grow in Christlikeness without the Spirit. We also are impotent to put to death the misdeeds of the body without the Holy Spirit. All other ways of killing sin are vain; it can only be done by the Spirit.

You may appeal to yoga, for example, to kill your sinful nature. Or you may engage in solitude by dwelling in an isolated cottage on top of a Welsh mountain. Or you may beat yourself with a whip until the blood flows. But nothing other than the grace of the Spirit will overcome your sins. In the Old Testament prophecy of Ezekiel (11:19 and 36:26), God promises His people that the Spirit will come and remove all elements of proud, stubborn, rebellious unbelief from their hearts. That work of mortification is a gift of the Spirit of Christ. Only through Him will we be delivered from sin and receive the power to become like our Lord Jesus Christ. There is no other way to this than by the Spirit. Conquering sin and increasing in love, joy, and peace is the work of God. So mortification is a happy work. The very concept of it is His work; the continuance of it, His work; the consummation, His work. The Paraclete's task is to weaken sin and strengthen Christ in us. Only He is sufficient for this work.

As you battle with the sin, never forget your duty is to "mortify the deeds of the body" (v. 13). Do not lie back and wait for the Spirit to do it. You must put to death the misdeeds of the body, but in the power, love, and wisdom of the Spirit.[4] Here are specific ways the Spirit helps you do that.

---

4. See Kris Lundgaard, *The Enemy Within: Straight Talk about the Power and Defeat of Sin* (Philipsburg, N.J.: P&R, 1998), 147ff.

1. *The Spirit convinces you of sin.* A sin may seem so beautiful, natural, and rational to us that we ask, "Who could possibly consider it to be sin?" For example, Jonah went to the port of Tarshish in defiance of God's command to go to Nineveh. In Tarshish Jonah found a boat on its way west. It had space for him, and he had the money for the fare. Weren't these signs of God's approval of Jonah's decision to go west rather than east to Ninevah?

We often use providence to support our rebellion. If left to our own wits, it may take a long time and perhaps some serious trials to bring us to the point of mortifying our pride, begging for forgiveness, and looking for salvation to the cross of Christ. Recognizing our rebellion as sin only comes when the Spirit speaks to our conscience, sounds an alarm, and doesn't stop ringing. If sin could be killed through state education and politically correct counsels, we might be hearing a lot more weeping over sin than we're hearing today. But conviction of the danger of sin comes only by the work of the Spirit.

2. *The Spirit reveals the power of Christ to deliver you.* Jesus tells His followers that if an eye offends them, they should pluck it out. The apostle Paul says in Romans 8:13: "but if ye through the Spirit do mortify the deeds of the body, ye shall live." They are all talking about the same thing: "Hear Christ the teacher." The Spirit brings to our remembrance what our Savior says.

What will happen to us in the future; where will we end up one day? Our God is the end of the journey, for as believers we will one day meet together at the feet of Christ in a place that is free of sin. We who have this hope must purify ourselves as God is pure. The Spirit constantly reminds us of the future God is preparing for us. As 1 Corinthians 2:8–10 says, God reveals it to us by His Spirit, for "eye hath not seen, nor ear heard, neither have entered into the heart of man, the things which God hath prepared for them that love him."

The love of Christ motivates us to put our sins to death. If you were to observe Paul on a normal day of self-sacrificing service to the Lord Jesus for the souls of men, you might see him drop exhausted at the end of the day. If you asked what insane passion drove him to work so hard, Paul might answer, "The love of Christ holds me in its grip. I stand in constant amazement that the Son of God loves me and gave Himself for me." As

Al Martin says, "This understanding of the fullness of Christ drove Paul with far more zeal than any legal motivation could drive a man."[5]

3. The Spirit sustains you in expecting help from Christ to overcome sin. Romans 6:5–7 says that as believers we are united with Christ in His death. Our old self was crucified with Christ so that the body of sin might be done away with. We are no longer slaves to sin because anyone who has died to sin has been freed from sin. Verse 11 goes on to say, "Likewise reckon ye also yourselves to be dead indeed unto sin, but alive unto God through Jesus Christ our Lord." The Holy Spirit convinces us of full provision in Christ.[6]

Jesus came to earth to justify and glorify you. He has freed men and women who were bound by lust and sin for many years, bringing them into the glorious liberty of the children of God. Look to Christ. Ask the Savior to finish the work He has begun in you and take you safely to the place where you will never sin again. All the fullness of grace is in Him, so all patience, gentleness, forgiveness, mercy, courage, endurance, and other graces are available for you. The Spirit sustains you in that hope.

4. The Spirit fixes Calvary in your heart with sin-killing power. "See your sin in the light of the self-emptying of Christ," says Al Martin. "Say to that particular sin, 'Is this that which caused him to leave the ineffable glory of his Father's presence, to come to the confines of the virgin's womb, to be born amidst the stench of a cow barn from the adoring wonder of angels to the rude, dumb stare of cows and goats? Has my sin demanded that self-emptying?'

"Bring those sins to the cross of Christ; hear the voice of the Son of God, 'My God, my God, why hast thou forsaken me' and in your own minds hear the Father answering, 'My son, my son, I have forsaken you because of that sin of your sin.' Name your sin and dare to bring it into the blazing light of that awful darkness. There is no light like that darkness to show sin in its true colors. Keep the conscience sensitive to the guilt and danger of your specific sins by bringing them to the cross of Christ."[7]

---

5. Al Martin, "Practical Helps to Mortification of Sin," *Banner of Truth* (July–August 1972): 25.

6. Martin, "Practical Helps," 31.

7. Martin, "Practical Helps," 28.

The Holy Spirit brings the Christian into communion with the crucified Christ. The Spirit brings the cross of Christ into the heart of the sinner by faith, and gives him fellowship with Christ in His death and sufferings. So the believer fights sin with the blood of Christ and by virtue of Christ's cross. Galatians 6:14 says, "But God forbid that I should glory, save in the cross of our Lord Jesus Christ, by whom the world is crucified unto me, and I unto the world." The Holy Spirit helps us fight sin with the mighty weapon of the cross.

5. The Spirit is the author and finisher of our sanctification. The Spirit puts to death our sin, first, by using the law of God. This is the great theme of Romans, which says, "By the law is the knowledge of sin" (3:20); "the law entered, that the offence might abound" (5:20); and "I had not known sin, but by the law" (7:7).

If you want people to be ignorant of sin, do not talk to them about the law of God, for the Spirit uses the law to convict people of sin. The Spirit uses Exodus 20 and the Ten Commandments, certainly, but he also uses Jesus' exposition of the law in the Sermon on the Mount in Matthew 6 and Paul's exposition of it in Romans 12. He teaches people that God will no longer be trifled with, and they can no longer scoff at sin. People do vile actions, and Christians try to brush those sins under the carpet and forget about them, but the Holy Spirit keeps bringing to light things done in darkness and helps us to deal with them. How amazing is the grace of the Holy Spirit to probe into such foul and filthy hearts that build dunghills of vile attitudes, words, and deeds. What a loathsome work that is for the *Holy* Spirit to perform!

Second, the Holy Spirit transforms us "into the same image from glory to glory, even as by the Spirit of the Lord" (2 Cor. 3:18). The Spirit puts to death the energies and restless ambitions of sin by making us increasingly conscious that true life is found only in Jesus Christ. He shows us Christ's perfect loveliness, beauty, and righteousness, which have been imputed to us. We see Him willingly taking the form of a servant and being obedient to death, even the death of the cross. He did that for you. Isn't that the most wondrous, blessed, and glorious gospel in the whole universe? Behold the Lamb of God, who takes away your sin. How can you live one moment longer under the grip of sin? The Spirit's work is to sanctify you. He mortifies your sins by the law and the gospel.

THE HOLY SPIRIT INTERCEDES FOR US

Romans 8:26–27 tells us the Spirit helps us in our weakness, specifically in praying. "Likewise the Spirit also helpeth our infirmities: for we know not what we should pray for as we ought: but the Spirit itself maketh intercession for us with groanings which cannot be uttered," these verses tell us. "And he that searcheth the hearts knoweth what is the mind of the Spirit, because he maketh intercession for the saints according to the will of God."

Our prayer life is so weak. Days can go by without earnest private devotions. What ought to be the honorable and delightful privilege of addressing Almighty God becomes an irksome and neglected task. When we do pray, our mind wanders from what we are praying about within minutes. Coldness of heart, a sense of unreality about the things we are talking about, lack of conviction about bringing our petitions to God, and the absence of joy and reverence turn our prayers into a mass of confusion and failure.

Yet the Spirit intercedes for us. He comes to us as the Spirit of grace and supplication and as the author of every spiritual desire, every holy aspiration, and every reach of the heart after God. Every thought of holiness comes from the Spirit. He who leads the Christian knows what that Christian should pray for and encourages such prayers. We would find it impossible to pray for strength to pluck out an offending right eye or cut off an offending right hand, as our Lord commands. We would find it difficult to pray for strength to put to death our remaining sin. We might find it irksome to pray for poverty of spirit, grief over sin, hungering and thirsting after righteousness, or contentment with the will of God, especially if that brings loneliness or loss of someone we love best, but the Spirit always intercedes for us in accordance with God's will (v. 27), saying, "Almighty God, give her those graces." He also gives us the strength to pray with increasing discernment and increasing vehemence.

The Spirit intercedes for us "with groanings which cannot be uttered" (v. 26). His groaning registers in our hearts, not in articulate speech in the form of sentences and paragraphs with commas and periods. His intercession transcends our speech; nevertheless, His groaning has meaning and purpose. We sense the Spirit's intercession in our hearts, but we cannot say, "This morning the Spirit interceded in my heart and this is what He said." Our words cannot express what the Spirit says.

God, however, searches our hearts to know the mind of the Spirit. Hannah went to the house of God and prayed. We are told, "She spake in her heart; only her lips moved, but her voice was not heard: therefore Eli thought she had been drunken" (1 Sam. 1:13). Even the high priest of Israel was incapable of understanding what the Spirit was prompting Hannah to pray, but God knew what she longed for. The Lord knows the cause and content of the Spirit's groaning. God knows the groans of the Holy Spirit's intercession. These groanings are wholly intelligible to him, and they are consistent with God's will. So Romans 8 offers us the extraordinary assurance that every day, the hearts of millions of Christians all over the world are filled with groans of the Spirit of God that are ascending to the throne of God. This will continue on until the Savior finally appears. Then the Spirit's groanings will finally cease. As George Rawson (1807–1889) so beautifully wrote,

> Gentle, awful, holy guest,
> Make Thy temple in our breast,
> There supreme to reign and rest,
> Comforter divine.
>
> In us, for us, intercede,
> And with voiceless groanings plead
> Our unutterable need,
> Comforter divine.

I saw my former seminary president, Edmund P. Clowney, a few years ago in California. He invited me over for coffee. During our visit together, he told me that for forty years since I graduated from seminary, he has prayed for me every day. "It gets a little disheartening asking God to bless Geoff Thomas," he said. "Are there particular needs I can pray for?"

I was mightily humbled and cheered that this man prayed for me every day. It made me wonder whether I had prayed for myself every day. We are touched by friends and family members who constantly pray for us, but there are two more glorious persons who constantly pray for us: the Lord Jesus above, at the right hand of God, who makes intercession for us; and the Holy Spirit below, who prays so mysteriously in us. What encouragement we have that God "is able to do exceeding abundantly above all that we ask or think" (Eph. 3:20) in constantly praying for us. Our weakness in praying does not define the limits of God's immeasurable grace, but rather increases the knowledge, love, and wisdom of the Son and the Spirit.

The intercession of the Spirit "helpeth our infirmities" (v. 26), but it does not discourage us from praying. Nor is the Spirit's intercession the reason or rule for our prayer. Some people refuse to pray unless they are assured that the Spirit moves them to do so. That is wrong. The Spirit helps us in the performance of our duty, not in the neglect of it. The rule is that we must always pray and not faint. The rule is that in everything, by prayer and supplication, we must make our requests known to God. You may start praying by saying, "Help me, Lord." But then do not think that coldness of feeling or lack of words is proof that the Spirit is not helping you. Keep praying! In communal gatherings for prayer that feel as cold as ice, confess to God, "Lord, we feel so cold and far from Thee." That confession will immediately warm up believers and raise their spirits as the Spirit comes to lead you. The Spirit kills our misdeeds and intercedes for us.

CHAPTER FIFTEEN

The Gifts of the Holy Spirit

Now concerning spiritual gifts, brethren, I would not have you ignorant.
Ye know that ye were Gentiles, carried away unto these dumb idols, even
as ye were led. Wherefore I give you to understand, that no man speak-
ing by the Spirit of God calleth Jesus accursed: and that no man can say
that Jesus is the Lord, but by the Holy Ghost.
                                                —1 Corinthians 12:1–3

The Corinthian congregation probably sent a list of questions to Paul, and one by one he addressed those questions in the first eleven chapters of 1 Corinthians. He dealt with divisions in the church, false teachers, a Christian living in immorality, lawsuits among believers, issues of marriage, idol feasts and the Lord's Supper, and then spiritual gifts. Judging by the amount of space Paul devoted to the use of spiritual gifts, it seems to have been a critical issue in the church at Corinth.

Indeed, the issue involves critical questions such as these: What is true spirituality? What do we look for in a spiritual person? Can we test the spirituality of a Christian? Do we trust a woman's spirituality because of her glowing face and shining eyes or a man's gifts by how he teaches or prays? What are the marks of spirituality? How do we become a congregation of the Spirit? Paul addresses those questions in 1 Corinthians 12. Spiritual gifts were present in every New Testament church during the time of the apostles, but they became a problem in the Corinthian congregation. Thus we have the valuable and essential teaching of Paul on this matter.

THE TRULY SPIRITUAL PERSON FOCUSES ON CHRIST
Paul begins his teaching on spiritual gifts by getting right at their foundation. He reminds the new Christians at Corinth of their pagan past

and how they were influenced and led astray by mute idols (v. 2). Before they became Christians, the Corinthians found little intellectual stimulation or ethical teaching to feed on in pagan temple services. They were more emotionally lured into those services by drums, rituals, cries, and swooning before mute idols. They were psychologically manipulated by the choreography of pagan worship.

Paul thus begins by contrasting pagan rituals with Christian worship. He says the experience of being carried away is not the essence of true spirituality. Fanatic orators such as Adolf Hitler or Jim Jones can orchestrate that kind of response. But being swept away by emotion is no proof that the Spirit of God is present in a church. Neither does it prove that what you hear is true. Think of millions of people who mass together in different parts of the world to find enlightenment. So Paul begins his teaching on spiritual gifts with a warning against the emptiness of being carried away.

What then is the mark of the presence and operation of the Holy Spirit? Paul says, "No man speaking by the Spirit of God calleth Jesus accursed: and that no man can say that Jesus is the Lord, but by the Holy Ghost" (v. 3). The essential proof of the Spirit's presence in someone is his confession that Jesus is Lord. If you have experienced the regenerating work of the Spirit and have been truly born again, you will testify that Jesus is Lord.

You make a statement of belief but also of intellect. Your confession is not prompted by a tide of emotion. Your mind puts words and concepts together in sentences, which is typical of the Bible's approach to spirituality. Scripture offers the revelation of God in prophecies, psalms, gospels, visions, letters, and other profound pieces of writing. For example, true spirituality is explained in the letters of Paul to the churches in Rome and Ephesus. The connection between the Spirit and what the apostles have written and how we respond to that writing is essential for true spirituality.

The basic evidence of the work of the Holy Spirit is His inspiring apostles into all truth in their preaching and writing. The Spirit then creates trust and obedience in Christians as they read the words of the apostles. And then Christian readers open their mouths and give their own confessions that "Jesus is Lord." They do not merely talk about themselves and their excitement as electric feelings run up and down their spines, tears burst out of their eyes, or laughter shakes their bodies. They do not have to mention the ecstasy or thrill of their experience.

Rather, true spirituality is shown by talking about Jesus Christ and confessing that He is your Lord and your God, then changing how you live in response to this truth. A spiritual person speaks and lives a Christ-centered life. Religious egotists were beginning to infiltrate the Corinthian congregation, but Paul said the truly Spirit-filled person preeminently talks of Christ as Lord. He confesses that Jesus of Nazareth is the incarnate God. He bears witness to the Lordship of the flesh-and-blood reality of the virgin-born carpenter from Galilee.

Before becoming Christians, the Corinthians believed the peak of their rotten old religion was the feeling that they were being carried away by spiritual forces. But Paul tells them that a true spiritual experience is being obsessed with the Lord Jesus Christ, honoring Him, glorifying Him, and worshiping Him. The person most full of the Spirit is the person most full of Jesus Christ.

SPIRITUAL GIFTS ARE GIVEN TO SERVE OTHERS

In 1 Corinthians 12:4–7, Paul says, "Now there are diversities of gifts, but the same Spirit. And there are differences of administrations, but the same Lord. And there are diversities of operations, but it is the same God which worketh all in all. But the manifestation of the Spirit is given to every man to profit withal. "

The greatest evidence of the Spirit in a person is his testimony that Jesus is God and his worship of Christ. However, "Jesus is Lord" is not a mantra that Christians must chant in worship. Rather, the Spirit is evident in various ways in the assembly of Christians. There are a variety of gifts, Paul says. He then changes his word for gifts from *pneumatika* (which presumably the Corinthian church has been using) to *charismata*.

The Corinthians were trying to bring the legacy of their previous spiritualism—the numinous, the exotic, the spooky, and the ecstatic—into the church of Jesus Christ. But Paul asked for something different. He stressed the gifts of *charismata*, meaning "graces," or "a present of grace," or "grace things." The Spirit creates new dimension and power in our lives through God's grace, Paul said. God in grace acts in us to form a new nature with new resources. The new life of the Christian is not due to education or natural talents or upbringing. The Christlike graces produced by the Spirit have little to do with our brains, talents, emotions, or psychological resources. By God's free grace, the Spirit works in all of us. Think of a cobbler like William Carey or a tinker like John Bunyan and how their gifts changed the world. That was solely due to the Holy Spirit's powerful work in them, equipping them with the gifts to communicate to others.

Every virtue we possess and every victory we win and every thought of holiness come from the Spirit. He gives *charismata* to the people of God for different kinds of service (v. 5), Paul says. He refers to corporate sanctification here, for one of the chief means of grace in preparing Christians for heaven is the mysterious influence one believer has over another. Of course preaching, worship, baptism, and the Lord's Supper influence believers, but "body life" or "body ministry" is also important. Think of all the verses in the New Testament that contain the phrase *one another*. Paul says spiritual gifts are given for different kinds of service.

We see how different those services are by considering passages that tell us to love one another, be devoted to one another, give preference to one another, be like-minded with one another, refrain from judging one another, build up one another, accept one another, greet one another, wait for one another, care for one another, refrain from challenging one another or from envying one another, bear the burdens of one another, bear with one another, speak to one another, be subject to one another, highly regard one another, be truthful with one another, forgive one another, comfort one another, encourage one another, live in peace with one another, seek good for one another, exhort one another, stimulate one another, refrain from speaking against one another or complaining to one another, confess your sins to one another, pray for one another, be hospitable to one another, and serve one another.

How overwhelming our responsibility is to one another in church. How are you doing in serving fellow Christians? They will not get such service from the world, only from fellow believers. You say you are too weak or busy or deficient in certain gifts. By nature you may not have the gifts, but you do have the Holy Spirit, who gives you a rich variety of gifts that enable you to serve one another, because every Christian has them.

When God gives gifts to His people, they are not a mark of exalted spiritual privilege. They are not given to give you status as a minister or for your personal edification, enjoyment, or distinction. Spiritual gifts are given to make you better servants of other Christians in your congregation. "The greatest among you shall be the servant of all," says Jesus, and He sends the Holy Spirit to enable you to serve.

Paul amplified that by saying the ministry of the Spirit in us is for *working* (v. 6). So a spiritual gift is divine empowering from our heavenly Father to enable us to work sacrificially, lovingly, patiently, and to keep going, no matter what the challenge. After regeneration, you soon discover that you have a new energy source because you, by faith, have been plugged into the Spirit of God. The Spirit gives you gifts so you can serve one another. You can get down on your knees with a basin of water and towel to wash the feet of fellow disciples.

Paul concludes that "the manifestation of the Spirit is given to every man to profit withal" (v. 7). What an extraordinary statement. What do you expect after reading "the manifestation of the Spirit here": a rushing, mighty wind and cloven tongues of fire resting on the heads of people, people swooning or jumping or crowing like cocks? No, Paul goes on to say that the manifestation of the Spirit is given for the common good. Christians are gifted to serve others who are in need. The fruit of the manifestation of the Holy Spirit of God is not an emotional high; it is service in the fellowship of believers.

SPIRITUAL GIFTS ARE DISTRIBUTED AS THE SPIRIT DETERMINES

The Spirit gives various gifts: wisdom, knowledge, faith, healing, miraculous power, prophecy, distinguishing between spirits, speaking in tongues, and the interpretation of tongues. "But all these worketh that one and the selfsame Spirit, dividing to every man severally as he will" (vv. 8–11), Paul says.

Notice that the first gifts named are the message of wisdom and of knowledge. Gifts of intelligent and thoughtful utterance proceeding out of wise and knowledgeable lives are given for the common good of the congregation. Thank God if you have those gifts in your church. Thank God if your elders and deacons are blessed with the grace to give wise words both privately and publicly. We each have been given the gifts to offer words and deeds of wisdom as well as to receive them from others. How that benefits the entire congregation!

Of course that is also true of the other gifts Paul mentions. However, those gifts of grace would be valueless without wisdom, understanding, and knowledge. All the gifts are given to edify the congregation. For example, the gifts of miraculous powers and healing may lift the spirits of a congregation as they are used to restore a desperately ill church member to health. The spiritual gifts are given for the common good of the congregation. They all come from the Spirit, and He gives them to each Christian "as He wills." You cannot name a spiritual gift and claim it for yourself. Even in the first century, when some of these gifts were given to confirm the truth of the apostles, you could not say to the Holy Spirit, "Grant me the gift of miraculous powers, or the gift to speak a Celtic language." The Spirit was and continues to be sovereign in granting to each Christian what gifts He chooses.

THE SPIRIT BAPTIZES EVERY CHRISTIAN INTO THE BODY OF CHRIST

Paul says we are all baptized by one Spirit into one body and are all given the same Spirit to drink (1 Cor. 12:12–13). He gets close to saying "baptism in the Holy Spirit," but like every other New Testament writer never uses that phrase. Scripture always refers to baptism as *with* or *by* the Spirit.

The theme that Paul returns to in this verse is the wonderful privileges that all believers in the Corinthian congregation have received in Christ. The apostle greets them by declaring to them their glorious privileges. They are all members of one body and have all been baptized by one Spirit into this body and been given one Spirit to drink. There are not two bodies, one for those who have made a profession of faith and another for those who have not. And there is only one baptism, for baptism into the body of Christ is not a Spirit-less activity which later needs to be upgraded into Spirit baptism. One Spirit baptizes every one of us in regeneration. We are dry and thirsty sinners with nothing in the world to quench our thirst. "Drink the Spirit!" Paul commands us. So receive Him into your life, for refreshment and new life come from Him.

This baptism is also not for people as a second blessing. Baptism is the privilege of every person in every place who calls on the name of our Lord Jesus Christ. We are baptized by one Spirit into one body, and that is true for the weakest lamb in the flock of Christ, for the newest Christian, and for the backslider who has returned in repentance to Christ. It is also true of a Christian who has committed a terrible sin, for committing a particular sin does not amputate him from the body of Christ or disconnect his membership. What should be done with you who have behaved in a particularly abominable sub-Christian manner? I will take the wonderful privileges that the Spirit has given you, and I will beat you with them. How can you who died to the dominion that sin once had over you go back and live one moment longer in that sin? So repent of your sin, change your ways, and return to Christ.

VARIETY AND HARMONY EXIST IN THE BODY OF CHRIST

The final section of 1 Corinthians 12 describes various organs and limbs of the human body. Some of them are more prominent than others, but that is purely due to their functions. The point is that every part of the body is necessary, particularly the less aesthetically pleasing parts. Let none of the seemingly less attractive parts of the body feel inferior to more significant parts, and let none of the more spectacular parts of the body feel superior to less impressive parts. God has designed and arranged every organ in the body (v. 18). Each part needs every other part. The parts do not compete with each other; rather, they complement and supplement each other. If the body was all nose, what would digest its food and remove its waste products?

In talking about the different gifts the Lord gives to members of the church, Paul concludes with another list, this time of persons rather than gifts (vv. 28–30). This list includes the gifts of apostle, administrator, and those who help them. Neither list is complete and incapable of adjustment. Some of the gifts are present in every church, while others are not. Note that in both lists, speaking in tongues and interpreting those tongues comes at the very end. Also, immediately after mentioning those gifts, Paul warns us to "covet earnestly the best gifts" (v. 31). The analogy of the inequality of body parts seems particularly applicable in this warning.

CLOSING APPLICATION

Let us conclude this chapter on the gifts of the Holy Spirit with the following reminders:

1. Note the difference between the gifts of the Spirit and the fruits of the Spirit. The fruits of the Spirit are those graces that the Holy Spirit creates in every true Christian. They are the divinely begotten virtues which make us like Christ and other believers. The preeminent fruit of the Spirit is love, which Paul explains in detail in the next chapter. If someone who professes to be a believer is characterized by a lack of love, it is difficult to see the Spirit of God dwelling in him. The apostle John emphasizes this point by saying, "every one that loveth is born of God, and knoweth God" (1 John 4:7). If you see this love in a person, you can conclude that he has been born of God. So the fruit of the Spirit is what makes us like Christ and fellow believers.

The gifts of the Spirit are different. Although they too originate in the Holy Spirit, His gifts make us different from one another. The analogy for these gifts is the body, which has many organs, all different from one another. As 1 Corinthians 12:18–20 says, "But now hath God set the members every one of them in the body, as it hath pleased him. And if they were all one member, where were the body? But now are they many members, yet but one body."

Paul lists many spiritual gifts, asking of each, "Are all apostles? Are all prophets? Are all teachers? Do all work miracles? Do all have gifts of healing? Do all speak in tongues? Do all interpret?" The answer to each of these questions is, of course, no. These gifts distinguish one Christian from another. Thus it is wrong to choose one of the Spirit's gifts and make that gift the defining evidence for the presence of the Spirit in everyone else's life. The Holy Spirit gives some gifts to one person while refusing them to others. All Christians are given gifts by the same Spirit, but those gifts differ according to the Spirit's choosing. But every Christian is given the Spirit's fruit, especially love.

2. The gifts of the Spirit are from Almighty God. The creator and sustainer of the cosmos, who is infinite, eternal, and unchanging in His being, wisdom, power, holiness, justice, goodness, and truth, is the giver of gifts to His chosen ones. The Spirit is God. This is strikingly seen in the Trinitarian structure of 1 Corinthians 12:4–6. The order of the persons of the Godhead here is not the baptismal formula of Father, Son, and Holy Spirit. Rather, verses 4–6 refer to the Spirit of God first, then to the Lord Jesus, and last of all to the Father in saying that there are different kinds of gifts but the same Spirit. There are different kinds of service but the same Lord. There are different kinds of working, but the same God works all of them in all men.

Some people claim to have a spiritual gift and say, "This is mine because Almighty God, the maker of the Milky Way, has given it to me." That is a staggering claim, and if it is true, I have to accept it and be silent. Yet I do ask that we consider what the marks of the indwelling of God in the Christian are according to the New Testament. I too make the audacious claim that this Almighty God has called me and gifted me to be a pastor and preacher. The criteria for the truthfulness of that claim must transcend my own personal feelings that it is true.

Those feelings may be important for me, but we must go to the Bible to see what the marks are of a man who is called by God into the ministry. What are the life and ethics and theology of such a person? What are his required duties and needed energies? My life as well as the life of every true preacher must be examined in the light of Scripture. If there are no criteria to explain what some of these gifts are and what the stewardship of them consists of, we must be silent about our claims to have such gifts. There is no call of the Creator without the integrity of His requirements, and these are spelled out in the Word of God.

Consider Neil Babcock, who spent years with groups of people who claimed to receive messages directly from the God of the universe. Increasingly Babcock became less comfortable with these claims. He said, "'Thus saith the Lord.' How I struggled with those words! As Jacob wrestled with the angel in the dark of the night, so I wrestled with those words. As the angel wounded Jacob, so those words wounded me. And as Jacob's defeat became his victory, I thank God those words, so right and unfathomable in their significance, defeated me.

"The moment of truth came when I heard a prophecy spoken at a church I was visiting. I was sitting in the church trying to worship God while dreading the approach of that obligatory moment of silence which signalled that a prophecy was about to be spoken. The silence came, and soon it was broken by a bold and commanding 'Thus saith the Lord!' Those words triggered an immediate reaction. Conviction, like water rising against a dam, began to fill my soul.... Until finally, the dam burst: 'This is not my God,' I cried within my heart. 'This is not my Lord!'"[1]

3. *Some of these gifts ceased before the end of the first century.* The first gift (v. 29) is the gift of apostle. Could anyone apart from the twelve who were called by Christ and set apart by the church claim to be an apostle? Could you aspire to be one? Could you put your name forward for the church to

1. Neil Babcock, *My Search of Charismatic Reality* (London: The Wakeman Trust, 1992), 58–59.

vote on your becoming an apostle? Could a congregation claim that their minister had grown to the status of apostle?

In Acts 1:21–22, Peter talks to the church about the qualifications of an apostle. He says, "It is necessary to choose one of the men who have been with us the whole time the Lord Jesus went in and out among us, beginning from John's baptism to the time when Jesus was taken up from us. For one of these must become with us a witness of His resurrection."

To qualify as an apostle, a person must have walked with Christ during His earthly ministry and must have been present when the resurrected Christ revealed Himself. It is thus impossible for people after the time of the apostles to become apostles, because the Lord Jesus is now in heaven. No one has seen Him in the flesh since the first century.

You may ask, "What of the apostle Paul? He didn't see the risen Jesus Christ, did he?" Yes, he did. Paul says that on the road to Damascus, he saw the real, living, glorified Jesus who stepped through the veil and met with Paul.

The spiritual gift of apostle has now ceased. That gift was a foundation-laying work of the church, and that function is done. The gospel church has always been cessationist in viewing the gift of apostle and prophet. That office was given at one time in the history of redemption; it was not intended to be a constant flowing gift of the Spirit into the life of the church. Apostleship was a foundational gift. Today the miraculous God-breathed Bible that the apostles completed is the permanent spiritual gift of God to every gospel church.

In his book *Authority*, Martyn Lloyd-Jones says apostleship is the only, final authority. "It cannot be added to because there cannot be any successors to the apostles," he says. "By definition they cannot have successors.... Those originally chosen have had no successors. There have been no others who have been especially called and endowed and inspired to speak and to teach authoritatively by the risen Lord himself directly. The thing is impossible. There is to be no fresh revelation. There is no need of any. It was given and given finally to the apostles (see Jude 3).

"The church is built upon the foundation of the apostles and prophets. We must therefore reject every supposed new revelation, every addition to doctrine. We must assert that all teaching and all truth and all doctrine must be tested in the light of the Scriptures. Here is God's revelation of himself, given in parts and portions in the Old Testament with an increasing clarity and with a culminating finality, coming eventually 'in the fulness of times' to the perfect, absolute, final revelation in God the Son."[2]

So God gave some gifts for the foundation of the church. This was especially so of the testimony of the divinely appointed apostles and the prophets with whom they were identified. These were channels of God of truth to His people for the foundation of every gospel congregation. But God also gives other superstructural gifts, which continue in the church today. We ask for those gifts of the triune God to spread the gospel of Christ throughout the world and to build His church until the second coming of Christ.

---

2. D. Martyn Lloyd-Jones, *Authority* (Edinburgh: The Banner of Truth Trust, 1984), 59–61.

CHAPTER SIXTEEN

The Most Excellent Way of Love

Though I speak with the tongues of men and of angels, and have not char-
ity, I am become as sounding brass, or a tinkling cymbal. And though I
have the gift of prophecy, and understand all mysteries, and all knowl-
edge; and though I have all faith, so that I could remove mountains, and
have not charity, I am nothing. And though I bestow all my goods to feed
the poor, and though I give my body to be burned, and have not charity,
it profiteth me nothing. —1 Corinthians 13:1–3

The great Bible chapter on the theme of love is sandwiched between a
chapter that ends with the words "covet earnestly the best gifts" and
one that begins with the words "desire spiritual gifts." Chapter 13 says
the only way spiritual gifts can be pursued and used is in love. Love is
thinking of others with care, honor, and respect to build them up in the
church. Lack of love seems to have been the greatest weakness of the
Corinthian congregation.

THE HOLY SPIRIT'S GIFT OF LOVE

Love is the supreme grace given to every believer. If the church is the fellowship of the Holy Spirit, it is also the grace of the Lord Jesus Christ and
the love of God. It is the community in which our delight is to keep the
greatest commandments to love God with all our hearts and to love our
neighbors as ourselves, because we are full of Christ's grace. To fall short
of love is to break the greatest of all commandments.

Notice that Paul begins chapter 13 with the gift of tongues, which
is beloved by the Corinthians. He progresses to the gifts he personally
esteems, prophecy and faith, then moves to the gifts valued by the pagan
culture of Corinth, giving up everything you own for the poor or giving

up your life as a martyr. Then Paul says love transcends everything; it is greater than every other gift of the Holy Spirit.

Paul begins by talking about the tongues of men and of angels. He says that if you have developed your gift of tongues to such heavenly heights that you speak like an angel, but you lack love, everything you say is as empty as the banging of a pagan gong to summon gods to the temple or the clashing of cymbals to drive off evil spirits.

Paul next talks about having such a great gift of prophecy that you understand the secret things that belong to God alone. A person with this gift could explain where sin came from, announce the date of the second coming, and show how the Holy Trinity works. All mysteries and all knowledge belong to a person with such a gift. In addition, this person has such great faith that he can speak to a mountain, and the mountain will move. A person with such prophetic powers and mountain-moving faith must surely be a spiritual giant! "That isn't necessarily so," Paul says. Without love, a person of great prophecy and faith is nothing.

Next, Paul talks about giving away everything one owns to the poor. Surely such a person deserves front-page headlines. So does the person who is so staunch a believer that he gives up his life for what he believes. Surely this person would merit a statue in the gallery of people of faith. But Paul says generosity or martyrdom without love is nothing.

You can give away everything, even your body, for your beliefs, but what is your motive for doing so? Is it for praise, honor, attention, or rewards in the afterlife? Our world is terrorized by suicide bombers who are willing to blow up themselves because of their faith. Without love, their deaths mean nothing. Furthermore, such a person may also surrender his body so he may boast, but true love excludes boasting.

Paul goes on to define what love is. He says, "Charity suffereth long, and is kind; charity envieth not; charity vaunteth not itself, is not puffed up, doth not behave itself unseemly, seeketh not her own, is not easily provoked, thinketh no evil; rejoiceth not in iniquity, but rejoiceth in the truth; beareth all things, believeth all things, hopeth all things, endureth all things" (vv. 4–7).

Love is not primarily emotional, passionate, and fiery; it is patient, Paul says. Are you disappointed in this definition, which presumes taming your emotions, stretching yourself for others, and lengthening the time before you respond to a person who may provoke you or try your patience? Love is not essentially a feeling or affection; it is a way of behaving, Paul says. It probably starts as a feeling but then develops into actions. Love does things; it gives to others.

For example, the Jews hated the Samaritans. So a Samaritan man lived his entire life knowing he was despised by his Jewish neighbors. But one day this Samaritan came across a Jew who had been robbed, beaten up, and left for dead on the side of the road. Jewish leaders saw the body but hurried past it to go on and do their business.

Love does not pass by a wounded person. It stops and does something. Love is kind, says 1 Corinthians 13; it is not self-seeking, keeps no record of wrongs, and does not delight in evil. Rather, it always protects and always perseveres. The Samaritan loved the wounded Jew, not emotionally or with infatuation, but in his actions. He addressed the man's wounds, then took him to a place of safety where he could heal.

Finally, verse 8 says, "Charity never faileth." Some gifts, such as prophecy, tongue-speaking, and knowledge will cease. Perfection will come, and the imperfect will disappear (v. 10). This perfection may refer to the time after the death of all the apostles and their gifts. When that time comes, the fullness of revelation, which is the apostles' eternal legacy to the church, will be evident in every congregation. We should not dismiss that viewpoint too readily, though it is a minority view, for this letter to the Corinthians is probably the first piece of New Testament Scripture in the church.

No gospels had been written at the time the Corinthian church received their first letter from Paul, nor had any epistles to the Romans or Ephesians. Letters to James and the Thessalonians and Galatians may have been written, but they may not yet have come to Corinth. At the time 1 Corinthians comes to the church of Corinth, the congregation possesses gifts of revelation, wisdom, knowledge, tongues, prophecies, and interpretations, but it does not yet have the New Testament. The church is spiritually impoverished.

So some scholars argue that *maturity* (*teleios*) in verse 10 refers to the time when the twenty-seven books of the New Testament become the blessed possession of every church, complementing the thirty-nine books of the Old Testament. Combined, those two testaments become God's Word for the church until the end of the age, enabling believers to become complete and fully furnished for all good works God gives them to do. However, others do not accept this view but believe that *perfect* or *mature* refers to the end of time, when God will be seen "face to face" (v. 12).

Either way, Paul's concern in these verses is to edify believers in Corinth who think they are super-Christians because they have certain gifts of the Spirit. "You must grow in love," Paul tells them. However mature we are right now, we are still childlike in our faith. We will attain full maturity only after we get to heaven.

With all their gifts, the Corinthian Christians are looking at themselves as though dimly in a mirror. They haven't yet received a single gospel, much less the revelation of Christ in the gospels, Acts, letters, and Revelation. They are certainly not yet in the presence of the Lord Jesus in glory. Faith, hope, and love are not transient graces; they will all endure, but the greatest of them is love, Paul says.

THE HOLY SPIRIT'S GIFT OF PROPHECY

Paul begins chapter 14 with the commands to "follow' and "desire." He wants the ardor of believers to be channeled into the way of love, particularly through the gift of prophecy. The goal of prophecy, according to verse 3, is to strengthen, encourage, and comfort others.

What prophecy does first is to *strengthen* others. This word is repeated a number of times in this chapter in verses 4, 12, 17, and 26. Sometimes this word is translated as *edify, build up,* and *strengthen.* So the purpose of prophesying is to edify, build up, and strengthen.

The gift of prophecy helps people, Paul says in verse 3, which is the essence of a gift: to be wonderfully useful in serving others. So Paul teaches us to eagerly desire the gift of prophecy. The original word for *prophecy* is not easily translated into English, but other possibilities, such as "speak thoughtfully" or "counsel" or "express the will of God" aren't much better. Neither is "preach," because the gift of prophecy is exercised more outside the pulpit than from it.

For example, in our church's meeting of officers, participants are asked to address an issue, then pass the wisdom of their decisions to the congregation to strengthen and encourage and comfort people. In the "experience meetings" in Wales after the Great Awakening of the eighteenth century, Christians would prophesy in thoughtful speech to one another. A group of spiritual leaders in the Highlands of Scotland had the gift of explaining the will of God in a certain situation so that Christians were built up, strengthened, and comforted. These are all examples of the gift of prophecy.

THE HOLY SPIRIT'S GIFT OF TONGUES

The gift of tongues appears to be a lesser gift because Paul says, "For greater is he that prophesieth than he that speaketh with tongues" (v. 5). But is that really what he means? Let us examine the gift of tongues in more detail, answering four questions: What precisely is this gift? To whom is it directed? How do unbelievers respond to it? How should it be used in church worship?

1. *What exactly is this gift?* Acts 2 is the first place in the New Testament where we read of the gift of tongues. Under the direct influence of the Holy Spirit, this gift allows believers to speak in languages they have not previously known. They use these languages in prayers of thanksgiving or singing and in speaking about the great works of God in the gospel. The same Greek word for "tongue" in 1 Corinthians 12:5 is used in Acts 2, and elsewhere in the New Testament the word refers to an existing language.

During Pentecost in Jerusalem, the Holy Spirit gifted 120 believers with tongues. People from many Gentile nations heard those believers speaking and said in amazement, "We do hear them speak in our tongues the wonderful works of God" (Acts 2:11). Luke, who wrote Acts, tells how Paul and Apollos then went to Corinth, where they started a church. From this we may conclude that the gift of tongues in Corinth was the same gift given at Pentecost.

Of the three great signs at Pentecost—the mighty, rushing wind; the appearance of flames on believers; and the gift of tongues, the most mobile and useful gift in the mission church is tongues. This gift is used in Samaria, in Cornelius's household, and in Ephesus. Its presence says, "The Spirit at work here is the same Spirit that was poured out on Pentecost. We are one in the Spirit."

Paul gives no indication that when the gospel reached Corinth another kind of tongue, or "ecstatic utterances," emerged in the church. Rather 1 Corinthians and other passages in the New Testament always refer to the gift of tongues as articulate, verbal communication. From the beginning of creation, God and angels have clearly spoken to humans in their own language. God speaks to many of us in English, He speaks to my Welsh wife in her Welsh Bible, and He speaks to others in their native language. Whatever language God uses to speak to men and women is a true, living language.

If the gift of tongues in Corinth was different from the gift of tongues in Ephesus or Samaria or Cornelius's household or Jerusalem, surely Acts or 1 Corinthians would have given some description or explanation of that change, but they do not. Consistently, the gift of tongues in the New Testament refers to languages. Phil Roberts wisely says, "Ecstatic utterances are the product of altered states of consciousness or of mindlessness. As God is a supremely rational being and constantly lays stress upon the place of our rational faculty in spiritual activity, it would seem contrary to all we know to believe he would employ mindless communication, that is, that which has no rational basis and indistinguishable from gibberish."[1]

The gift of tongues was to be used in Christian worship, quite unlike that of the worship of pagans in which people were carried away by spectacle and sound (1 Cor. 12:2). In gospel worship, all gifts were to be used with this acknowledgment that "the spirits of the prophets are subject to the prophets" (1 Cor. 14:32), and in obedience to the teaching, "Let all things be done decently and in order" (1 Cor. 14:40).

The gift of tongues actually has three aspects: the gift of speaking an unknown language, the gift of the speaker to understand and interpret what he says, and the gift of people who can deliver the correct interpretation of those words to others. Paul thus says to the church:

> Wherefore let him that speaketh in an unknown tongue pray that he may interpret. For if I pray in an unknown tongue, my spirit prayeth, but my understanding is unfruitful. What is it then? I will pray with the spirit, and I will pray with the understanding also: I will sing with the spirit, and I will sing with the understanding also. Else when thou shalt bless with the spirit, how shall he that occupieth the room of the unlearned say Amen at thy giving of thanks, seeing he understandeth not what thou sayest? For thou verily givest thanks well, but the other is not edified (vv. 13–17).

So, above all, the gift of tongues is to be used to benefit others.

2. To whom is this gift directed? The gift of tongues is directed to God (v. 2), Paul says, and declares how great God is in creation and redemption. The gift of prophecy is directed to people. The strength of prophecy is

---

1. Phil Roberts, *The Gift of Tongues* (Stoke-on-Trent, U.K.: Tentmaker Publications, 1991), 5.

that everyone in the church may hear it, understand it, and be edified by it (v. 4), whereas the words of a foreign language spoken by a person with the gift of tongues are limited in usefulness, particularly if no one understands them.

Paul views the gift of tongues in Corinth as a true gift from God, but he wishes that all the Corinthian believers might enjoy this gift along with every other spiritual gift. He does not direct Christians in any congregation to seek the gift of tongues. "I would that ye all spake with tongues but rather that ye prophesied," he says. "For greater is he that prophesieth than he that speaketh with tongues, except he interpret, that the church may receive edifying" (v. 5). Gifts are given to edify and strengthen the church, so Paul says, "I thank my God, I speak with tongues more than ye all: yet in the church I had rather speak five words with my understanding, that by my voice I might teach others also, than ten thousand words in an unknown tongue" (vv. 18–19).

When you say, "Christ died for our sins," those five words could bring salvation and comfort to a hearer. But if those words are spoken in a language that a listener does not understand, they will not profit him at all. In the scale of gifts, the most useful is the one that edifies and strengthens people, whereas the least is one that is used more for self-interest than for the benefit of others.

3. How do unbelievers respond to this gift? If unbelievers come to a worship service in Corinth where everyone speaks in tongues at the same time, they might conclude that believers are out of their mind, Paul says (v. 23). The doubts of visitors about Christianity might only be confirmed by what they see.

By contrast, how different their response might be if one by one people in the church prophesy to one another (cf. v. 31), praising God for His goodness to them. Paul says the result of such testimony might be that a stranger "is convinced of all, he is judged of all: and thus are the secrets of his heart made manifest; and so falling down on his face he will worship God, and report that God is in you of a truth" (vv. 24–25). The testimony and the teaching of one person might then have a profound impact on unbelievers.

The gift of tongues can be as unproductive to unbelievers as trying to mix oil with water. Tongues may actually harden an unbeliever against faith in God. To illustrate, Paul quotes from Isaiah 28:11–12: "In the law it is written, With men of other tongues and other lips will I speak unto this people; and yet for all that will they not hear me, saith the Lord" (v. 21).

Paul wisely says that the marks of conversion become evident when a person comes into a worship meeting, understands the message of the gospel, and is convinced that he is a sinner. The secrets of his past life seem to be known by everyone who speaks. Overwhelmed with the reality that God is among these people, the sinner falls to the ground. He is not so much fascinated by the gifts as he is convinced of the great giver. He falls at the feet of the living God as one dead. That is the mark of successful evangelism.

4. What part do tongues play in a worship service? Paul begins the next section with a description of a typical worship service in Corinth, which is pretty chaotic. "When ye come together, every one of you hath a psalm, hath a doctrine, hath a tongue, hath a revelation, hath an interpretation" (v. 26), he says. Everyone is sitting on the edge of their seats waiting to make their contribution, so the meetings are long and full of words. Paul returns to the teaching that the Corinthian believers must judge what the best gifts are for helping people in worship. "Let all things be done unto edifying" (v. 26), Paul says. Let nobody think that congregational worship is a platform for one person or another to exhibit his gifts to the church. Do not join a certain church because it allows you to talk more than in another church. The purpose of worship is to strengthen people in their walk with Christ. Judge the usefulness of worship practices not by how many people can contribute in an hour but by how the congregation is strengthened in that worship.

Paul introduces guidelines for the exercise of spiritual gifts in worship. Two people (well, maybe three) may speak in tongues, and that is it. No more. Then the person with the gift of interpretation must speak. If a person with that gift is not present, the tongue speaker must be silent. So too, two people with the gift of prophecy (at the most, three) are enough for any congregation to hear and digest and carefully weigh. People should patiently wait their turn to speak or prophesy, for, as Paul explains, "God is not the author of confusion, but of peace" (v. 33). He concludes this chapter by saying, "Let all things be done decently and in order" (v. 40). Women should remain silent, for they do not have the authority to speak publicly to the entire congregation. Taking a role of headship within the church is forbidden them.

It is all right for them to speak on other occasions and places when people gather together to study and pray. A family or a group can encourage women and novices to pray on those occasions. But in the midweek meeting, the congregation must exercise caution to preserve some biblical order so that while men take the leadership in intercession and women wait before praying for men to lead the congregation in prayer. That is what every godly woman desires.

Those are the comments on worship the apostle Paul gives us. They are inspired by the Spirit of God in a chapter in the Bible that speaks most clearly of the exercise of spiritual gifts within a congregation. This passage is one of the most difficult chapters in the Bible to exegete. The great preacher Chrysostom, born in 344, wrote of this chapter, "This whole place is very obscure, but the obscurity is produced by our ignorance of the facts referred to and by their cessation, being such as then used to occur but now no longer takes place."[2]

There are opportunities every week in a midweek service for sharing the church's needs and blessings and for members in good standing in the congregation to address people in prayer, but very rarely is an ordinary church member called to offer a message to the whole gathering, even in the most spiritual of churches. The situation today is different from that in the church at Corinth. Today we all have the Bible, and our worship is led by a person gifted and appointed by God who, with the inspiration of the Holy Spirit, declares the Word and its implications to the congregation. He does this just as Christ did in the synagogue of Nazareth. We are helped by words we read in Scripture in the discipline of private devotion, but there is a difference between the Spirit's ministry to us in a quiet place, and our public expression of what we have learned to the whole congregation. Few personal blessings are designed to be transferred to public messages that are delivered to an entire assembly.

---

2. Chrysostom, "Homily 29 on 1 Cor. 12:1–2," in *Nicene and Post-Nicene Fathers of the Christian Church*, ed. Philip Schaff (Grand Rapids: Eerdmans, 1989), 12:168.

THE HOLY SPIRIT'S GIFT OF THE WORD

As Paul brings this chapter to a close he asks, "Came the word of God out from you?" (v. 36). Of course it did not. The Word of God originated in heaven and came to the church via apostles who were called, gifted, and equipped. It did not come from nineteenth-century Germany, where modern higher criticism originated. It did not come from Rome, where Roman Catholic traditions originated. It did not come from Geneva in the fertile preaching and writing of John Calvin. It did not come from the Mormon Church in Utah. It did not come from Welsh Calvinistic Methodism. The Word of God originated in heaven and stands above every denomination and cult and church, insisting that every Christian hide it in his heart so that he does not sin against God.

Paul also asks, "Came it unto you only?" (v. 36). If you stood in the Vatican and witnessed the confidence and authority of the papacy, you might also sense the Roman Catholic Church's conviction that it is the only true church of God in the world, and its doctrines are what you must believe, and its traditions are the way you must do things. It believes it is the only one the full Word of God has reached.

If you went to Salt Lake City and walked around the temple of the Church of the Latter Day Saints, you might be aware of the same confidence that this is the true church, the only one to have received the final revelation of God on gold tablets. People in ten thousand tiny independent congregations have the same attitude. They believe they are the only ones who are preserving the truth, which has not reached any other group. They broke away from other churches, believing, "We are the only people to whom the Word of God has been revealed."

The answer to both questions Paul asks is no. The Word of God comes to us; it does not originate with us. It comes from God, and we are certainly not the only people it reaches. The gift of tongues the Corinthians experience have also been spoken in Ephesus, Cornelius's household, Samaria, Jerusalem, and many other places in Greece and Asia. So Paul says, "The gospel has spread to the whole eastern Mediterranean basin, but if you are going to continue to be a part of the people of God, you had better maintain the unity of the Spirit in the bonds of peace, and that comes about by knowing and doing what God says in His Word." The Scriptures are the foundation for the whole church—not the Bible plus the sacred traditions of Rome nor the Bible plus the Book of Mormon nor the Bible plus modern criticism. Paul warns, "If any man think himself to be a prophet, or spiritual, let him acknowledge that the things that I write unto you are the commandments of the Lord. But if any man be ignorant, let him be ignorant" (vv. 37–38).

This is a striking statement. What Paul writes in this chapter, in this entire letter, and in all his writings is the Lord's command. Not only the apostle Paul but other apostles write other books of the New Testament or stand behind Mark (as Peter does) or Luke (as Paul does). They write with the Spirit's assistance and at the Lord's command. Every church must acknowledge this. If some practices or beliefs in a church are not in agreement with what is written in Scripture, they must be changed until everything matches what is written.

Likewise, the preachers Jesus Christ sends into the world do not have the option to choose practices they like, such as special vestments or ideas they agree with. The Lord does not grant them that option. For two thousand years, the gospel has gone out into the whole world. Both the world and the church belong to the Lord, and the church has the right to insist that its preachers bring them God's Word. Every other idea (whether it comes from learned academics or individuals who claim to be prophets) must be measured against Scripture. If no biblical support can be found for this idea, no person's conscience is bound to believe it.

Do not ignore this warning, for if you do, *you* will be ignored. In the great day when all people in the world are gathered before the judgment seat of Christ, those who stood and spoke in the name of Christ will be under special scrutiny because of the influence they have had. They will be tested whether they acknowledge that what the apostle Paul wrote was the Lord's command. If they did, they will be welcomed to the joy of their Lord, but if they did not, they will be ignored. That is the essence of 1 Corinthians 14 on the gift of tongues and prophecy.

CHAPTER SEVENTEEN

The Sealing of the Holy Spirit

In whom ye also trusted, after that ye heard the word of truth, the gospel of your salvation: in whom also after that ye believed, ye were sealed with that holy Spirit of promise.
                                                                    —Ephesians 1:13

A Christian is not a loner. Our family, friendships, leisure time, home, and money, indeed everything about us, is inseparably linked to the Lord Jesus Christ. The Savior affects everything in the lives of His people. In Ephesians 1:13, Paul tells us the Christian is included in Christ. According to our text, three things must happen for that to be true.

1. You hear the word of truth. Christianity claims you should become a Christian because Christianity is true. Christianity is not a myth or an elaborate hoax, or a "cunningly devised [fable]" (2 Peter 1:16). What it says is absolutely true. Before you can be included in Christ, you must hear this truth. If you want to hear this truth proclaimed, you must go to a church that explains the Bible and the consequences of applying its words to your life. You must hear the word of truth because it is utterly indispensable to your salvation. You cannot be included in Christ without hearing the truth, which Paul describes as "the gospel of your salvation." The word of truth offers good news about sinners like you: you may be saved from your guilt and God's holy condemnation of your sins. Have you listened to the Word of God? If not, how can you dismiss as rubbish what you've never thought about? The blessed message of Christianity speaks about the good news of salvation.

2. You believe what you hear. You must trust the message about Jesus Christ and entrust yourself to Him. A woman who is about to marry knows that from the time she is wedded, her life will be included in the life of her husband. The two will become one. He will care for her and for the children God gives them. She trusts in him and everything he tells her. A husband also trusts his wife. That is the kind of faith written about in our text. It speaks of believing in someone you love so you may be committed to that person. So, you must first hear the word of truth, then believe it enough to entrust yourself to the Lord Jesus.

3. *You are sealed with the Holy Spirit.* Prophets such as Ezekiel and Joel promised that the Holy Spirit would one day be poured out on every person who believed. Since the day of Pentecost, the Spirit has come upon every Christian. We are born into new life in Christ by the Spirit of God. That is why we believe that God's Word is true. That is why we entrust ourselves to Jesus Christ and are included in Him. The Holy Spirit seals our belief that we belong to God.

These three steps of faith define a person as a Christian. Let us now more closely examine the third step of being sealed by the Holy Spirit and what it means. The Authorized Version of the Bible says: "After that ye believed ye were sealed with the holy Spirit of promise." Assisted by that translation, some people have said a person can be an unsealed Christian and can live many years without being sealed with the Spirit.

I cannot accept that interpretation, first, because a close relationship exists between faith and sealing. Only believers are sealed; unbelievers are not. Second, the Authorized Version of the Bible is not the best translation of this particular verse. A similar construction of this verse often occurs in the gospels, where we are told, "Jesus answering said,... You believing were sealed." You wouldn't say, "After Jesus had answered, he said..." Certainly you would not think the phrase in the gospels means that many years after Jesus answered, He said something else. So it is equally unhelpful to translate the construction in Ephesians 1:13 as the Authorized Version does. What Paul says is aptly translated as, "Having believed, you were marked in him with a seal, the promised Holy Spirit" (NIV 1984).

THE SEALING OF THE SPIRIT

There is no doubt that after we become Christians, we may experience memorable blessings from God. Yet many Christians cannot state the actual time they became followers of the Lord Jesus Christ. They may be unsure of the year that they experienced regeneration by the Holy Spirit.

Regeneration is the greatest change a person can know, for in it he is given the life of heaven. His old heart of stone is replaced by a heart of flesh, his sins are forgiven, and the righteousness of Christ is imputed to him. He is adopted into the family of God and joined to Jesus Christ, yet, quite astonishingly, he is unaware of precisely when this extraordinary transformation took place. "I once was blind but now I see," is all he can say.

Since many Christians cannot pinpoint the time of their regeneration, subsequent experiences of God's blessing in their lives may be more memorable than the time when they became Christians. A believer will surely remember when his spirit was affected by certain sermons or when he was surprised while singing the words of a hymn or enlightened in a prayer meeting when he experienced the presence of the Lord in a precious way. A believing woman might enjoy the glory of her Creator God as she watches the sun go down, or a farmer might stop his tractor as he is overwhelmed with God's love for a sinner like himself. One night he may have a vivid dream. The details of the dream slip away, but the impression of radiance and splendor live on. In a camp or in a conference or on a Sunday evening in church, a believer may feel the Lord's nearness. He may be preaching or praying and feel captivated by the Lord Jesus. Such experiences impress a believer with God's nearness. He humbly seeks those experiences and accepts them with joyful thanksgiving.

How do Christians explain these times? One might modestly say, "I had a blessed time in my little room that day," and call this experience a visitation from God, a blessing, a baptism, a sealing, a filling, or a coming upon him.

Alvin Plantinga, one of the world's leading philosophers, has taught at Yale, Harvard, the University of Chicago, Calvin College, and Notre Dame. His powers of logic are staggering. Plantinga said he left home as a young man to go to Harvard University. There he was struck by the enormous variety of spiritual and intellectual opinions. He spent much time arguing about the existence of God. "I began to wonder whether what I had always believed could really be true," he said.

Something then happened to Plantinga on that campus at Harvard. He wrote, "One gloomy evening I was returning from dinner. It was dark, windy, raining...nasty. But suddenly it was as if the heavens

opened. I heard, so it seemed, music of overwhelming power and grandeur and sweetness. There was light of unimaginable splendor and
beauty; it seemed I could see into heaven itself. I suddenly saw or perhaps
felt with great clarity and persuasion and conviction that the Lord was
really there and was all I had thought."[1]

The experience affected Plantinga for a long time. Though he was
still caught up in arguments about the existence of God, they seemed
merely academic and of little existential concern.

Please do not sniff at this experience as mere emotionalism. I believe
that the Bible affirms such experiences. For example, we are told that the
disciples were filled with joy and the Holy Spirit. Surely that says more
than that they were regenerate. Or in the Psalms, King David writes that
God "is the health of my countenance" (Ps. 42:11). David had been conscious of his spiritual disintegration and coldness, but God delivered him
from that. Again, Peter speaks of an experience of "joy unspeakable" that
was "full of glory" (1 Peter 1:8).

Many believers have had moving religious experiences, but we hesi-
tate about referring to them as a sealing of the Spirit because some people
can have such experiences and yet go to hell. These experiences are not
the sole prerogative of evangelical Christians; all kinds of Buddhists and
cultists have religious experiences, whereas those who have been sealed
by the Spirit will never perish. Jesus says many will say to Him on the
last day, "We have eaten and drunk in thy presence" (Luke 13:26), yet He
will say to them, "Depart from me, all ye workers of iniquity" (v. 27).

C. R. Vaughan took a different approach to the sealing of the Spirit. In
The Gifts of the Holy Spirit, Vaughan said the Spirit seals the believer with a
variety of blessings and activities that characterize the mature Christian
life.[2] Vaughan encouraged us to desire the sealing of God's salvation, the
sealing of all spiritual necessities, the sealing of the great doctrine of the
covenant, the sealing of the spirit of prayer, and the sealing of evidences
of conversion in the renewed heart. We are to ask God for the sealing of
all energies of grace and every vital driving spiritual force in our regenerate souls as well as the hope of heaven. Vaughan believed that the

---

1. As cited in David Feddes, *Radio Pulpit Ministry of the Back to God Hour* 40, no. 3
(February 1995): 19.

2. C. R. Vaughan, *The Gifts of the Holy Spirit* (Edinburgh: The Banner of Truth Trust,
1975), 259–75.

sealing of the Spirit is the means by which Christians attain assurance and renewing energy in the blessings of our life with God.

He put the sealing of the Holy Spirit firmly in the category of progressive sanctification. He did not believe that one supreme religious experience brings all these blessings into a Christian's life. Rather, he urged, "Go on being sealed by the Spirit in the whole range of your walk with God." The Christian should grow in assurance and usefulness, and this is attained by the work of the Spirit in our lives, he said.

Personally, I consider the experiences of God's nearness in my life as the presence of God and insist that such experiences must be structured by the biblical motifs of ruin, redemption, and regeneration by grace alone, faith alone, and Christ alone. Otherwise religious experience (which is not uncommon) can give religious unbelievers false grounds of hope. Vaughan's emphasis on experiential growth due to the Spirit's work in our lives is grand, but I would not use the words *sealing* or *baptism* to describe those attainments. I do not think either word is used that way in the Bible. I would use the word *sealing* in the initial definitive work of sanctification, which is the blessed privilege of every true believer rather than make it part of progressive sanctification.

The great word in our text is *seal*. In the New Testament a seal was a sign of ownership. It was an authentication and guarantee of the genuineness of a particular article or document. It was a certificate of trustworthiness saying, "This is authentic." It was also a medium of proof. The seal granted authority, gave a commission, and delegated power. The seal on the stone of the tomb of our Lord said, in effect, "This tomb is now under Caesar's authority; back off."

Likewise, Paul says to the Corinthians, "For the seal of mine apostleship are ye in the Lord" (1 Cor. 9:2). The apostolic gifts Paul bestowed on the Corinthians, and the life of Christ that those gifts displayed, were a seal that Paul was called to be an apostle and was sent to preach to the people of Greece by the Son of God. Likewise, the lives of Corinthian believers were seals of Paul's ministry. They were guarantees of his divine authenticity.

So in our text the sealing of the Spirit is a guarantee that men and women believers are joined to the Lord Jesus Christ. The gift of the Holy Spirit authenticated that these people were the beneficiaries of God's union with them through His dear Son. The seal proved they were forgiven sinners, not because they noisily claimed that but because the

Spirit of God affirmed this truth. His presence in them affirmed that they believed in God.

If someone asked, "How can I know that I am a true Christian?" Paul would say that trusting in Christ indicates that you have been sealed by God, and the seal is the Holy Spirit who is now in you. The seal is not what the Holy Spirit does, such as make you cry or laugh or jump for joy or speak in tongues (*glossalalia*). The seal of the Spirit is not a particular experience that results from the indwelling of the Spirit. The seal that God gives to every Christian is the Spirit Himself. The seal is not a second blessing, either; it is the person of the Holy Spirit that indwells every Christian believer. The presence of the Holy Spirit testifies that God blesses a believer with every spiritual blessing in Christ.

There are several ways to know that we have the seal of the indwelling of the Spirit:

1. The Holy Spirit ministers to me. I increasingly find delight in the presence and conversation of those who have the Spirit. I delight in the Lord's Day, the time of worship, the activities of preparation and contemplation, and the structure of the day. I love hearing the Bible preached with the Holy Spirit sent down from heaven. If a person called by God is leading a meeting in which the Word of God will be taught, I will be at that meeting. I believe the Bible is inspired by God. I pray for myself and those I love, such as friends, family, and acquaintances. I long for such people to know God and to give their lives to glorify and honor Him. I am sorry when I sin; I feel the need to confess my sin to God. I want to please God in all I do, so I present my body a living sacrifice to Him. I pray, "Take my life and let it be consecrated, Lord, to Thee." These delights are marks of my sealing; they are consequences of the Holy Spirit in my life. There is no other explanation for behavior that is so contrary to worldly appetites other than that God has been at work in my life.

2. The fruit of the Spirit is evident in my life. Galatians 5:22–23 says, "But the fruit of the Spirit is love, joy, peace, longsuffering, gentleness, goodness, faith, meekness, temperance: against such there is no law." Those fruits are not yet perfected in me. When my elderly mother lived with us, she suffered from dementia. She asked the same question every few minutes for several hours, night after night. I should have been more patient and kind with her. I should have shown more self-control. Yet, this fruit is not totally absent in me. I have the divine love, joy, and peace that Paul lists, even in times of deep distress. I would be far more unpleasant, selfish, and unforgiving without the Holy Spirit's work in my life.

3. *I know the blessing of the Spirit.* I was called to the ministry in 1963, and for forty-four years I have preached the Word of God. Has that been one long ego trip? I do not deny the possibility. Standing in front of a hundred people and preaching the Word of God week after week can satisfy some egos, but I have instead known time and again help beyond myself in preparing and preaching the Bible. Many wonderful men from this congregation have subsequently been called into the ministry. Believers of very different backgrounds and personalities tell me that they are helped by my sermons. That is only possible through the Holy Spirit's gifts to me in teaching, pastoring, and leadership.

4. *I see the Spirit's leading in my life.* God has led me in paths of righteousness. That has been the overwhelming direction of my life. I have sinned every day and have had significant stumbles; God has had to pick me up several times. Every day I have known forgiveness. I have never experienced a day when I did not know that Jesus Christ was my Savior and that I should be walking closer to Him. He has led me in serving others, turning my cheek to insults, self-denial, and worshiping the King of heaven.

So I know the Holy Spirit is in my life because God says the Spirit is in the life of everyone who believes in His Son. Through the marks of the Spirit, I see God's confirmation that His promises are true. That is the seal of the Spirit of God. Have we been marked in Christ with this seal? Are the fruits of the Spirit visible in your life? Do others recognize those gifts in you? Are you being led year after year by the Spirit? Does that, in turn, lead others to Christ?

Such questions are not about your orthodoxy. They are not even about your feelings and emotions. They are about your spirituality. That word has become a very common word today. Young people claim they seek spirituality rather than materialism in their values. I wonder about that. The spirituality that is pleasing to God is the result of the Spirit's work in our lives. It bears holy fruit along the narrow path of serving others in the name of Jesus Christ. True spirituality is created and sustained by the Spirit of God. Have you been marked in Christ with the seal of the Holy Spirit?

TO WHOM THIS SEAL BELONGS

Ephesians 1:13 tells us, "In whom ye also trusted, after that ye heard the word of truth, the gospel of your salvation: in whom also after that ye believed, ye were sealed with that holy Spirit of promise." Paul is writing here to the congregation at Ephesus, specifically to those who have made a credible profession of faith and are included in Christ. They have heard the word of truth, believed it, and were marked with a seal. The *you* that Paul addresses here is the entire congregation at Ephesus. He does not say everyone in the congregation has heard the Word and believed and been sealed, but that those who heard and believed were also sealed. Paul does not say that the Ephesians were super-Christians marked with a divine seal. No. God has put His hallmark on every single Christian by giving him or her the Holy Spirit. He is the seal. That mark proves all Christians are owned by God. They all have this guarantee. Without it they are not Christians at all. The whole point is that you can tell a true Christian by looking for the seal.

Now if many true Christians are not yet sealed, this criterion of being sealed, as I have described it, is of no use whatsoever in judging whether someone is a true believer. The Spirit of God, the third person of the Godhead in His ministry, His fruits, and His gifts is the mark that distinguishes the true believer from the atheist, the agnostic, the humanist, and the merely religious person. The presence of the Spirit shows us whether a person is a son of God.

In the world of commerce you look for a hallmark such as a seal, a signature, a guarantee, a watermark, or an imprint to prove that an article is genuine. That is the idea here. We know that a person is a true Christian because his life includes attitudes and actions, words and deeds that can only be explained by the presence of the third person of the Godhead in his life. If a person does not bear God's seal, he is not a child of God. Let us look now at three pairs of words in this verse for further understanding.

1. *In whom.* Verse 13 says, "in whom...ye were sealed." By this Paul is saying that a Christian is no longer a loner. In *L'Etranger*, Camus describes a person who is an outsider, a stranger, and an outcast, but as a believer in Christ you are *included in Christ.* You have been joined together with Christ; you are a branch of His true vine, and His life constantly nourishes you. His status is also yours; you are chosen in Him, adopted as a

son or daughter in Him, accepted in Him, redeemed in Him, forgiven in Him, and sealed in Him.

You understand how incredible we find the interpretation that whereas all Christians are chosen and adopted and redeemed and forgiven in Christ, they are not all sealed! That simply cannot be, because if you are in Christ, "ye were sealed with that holy Spirit of promise" (v. 13). All these blessings stand or fall together; all the accepted ones and the united ones and the reconciled ones and the pardoned ones are also the sealed ones. It is impossible to be in Christ without being predestined; it is impossible to be in Him without having the righteousness of Christ imputed to you; it is impossible to be in Him without everything working together for your good; it is impossible to be in Him without God supplying all your needs, and it is equally impossible to be in Him without being marked with a seal. No person can be *in* Christ but *out of* the seal.

Let me go further; we cannot possibly be in Christ without also being in the Spirit because Christ and the Spirit are indissolubly one. A twenty-pound banknote has the seal of the Bank of England; on one side is Adam Smith and on the other is Queen Elizabeth. You cannot have a twenty-pound note that has only the picture of the queen and not of Adam Smith, and vice versa. If the note is genuine, it has both portraits.

So it is with the Christian; he has Christ and the Spirit. You cannot have one without the other. They are so closely identified that Paul says to the church at Corinth, "The Lord is that Spirit" (2 Cor. 3:17). He is not confusing the distinct identity of these different persons, for the Holy Spirit did not become incarnate and die for our sins. Paul is merely stressing the utter merger of their work in the economy of redemption. The Spirit does exactly what the Lord does. The Spirit's work is not a special work *beyond* the Lord's. The Spirit is the Lord at work. So the seal of the Spirit and the Son of God belong to every Christian. The weakest lamb in the flock of Christ has both Son and Spirit, and, of course, the Father too.

2. *Ye also.* The two words at the beginning of our text refer to the sentence that precedes it: "That we should be to the praise of his glory, who first trusted in Christ. In whom ye also trusted..." (vv. 12–13). Paul is saying that "we Jews" were first to hope in the Messiah, but now Gentiles have also been included in Christ. Once the Gentiles were without God, without His covenants and promises, without the Ten Commandments and the Scriptures, without temple sacrifices, and without the hope of the

Messiah who would crush Satan's head. They were in the dominion of darkness, ruled by the god of this world, but now "ye also" have heard the good news and believed it and were sealed with the Spirit.

This is a particular reminder to Christians in Wales to never lose sight of the glory and marvel of God's grace to them. Recent archaeological digs in primitive sites in Wales have confirmed how horrific life was before the gospel came. Human sacrifices were not uncommon. The gospel delivered the Welsh from such druidic barbarism.

So we too have heard the word of truth. In spite of all that we are, and all that we've been, and all that we know about ourselves, and most of all what God knows about us, He in stupendous grace has marked us with the seal of the Spirit. "They shall be mine," says the Lord, and the day that we cease to wonder about that is the day that the savor disappears from our Christian life. I am not sure whether much of our lukewarmness and worldliness in faith and the artificial excitements in our worship services do not stem from our being too used to the idea that God loves sinners like us. Somehow we are taking for granted the privilege of our adoption and the glory of being sealed with the Holy Spirit of God. Paul thus says to us, "Ye also," who sometimes were afar off, alienated and enemies in your minds by wicked works, God has brought you near. I say this to myself as well. I too am being loved with everlasting love by the Maker of the universe. I am chosen by Him, adopted into His family, redeemed from the slavery of sin, forgiven of guilt, and kept from its power!

3. *Promised Spirit.* Every Christian has the Holy Spirit because God has promised Him. We are sealed because God has promised it. I emphasize this because some people say we must do certain things to wrest this sealing from the hands of God. You have to earn the sealing by prolonged sessions of prayer, by dealing with your sins and renouncing them and earnestly beseeching the Lord for many years until you feel your life is in order and you have risen to a higher plane. You have amputated all that is wrong from your life so that at long last you may experience the sealing of the Spirit.

Certainly as Christians we must pray more earnestly and humbly; we have to take up our cross and deny ourselves and follow Christ. We experience suffering in our body and soul because Christ has also suffered. If our eye causes us to fall into sin, we are to pluck out that eye. We must keep bodily desires in subjection lest they lead us astray. All those disciplines are part of the Christian life, but they are all done by the power of the Spirit who has already sealed us. They are not done to obtain the sealing.

How does someone obtain the seal of the Spirit? We must believe in the Lord Jesus Christ. We must look to Him and be saved. That is the glory of the gospel. The conditions of the sealing of the Holy Spirit are precisely analogous to the condition of justification, by which Jesus comes into our lives by grace alone through faith alone. You must receive into your heart the Son of God. At that moment you will be marked in Him with the seal of the Holy Spirit. The Gentile Christians in Ephesus did not have to fulfill certain conditions to receive the seal of the Holy Spirit because God had already promised to give the Spirit to all who believed in His Son.

THE INCONSISTENCY OF SOME BELIEVERS

"Look how that Christian behaves," some say. "Are you saying that in his weakness, failure, and utter ordinariness, that person is sealed with the Holy Spirit of God?" I ask in response: what is the legitimacy of pragmatic arguments in the face of plain statements of the Word of God? The same argument applies with equal force to the claim that a Christian is a "new creation in Christ Jesus" or that he is "blessed with every spiritual blessing in the heavenlies in Christ Jesus."

Imagine you are worshiping at the Antioch congregation and notice the apostle Peter sitting in the midst of the Jewish section of the congregation. During lunch he is passed dishes of kosher food, and noisy comments are made about the importance of clean versus unclean food. It becomes clear to you that in the matter of food, Gentiles are being denigrated as second-class Christians and Peter is helping to widen this crack by eating only kosher food.

Do we accuse the apostle of never having had the sealing of the Holy Spirit? No. We should not minimize the glory of each Christian. Rather, we should maximize the glorious privileges and status of God's people, and charge them with living far below their privileges. We might say to Peter, "What are you doing by keeping yourself away from Gentile believers in this congregation? You have been sealed with the Holy Spirit. You are indwelt by the Lord Jesus. You have been chosen, justified, redeemed, forgiven, adopted, joined to Christ, sanctified, and glorified. Today your behavior towards your fellow believers has been inconsistent with your beliefs and your love for them in Christ! Shame on you, Peter!"

Our problem is that we have not been mastered by the glory and privileges of the Christian life. We are too rarely lost in wonder, love, and praise at what God has done for us in redemption. Are we excusing our conduct by claiming that God hasn't baptized or sealed us with the Spirit? I must realize that not for one moment of my life, even in the midst of all my temptations, my falls, and my shame for my sin, I am disconnecting myself from Jesus Christ. But even in backsliding, I do not cease to be a regenerate man or to be sealed with the Spirit.

The wonder is that a believer's wickedness does not suspend even temporarily his status and privileges. He may try to excuse himself by claiming that he never was sealed, but he is deceived. His sealing is rather abused by his reprehensible behavior.

My friends, we must live according to our privileges and under the seal of the Holy Spirit. If we let the plain truth of the gospel be true for our daily lives, then as ransomed, sealed, adopted, and forgiven children of God, who might better sing the praises of Christ?

CHAPTER EIGHTEEN

The Love of the Holy Spirit

Ye adulterers and adulteresses, know ye not that the friendship of the world is enmity with God? whosoever therefore will be a friend of the world is the enemy of God. Do ye think that the scripture saith in vain, The spirit that dwelleth in us lusteth to envy? But he giveth more grace. Wherefore he saith, God resisteth the proud, but giveth grace unto the humble. Submit yourselves therefore to God.　　　　—James 4:4–7

James 4:5 is the only verse in the epistle that seemingly refers to the Holy Spirit. The sentence can be translated a number of ways. The NIV translates this verse as "the spirit he caused to live in us envies intensely." In other words, the reference to the spirit is to our own spirits. But the textual notes on this verse suggest two other translations. I believe the second is the best translation: "the Spirit he caused to live in us longs jealously." To understand these words, let us look at their context.

THE WANING LOVE OF EARLY BELIEVERS

Some people in the early church were cooling in their love for Christ as they took lingering glances at the world. James is extraordinarily straight in addressing these New Testament Christians. He said to them two verses earlier, "Ye lust, and…kill…ye fight and war…. Ye ask amiss." Now he addresses them as "adulterers and adulteresses" (v. 4). These believers must have highly respected this man who was the half-brother of Christ to have so meekly accepted what he preached to them. As a preacher, I am as much under this apostolic indictment as anyone else. I don't choose to be addressed as an adulterous person, but I do have to accept the issues that God wants to raise with His people in this chapter. We must all respect the apostolic word and respond by asking our Lord, "Is it I?"

James goes on to say, "Know ye not that the friendship of the world is enmity with God?" The world the Bible refers to here is the world created by God. He owns and rules this world and gave it to man to be subdued and enjoyed. But it has become a fallen world, disordered, rebellious, and aloof to God due to our father Adam's broken relationship with God. The world has become organized by sinful mankind under the power of the god of this world. It has been given over to unrighteousness and is hostile to the truth and the people of God. Wicked people have organized the world into a bad system that is hostile to God. It is dominated by "the lust of the flesh, and the lust of the eyes, and the pride of life" (1 John 2:16). Its motives are pleasure, profit, power, and promotion.

So, Scripture says the world is a subtle organization of man that operates according to laws, goals, and gods that are contrary to those of God the Father of our Lord Jesus Christ. The world crucified Christ. It declared in the languages of the leading nations of the world its enmity towards God on a placard above Jesus' head on the cross that said, "This is the king of the Jews." The world was friend to a murderer, Barabbas, and enemy to the blameless Son of God. It still is. The world will always choose a rogue above a righteous man. As Cyprian wrote to Donatus more than 1,700 years ago, we too must say that "it is a bad world, an incredibly bad world." And so a poet once said of the world:

> Man's mind reaches past the stars,
> Probes the atom,
> Measures waves of ether in the infinite spaces...
> But he still lives in an old house,
> An old house full of echoes!
>
> Tear down the rotted boards;
> Scrap the bat-haunted chambers;
> Stop the babbling of simian tongues
> Pretending to blabber wisdom!...
>
> I am tired of echoes...echoes...echoes
> In the old house.[1]

When I was a boy, I hung out with kids who would pass by a derelict mansion on the way to a park in Merthyr. Occasionally we would climb through a window and stand in the vast hall of the empty house. We

---

1. Elias Lieberman, "It Is Time to Build."

were afraid to climb the stairs with their rotten boards or enter any of the dark rooms. We would smell the damp and look at the fungus. It was silent and menacing.

Those who live in a world without God are like children walking through a condemned house. Some features of the world still remind us of its former glory, and occasionally bursts of creative energy and brilliance excite us. We cheer one another at political conferences or conventions by saying, "It's going to get better." The opening ceremony of the Olympic Games in China, the sight of two athletes running for the finish line, a rousing speech, or a great song can temporarily lift our spirits, but then the overwhelmingly destructive spirit of our age takes over again.

Some Christians in the early church were taking lingering looks at the world around them. A professing Christian named Demas is mentioned three times in the New Testament: the first in Paul's letter to Philemon, verse 24, where the apostle lists his fellow workers as Marcus, Aristarchus, Demas, and Luke; the second in Colossians 4:14, where Paul says, "Luke, the beloved physician, and Demas, greet you." The last time reference is in 2 Timothy 4:10, where Paul writes chillingly, "For Demas hath forsaken me, having loved this present world."

Demas fell in love with the decaying house of this world and deserted God. Do you think loving the world is still a danger today? Have people you once worshiped with and professed what you believe stopped coming to church? What happened to some of the teenagers who professed their faith? Did they once more fall in love with the attractions of the world? Did they find comic relief and thrills and purpose for living in the world rather than in things of the Lord? Perhaps they found boyfriends or girlfriends outside of church. Now they are ice-cold toward Jesus Christ. They live as if He never existed.

How is it with you? What way are you heading? Where does your mind turn when it is empty? In idle moments, what do you think about? What absorbs your affections? Are you falling in love with the world rather than loving and serving the Lord Jesus? Remember, friendship with the world is hatred towards God.

OUR ADULTEROUS LOVE FOR THE WORLD

James accuses worldly minded Christians of adultery. Christians are God's bride, so their longing, loving looks at the world are the beginnings of infidelity. Two loves in a relationship are one too many. Princess Diana once said, "There were three of us in this marriage so it was a bit crowded." Charles's relationship with another woman violated the vows Diana and Charles had taken in their wedding ceremony: "To have thee only unto me until death us do part."

Loving a world that scorns Jesus Christ breaches our betrothal to our Husband, God. That is why James addresses believers who love the world as adulterous people. A lover of the world is an unfaithful bride to God. B. B. Warfield, in a sermon on these verses titled, "The Love of the Holy Spirit," said, "We cannot have two husbands; to the one husband to whom our vows are plighted, all our love is due. To dally with the thought of another lover is already unfaithfulness."[2] We sing of Christ,

> From heaven he came and bought her
> To be his holy bride.
> With his own blood he bought her,
> And for her life he died.

The Son of God loved His people. They were given to Him by His Father, and Jesus came to earth from heaven to claim His bride. He took all her liabilities upon Himself and went to the cross for her, thereby paying off every debt she owed. Now, in heaven at God's right hand, Jesus prays for His bride without ceasing. He loves His church as His own body. Yet there are some in the church today who say they love the Lamb of God while they cast longing looks at a world that hates God.

Christ's affection for His people is taught in Scripture. James asks in verse 5, "Do ye think that the scripture saith in vain..." anything? It is a rhetorical question. James is stating as strongly as he can that no saying of Scripture is empty. He appeals to the extraordinary authority of the Bible to describe the special relationship between God and His people, and why loving the world is adulterous. In numerous Old Testament passages, the Lord expresses love for His people in terms of a groom's love for his chosen bride. God is a jealous God. He announces this in the Ten Commandments. He has the burning jealousy of a loving husband toward the tenderly cherished wife who has wandered from the path of fidelity. The prophets often take up this theme. For example, Jeremiah

---

2. Warfield, *Person and Work of the Holy Spirit*, 98.

3:14 says, "'Turn, O backsliding children, saith the LORD; for I am married unto you.'"

James now challenges us, asking whether Scripture speaks of these things without reason. We are the bride of Christ, and He is our loving husband. He has died for us so we may live for Him and one day go to the place He has prepared for us. He delights in us; that is the wonder of our relationship with the Lord. As you walk through life, remember that the Lord is walking alongside you with His arm around you. Francis Schaeffer picked up this theme in *The Church Before the Watching World*, where he compared Christianity with the stories of Eastern religions (which are now so chic in the media). "Shiva came out of his ice-filled cave in the Himalayas and saw a mortal woman and loved her," Schaeffer wrote. "When he put his arms around her, she disappeared, and he became neuter.

"There is nothing like this in the Scriptures," Schaeffer said. "When we accept Christ as our Saviour, we do not lose our personality. For all eternity our personality stands in oneness with Christ."[3]

So the Bible takes the great sin of adultery and shows us how serious it is by comparing it with our turning away from God to fall in love with the world. He says those guilty of such betrayal are "adulterers and adulteresses" (v. 4). Likewise, the prophet Isaiah cries out about the city where God's temple is set, "How is the faithful city become an harlot!" (Isa. 1:21). Jerusalem the golden has become a prostitute. In Ezekiel 6:9 the Lord cries, "I am broken with their whorish heart."

God is not indifferent about how we live day by day. "God is not just a theological term; he is not a 'philosophical other,'" Schaeffer said. "He is a personal God, and we should glory in the fact that he is a personal God. But we must understand that since he is a personal God, he can be grieved. When his people turn away from him, there is sadness on the part of the omnipotent God."[4] God is also jealous. Zechariah 8:2 says, "Thus saith the LORD of hosts; I was jealous for Zion with great jealousy, and I was jealous for her with great fury."

---

3. Francis Schaeffer, *The Complete Works of Francis A. Schaeffer: A Christian Worldview* (Wheaton: Crossway Books, 1985), 4:136.
4. Schaeffer, *Complete Works*, 4:142.

THE HOLY SPIRIT'S LONGING FOR GOD'S PEOPLE

Church members who love the world are guilty of spiritual unfaithfulness, and God is jealous when this occurs. James 4:5 says, "The Spirit he caused to live in us longs jealously" (v. 5 footnote). The language is intense and full of the hungry ache of love. God's Spirit longs for us, James says.

My grandson's fiancée is in Viet Nam for some months; she is teaching English as a second language while he is in London. The couple intensely longs for one another as they wait to be married at the end of the summer. This word *long* is the same verb the Greek translators of Psalm 42:1 use in saying: "As the hart panteth after the water brooks, so panteth my soul after thee, O God." James now turns that thought around so that we focus not on our panting after the Lord, but rather on God panting after His people.

Panting is used by Greek classical writers to indicate deep jealousy, but in James 4:5 it refers to the passionate love of God the Holy Ghost for us. It is the agony the Spirit experiences when a rival takes away the affection of someone He loves. The loved one turns away from the Spirit and loves His rival. Worse than that, the one she gives her love to despises the Spirit. Likewise, the church loves a world that has nothing but contempt for Christ, and the Spirit views this with longing jealousy. This is how God sees us when we dally with the world and its fashions, fads, rewards, and glittering prizes. God is jealous when our ardor for Him wanes and we begin to love the world. Did the world die for us, rise from the dead for us, and ever live to intercede for us? Did the world forgive our sins? If not, why have we transferred our love to the world? Our love should be pledged only to Christ, but now the Spirit perceives that we have abandoned our first love by withdrawing from Jesus and taking our love to the world. James says the Spirit is deeply unhappy about this and pants after us with jealousy.

Warfield wrote, "Let us not, however, refuse the blessed assurance that is given us. It is no doubt hard to believe that God loves us. It is doubtless harder to believe that He loves us with so ardent a love as is here described. But He says that He does. He declares that when we wander from Him and our duty towards Him, He yearns after us and earnestly longs for our return; that He envies the world our love and would fain have it turned back to Himself. What can we do but admiringly cry, 'Oh, the breadth and length and height and depth of the love of God which passes knowledge!' There is no language in use among men which is strong enough to portray it. Strain the capacity of words to the uttermost and still they fall short of expressing the jealous envy with which He contemplates the love of His people for the world, the yearning desire which possesses Him to turn them back to their duty to Him. It is this inexpressibly precious assurance which the text gives us; let us, without doubting, embrace it with hearty faith."[5]

THE HOLY SPIRIT'S LOVE FOR US

James emphasizes here that the Holy Spirit loves us. Of course God is love, and Father, Son, and Holy Spirit share the same substance or being. All are equally powerful, merciful, knowledgeable, and long-suffering. All equally love; the Spirit loves us just as the Father or Son loves us, but we have lived a long time as Christians without being conscious that we are also loved by the Spirit. We are more aware that God the Father so loved the world that He gave His only begotten Son to die for us.

"Behold, what manner of love the Father hath bestowed upon us, that we should be called the sons of God" cries the apostle John (1 John 3:1).

Scripture is filled with references to the Father's love and the Son's love for us: "The love of Christ, which passeth knowledge" (Eph. 3:19); "Hereby perceive we the love of God, because he laid down his life for us" (1 John 3:16); "Who shall separate us from the love of Christ?" (Rom. 8:35); "who loved me, and gave himself for me" (Gal. 2:20). We are encouraged by such truths. In our darkest days, these verses give us comfort. When the telephone rings and the news is bad, God's love for us is the bedrock of our peace.

Yet God the Holy Spirit, our blessed advocate and counselor, also loves us. Here are some assurances of that love.

1. *The Spirit's love is everlasting.* This love lasts without a break from eternity to eternity. We cannot get at the beginning of it, and we shall never see the end of it. It is from everlasting to everlasting, like God Himself. The love of the Spirit cannot be broken. If anything could break the love of the Spirit, man's sin might have done it. We know that the Holy Spirit can be grieved, but man's sin did not break the Spirit's love for us. Sin did

---

5. Warfield, *Person and Work of the Holy Spirit*, 101.

not break the love of the Spirit, but it did grieve Him and for a short time quenched its flow. Before this love could flow again, a new way had to be opened up, and that was done by the shedding of Christ's blood. As that blood flowed from the cross, the Spirit came flowing down from heaven, and it has flowed abundantly on all He loves ever since. He will continue to love them forever and ever.

2. The Spirit's love is unchanging. The context of this passage warns us how changeable our love is to the Spirit. We are like the sea that ebbs and flows. The love of the Spirit is not like that. The Spirit is the Lord who changes not, and neither does His love. Didn't He love His people with an unchangeable love while they were still unconverted? Yes. His love gripped them in their darkness. He brought Christians into their lives, who invited them to church and perhaps urged them to read a booklet. The Spirit caused that booklet to make an impact upon them. He illuminated their minds, brought them to conviction of sin, gave them life, then sealed them. The Spirit's love brought them to salvation. He could see nothing in them worthy of salvation, but He loved them nonetheless.

3. The Spirit loves freely. We cannot pay the Spirit to love us as much as He does. We cannot do anything to merit His love, either. Christ's death didn't buy God's love. The death of Christ wasn't the cause of God's love; it was the effect of His love. Jesus said, "God so loved the world, that he gave his only begotten Son" (John 3:16). So we can say, "God so loved the world that He sent the Holy Spirit to give life and faith and holy desires to all His people." Christ did not buy God's love; the Spirit did not buy God's love, and we cannot buy God's love. But what Christ did opened the way for the Spirit to love us.

4. The Spirit's love is sovereign. Jesus said in John 3:8: "The wind bloweth where it listeth…so is every one that is born of the Spirit." Why should God love Jacob, who was a cheat and liar? Why should he love Saul of Tarsus, who proudly persecuted Christians? Why should the Spirit love you or me? We are all ungodly, and the Spirit is under no obligation to love any of the human race, yet the Spirit showed to a company of people more love than any person could understand. He might have let all of them perish, but He breathed in them and gave them a new heart.

James speaks here of the Spirit's love, which is so great that He jealously yearns for you. Do you think Scripture says that without reason? Why is it important for us to learn that the Holy Spirit loves us? True, there are fewer references to the love of God the Holy Spirit in the New Testament than there are to God the Father or Son. For example, Matthew's gospel has only five or six references to the Holy Spirit, whereas it is full of references to God the Father and Son. The Father planned our salvation, the Son accomplished it, and the Spirit applies redemption to our souls. Each step is necessary, but each action is the purest expression of divine love.

Think again of the wonder of the Holy Spirit's loving you and coming to indwell you. Imagine that someone in London had problems with his drain and phoned Buckingham Palace to see if a member of the royal family would clean out the blocked sewer. You wouldn't do that, of course; you'd call a plumber to do the dirty work. So now think of the Holy Spirit coming into your desperately deceitful heart and cleaning up your life. The holiest being that has ever existed is coming into intimate contact with such depravity. As Warfield wrote, "The Spirit of all holiness is willing to visit such polluted hearts as ours, and even to dwell in them, to make them His home to work ceaselessly and patiently with them, gradually wooing them—through many groanings and many trials—to slow and tentative efforts toward good; and never leaving them until, through His constant grace, they have been won entirely to put off the old man and put on the new man and to stand as new creatures before the face of their Father God and their Redeemer Christ. Surely herein is love!"[6]

Now imagine that God summoned all the spirits into His presence and said, "We have a new Christian in mind. He'll never be special. He'll spend his entire life in the middle of nowhere in central Wales. Who would like to live in him and keep an eye on him for the next sixty years?" There might be a long silence as the assembled spirits think of all the people they would rather be with for the next decades, such as mighty preachers, heads of Christian organizations, doctors, politicians, revivalists, evangelists, or Christian athletes. Finally a junior spirit, with the greatest reluctance, says, "Go on then; I'll have a go." All the other spirits are most relieved that they did not have to volunteer.

---

6. Warfield, *Person and Work of the Holy Spirit*, 105.

Of course, that is not how it was with God's assignments. His work is not left to volunteers. James says, "God has caused the Spirit to live in us." The God who planned redemption and sent His own Son to accomplish it now sends the Spirit to throb with love in our very hearts.

Wouldn't you tremble for your salvation if you knew that a reluctant agent was inside you who constantly wished he were inside someone else? We know how cold we are. We sing, "Prone to wander, Lord, I feel it. Prone to leave the God I love." Where would we be without the help of the Holy Spirit? The world is constantly wooing us with its temptations. We fall so often that we cry, "O wretched man that I am, who shall deliver us from the body of this death!" We are so neglectful of God. Hours go by each day in which we never think of the Lord. What if you treated your spouse like that? How can the Spirit bear us? He does so because of His immense love; He is patient, kind, always protecting, always trusting, always hoping, always persevering, and never failing. He longs jealously for us despite all the stumbling blocks we put in front of Him.

The Spirit lives in us, James says. He doesn't just visit us on occasion to make an occasional inspection. He doesn't stop by from time to time for coffee. He doesn't come on approval like a renter putting a landlord on probation so that if he doesn't like his lodgings, he'll move on. No. Our life is now the home of the Holy Spirit for Him to settle, to stay, and to transform into His permanent dwelling place.

We are touched by the story of the brother of an American pilot who was shot down over Viet Nam and reported missing. The brother gave up his job and went to Viet Nam to spend months looking for his brother. He became known as the "pilot's brother." His love took him to village after village, talking to criminals and warlords and corrupt officials. He gave away his hard-earned money for any information that might lead to the rescue of his brother.

So too the love of the Spirit constrains Him to keep in step with us throughout our lives. If we fall into the gutter, He lies with us there. If we visit a brothel, He comes in there with us. We end up with a broken marriage, broken life, and broken heart, but He stays with us. If we go to jail, He enters the cell with us and spends years with us behind bars.

We cannot conceive of the foulness of sin as seen by God. Who then can imagine the love of the Spirit in coming into the desperately wicked human heart and dwelling there, not for Himself or for any merit to

Himself but that He might bring us to salvation and transform us into the bride of the Lamb? His love for us is so strong, mighty, and constant that it will never fail. When the Spirit sees us rushing toward destruction, He jealously hovers over us. When our own hearts despise themselves, the Spirit still labors with us in love. His love burns stronger because we so deeply need His help.

THE LOVING SPIRIT GIVES US MORE GRACE

The Spirit passionately loves us. He understands the pressures and temptations that belabor us. He knows our infirmities and sorrows. In one of her newsletters, Elizabeth Elliot wrote about a husband and wife who adopted nineteen children, ten of whom were seriously handicapped. Three more little boys have since joined the family. Twenty-eight people in all live in a well-ordered peaceful home "spilling over with sacrificial love, filled (of course) with joys and sorrows."[7] The couple began by adopting one handicapped child, then the number grew as God sent more children into their home. They now lavish love on all their children, washing and drying their clothing, helping them to eat and go to the bathroom—all in the name of the Lord Jesus Christ and with the strength that the Spirit provides.

How can such people do what they do? James tells us, God "giveth grace" (v. 6). As the number of children in a family increases, so does the grace to care for them. Likewise, as our sufferings increase, so the grace of strength increases. We might fear having an accident, a stroke, or some other physical calamity that could make us helpless pain-torn creatures. But we should not measure our ability to cope by our own limited resources. Rather, we should look to the Holy Spirit whose resources are endless. As Annie Johnson Flint says in her beloved hymn: "He giveth more grace when the burdens grow greater.... He giveth, and giveth, and giveth again!"

---

7. Elizabeth Elliot, "Count Your Blessings," *The Elizabeth Elliot Newsletter* (November/December 1998): 2.

CHAPTER NINETEEN

The Holy Spirit and Revival

*He saved us, by the washing of regeneration, and renewing of the Holy
Ghost; which he shed on us abundantly through Jesus Christ our Saviour.*
—Titus 3:5–6

Titus 3:5–6 offers us a picture of the outpouring of the Holy Spirit, not
in a few drops of rain, but in a generous downpour that drenches the
land. Paul experienced this downpour in the spread of the gospel during
his lifetime, as God lavishly poured out the Holy Spirit through Jesus
Christ our Savior. Many people were converted, cities and nations were
changed, churches were planted, and Christians were assured of their
interest in the Savior's blood as the fear of God fell on communities. This
indeed was evidence of revival.

PEOPLE OF HISTORIC REVIVAL

The history of the church was shaped by some great leaders and memorable spiritual breakthroughs, which, in turn, shaped the history of
nations. Think of Saint Patrick's work in Ireland in the fifth century and
Saint David's labors in sixth-century Wales. Patrick broke the back of hea-
thenism in Ireland, and David did the same in Wales.

In the eighth century, the Venerable Bede and his followers preached
in England. Here Bede translated the gospel of John into Anglo-Saxon. In
the fourteenth century, John Wycliffe translated the Bible into English,
and the Lollards, Wycliffe's followers, preached across the land. Many of
these preachers were imprisoned. Some were burned at the stake with
their Bibles tied around their necks. Girolamo Savonarola preached in
the fifteenth-century in Italy, where many people turned to God.

The greatest outpouring of the Holy Spirit since the apostolic era was the Reformation in the sixteenth century. In the seventeenth century, Puritans such as John Bunyan and John Owen preached and wrote extensively about the Scriptures, influencing many people for generations to come in Great Britain and North America. In the eighteenth century, the Great Awakening swept across Wales, Scotland, England, and North America.

In the nineteenth century, a new missionary movement sent the gospel into India. The twentieth century also incited spiritual awakening in South Korea, where many turned to Christ. Though there has been no specific countrywide revival in China, millions of people there have come to a saving knowledge of the living God.

Perhaps Jonathan Edwards was right in saying that the work of the gospel is most advanced by revivals. But consider the United States; in some ways, it is the nation most influenced by Christianity in the world today, with vast numbers of gospel congregations, seminaries, Christian colleges, Christian schools, Christian publishing houses, Christian radio networks, and thousands of missionaries going into all parts of the world. All this has been achieved without a nationwide revival. Meantime, liberal modernistic churches are seriously declining.

Similarly there have been regular harvests as well as years of drought in Europe, where we long for an enormous harvest. We have lived through a century of decline in Wales, where we have also watched the conspicuous work of God in a congregation in Sandfields, Port Talbot, under the ministry of Martyn Lloyd-Jones during the 1920s and 1930s. We have also seen a network of gospel churches planted across the country. We can do much without a great awakening, yet if we are to make any impact on our community for Jesus Christ and take the initiative against the gates of hell, we must also experience a mighty work of God through the outpouring of the Holy Spirit.

WHY REVIVAL IS SHUNNED

Why do Christians sigh when they hear that a sermon or sermon series will be on the subject of revival? Why should revival be a turn-off for people who believe in great awakenings and who long for a new work of the Holy Spirit in our land? Why are we unaffected by Lloyd-Jones's studies on the baptism of the Spirit when we have so often been revived by his preaching on the great themes of the gospel? Why are godly men and women so wary about messages on this theme? Here are some reasons for wariness about revival sermons.

1. *Revivals are poorly defined.* The word *revival* is not found in the New Testament. Thus people use the word to describe any event that makes them feel blessed. The problem is that some people describe a meeting where they experienced the nearness of God as a revival, while others who went to the same meeting felt it was dull and uninspired. One man's feast was plain soup to another.

2. *Revivals are illusive.* For a church member sitting in a pew, revivals never seem to be for the here and now. They appear to be events that happened a hundred years ago or that will occur sometime in the future. If they are occurring now, they are ten thousand miles away from where we live. So an ordinary Christian is restless about sermons on revival, believing that it is better to confront the reality of today rather than be overwhelmed with nostalgia for the past or fascinated with what is happening far away or longing for a future he may never see. There is some kind of betrayal of living New Testament Christianity in preaching for revival. We would not view the work of the Holy Spirit, true prayer, or gospel preaching as illusive—occurring in the past or in the future or someplace far away—rather than in the here and now. There is a real danger in living vicarious Christian lives through what we view as revival, and we know that is not right.

3. *Many revivals are not revivals.* Many people today claim to be experiencing revivals in places such as Toronto, Kansas City, or Pensacola, Florida. Those events, which we have watched on television or CDs, or have listened to on the radio, are, in our judgment, not revivals at all. Rather, they quench the Holy Spirit by driving the gentle dove away. We repudiate in the name of Jesus Christ the egotists who run those shows and strut their stuff before noisy audiences. "Blessed are the poor in spirit for theirs is the kingdom of heaven," Jesus said. We want to protect our congregations from such carnal influences. We want to save the fledgling church in Africa and China from exalting such meetings as role models to follow. They are not great awakenings of truth and godliness; they are not the outpouring of the Holy Spirit. People are being manipulated by

music, prolonged emotional appeals, fits of falling to the ground, fake healings, and false claims. What claims to be a revival is anything but and discredits the very term.

4. Many revivals seem nontheological. Many so-called revivals today appear to reject the theology of the Bible in exegeting the truth, and in the careful explanation and application of texts and passages of the Bible that are precisely written by God and humbly preached by ministers serving the Word of God. Why is there such an absence of preaching in the leaders of today's so-called revivals? Some Bible verses are quoted or alluded to, but they are incidental to the emotions of the hour. Who needs the Bible if the Holy Spirit brings mighty blessings on a group through a man whose greatest contribution is his sharing, his anecdotes, and his appeals?

5. Revival sermons are often depressing. Today's so-called revivals often begin with long descriptions of the horrific times in which we live and bleak statistics proving a nation's moral decline and collapse of faith. We do not enjoy having our noses rubbed in the follies of a fallen world; we see enough of that each day. Perhaps by the end of a revival message, our feelings are back to where they were when the service began, but often they are not. The theme "things are terrible and we need a revival" is not the most reviving experience.

6. True revivals make us afraid. Though we may be reluctant to admit it, we Christians in the twenty-first century are comfortable in our routines, thinking that the godliness we have attained in life is our limit. Do we really want a confrontation with God the Holy Spirit, which by the Word will break our pride and increase tenfold our zeal for serving Jesus Christ? Do we want the next years to be filled, night after night, in counseling guilty, troubled sinners and pointing them to the Savior? This commitment would demand much from us; it would take us away from pleasant evenings in the family room with our families. We want our churches to grow, but not through something that makes demands on our souls and our lives. If we are truly committed to praying for a mighty work of God in our hometown, it will cost us time, energy, and a bruising of our souls.

7. Gospel messages are better than revival messages. What we long for Sunday after Sunday are gospel messages preached in the power of the Holy Spirit. We want Jesus Christ to be exalted and sin to be exposed. Nothing can satisfy our souls but this, and a series of messages on revival or the second blessing or the baptism of the Spirit may actually detract from that. It is not the work of Jesus to give glory to the Spirit. The work of the Spirit is to glorify Christ, and that must also be our work. A chapter titled "The Holy Spirit and Revival" may raise questions, but let us press on, for that theme will yet bring Jesus to us in the power of the sovereign Spirit. Our hearts may then burn within us as we hear of the one whom our souls love.

Why should we speak of the Holy Spirit and revival? It is a biblical theme, which can be very encouraging to us at a time when true God-fearing congregations are shrinking and increasingly being marginalized in our society.

EXAMPLES OF REVIVAL IN THE BIBLE

Let us look at three examples from the Old Testament of large-scale turnings to God in revival.

1. Josiah's discovery of the Book of the Law. When King Josiah was twenty-six years old, an ancient copy of God's Word was found in the temple of Israel. For centuries, the Scriptures had gone missing, and no one, not even the priests, had seemed to notice. When the book of the law was rediscovered, it had a profound effect on the king, the priests, and all the people of Israel. We read in 2 Chronicles 34:14–21:

> Hilkiah the priest found a book of the law of the LORD given by Moses. And Hilkiah answered and said to Shaphan the scribe, I have found the book of the law in the house of the LORD. And Hilkiah delivered the book to Shaphan. And Shaphan carried the book to the king, and brought the king word back again, saying, All that was committed to thy servants, they do it. And they have gathered together the money that was found in the house of the LORD, and have delivered it into the hand of the overseers, and to the hand of the workmen. Then Shaphan the scribe told the king, saying, Hilkiah the priest hath given me a book. And Shaphan read it before the king. And it came to pass, when the king had heard the words of

the law, that he rent his clothes. And the king commanded Hilkiah, and Ahikam the son of Shaphan, and Abdon the son of Micah, and Shaphan the scribe, and Asaiah a servant of the king's, saying, Go, enquire of the LORD for me, and for them that are left in Israel and in Judah, concerning the words of the book that is found: for great is the wrath of the LORD that is poured out upon us, because our fathers have not kept the word of the LORD, to do after all that is written in this book.

Josiah then called together all the elders of Judah and Jerusalem, the men of Judah, the people of Jerusalem, the priests, and the Levites. All went to the temple, where the book of the covenant was read. Then King Josiah renewed the covenant Israel had made with God and vowed to keep all of God's commands, regulations, and degrees "with all his heart and all his soul." He then made everyone in Jerusalem and Benjamin pledge themselves to the law.

Josiah removed all idols from the territory belonging to the Israelites. He made everyone in Israel serve God. And, as 2 Chronicles 34:33 says, "All [Josiah's] days they departed not from following the LORD, the God of their fathers." The rediscovery of God's law provoked a national revival; it brought a king and his people to their knees in repentance and renewed their commitment to walk in God's ways.

2. Jonah's mission to Ninevah. God directed Jonah to preach repentance to Israel's arch-enemy, Ninevah. The prophet rebelled against that order by taking a ship in the opposite direction. But after nearly drowning, Jonah returned to the Lord and went to Ninevah, where he began to proclaim to the residents of that great city, "Yet forty days, and Nineveh shall be overthrown" (Jonah 3:4).

What was the response? "So the people of Nineveh believed God," says Jonah 3:5–10.

And proclaimed a fast, and put on sackcloth, from the greatest of them even to the least of them. For word came unto the king of Nineveh, and he arose from his throne, and he laid his robe from him, and covered him with sackcloth, and sat in ashes. And he caused it to be proclaimed and published through Nineveh by the decree of the king and his nobles, saying, Let neither man nor beast, herd nor flock, taste any thing: let them not feed, nor drink water: but let man and beast be covered with sackcloth, and cry mightily unto God: yea, let them turn every one from his evil way, and from the violence that is in their hands. Who can tell if God will turn and repent, and turn away from his fierce anger, that we perish not? And God saw their works, that they turned from their evil way; and God repented of the evil, that he had said that he would do unto them; and he did it not.

Again, the Word of God, rightly proclaimed, provoked the revival of a nation and its king.

3. The rebuilding of God's temple. The people of God had been in exile in Babylon for seventy years. Now, through God's miraculous intervention, specifically in the heart of Cyrus, king of Persia, many of the exiles had returned to Israel. But it was hard for these exiles to live for the Lord and support themselves in a ruined land that was surrounded by enemies who thwarted and sabotaged whatever they did. It took all their energy to look after themselves. Spiritually, things also began to slip.

When told they should rebuild the temple, however, the people claimed they were too busy. God's response to them through the prophet Haggai was firm. "Is it time for you, O ye, to dwell in your cieled houses, and this house lie waste?" he asked.

Now therefore thus saith the LORD of hosts; Consider your ways. Ye have sown much, and bring in little; ye eat, but ye have not enough; ye drink, but ye are not filled with drink; ye clothe you, but there is none warm; and he that earneth wages earneth wages to put it into a bag with holes.

Thus saith the LORD of hosts; Consider your ways. Go up to the mountain, and bring wood, and build the house; and I will take pleasure in it, and I will be glorified, saith the LORD. Ye looked for much, and, lo it came to little; and when ye brought it home, I did blow upon it. Why? saith the LORD of hosts. Because of mine house that is waste, and ye run every man unto his own house. Therefore the heaven over you is stayed from dew, and the earth is stayed from her fruit. And I called for a drought upon the land, and upon the mountains, and upon the corn, and upon the new wine, and upon the oil, and upon that which the ground bringeth forth, and upon men, and upon cattle, and upon all the labour of the hands.

Zerubbabel son of Shealtiel; Joshua, son of Jehozadak, the high priest; and the rest of the people listened to the Lord and worshiped Him. God stirred up the spirit of the people and their leaders, and everyone began working on the temple "in the four and twentieth day of the sixth month, in the second year of Darius the king" (Hag. 1:2–15).

The history of redemption offers many examples of revival that stirred a nation, renewed faith in the Lord, brought men and women to destroy idols and work for the Lord, and stirred many people to repentance. These examples from the Old Testament are not simply romantic folk stories. Nor do they offer an invariable pattern. For example, when Israel wandered through the wilderness, the people witnessed extraordinary blessings and miracles, such as the parting of the Red Sea, daily manna from heaven, water bursting from a rock, and the powerful preaching of Moses. Yet despite those wonders, the people did not experience revival, and every one of them perished in the wilderness.

Likewise, under the mighty ministry of Jeremiah, Israel did not turn as a nation back to God. Under the powerful ministry of Elijah, whose prayers were answered by God in sending fire to consume the prophet's sacrifice, the people of Israel did not turn back to God. So wonders from heaven do not necessarily bring people to national revival. Turning to God is totally the result of the quickening grace of God, the Holy Spirit.

REVIVAL IN THE NEW TESTAMENT

Let us turn now to some examples of revival from the book of Acts:

1. *Peter's sermon at Pentecost.* On the day of Pentecost, fifty days after the Passover, Peter preached to people in Jerusalem, declaring, "God hath made the same Jesus, whom ye have crucified, both Lord and Christ." The people heard this and were cut to the heart. They asked Peter, "What shall we do?" Peter told them to repent and be baptized, and they would receive the gift of the Holy Spirit. About three thousand people turned to Jesus Christ that day and were baptized (Acts 2:36–41). The impact on the land was great.

2. *Philip goes to Samaria.* We are told in Acts 8 that Philip went to Samaria to proclaim Christ there. Crowds of people paid close attention to what he said and witnessed his healings. Acts 8:8 tells us, "There was great joy in that city." Many men and women believed in the crucified Christ and

were publicly baptized in His name. Once more, the grace of God led to a great awakening.

3. *Paul's mission efforts.* Luke records the same phenomenon in the ministry of the apostle Paul. In Pisidian Antioch, Paul and Barnabas preached in the synagogue, then were asked to come back the following Sabbath. Acts 13 tells us that when the congregation was dismissed on that Sabbath, many of the Jews and converts to Judaism followed Paul and Barnabas, who talked with them and urged them to continue in the grace of God. On the next Sabbath almost the whole city gathered to hear the apostles preach. We are told, "As many as were ordained to eternal life believed. And the word of the Lord was published throughout all the region" (Acts 13:48–49). Likewise, at Iconium, Paul and Barnabas spoke so effectively in the synagogue that "a great multitude both of the Jews and also of the Greeks believed" (Acts 14:1).

The Word of God spread as God's blessing came upon the gospel as it was preached. Revival was not inevitable; it did not happen in Athens, although a small group of individuals there professed faith. The Holy Spirit's generous outpouring through Jesus Christ is the only explanation for revival. Let us now see how people within various congregations responded to the amazing work of God.

- Some needed to understand the Holy Spirit's role. Paul wrote to the church at Thessalonica how the gospel came to that congregation, saying, "For our gospel came not unto you in word only, but also in power, and in the Holy Ghost, and in much assurance" (1 Thess. 1:5). What stirring words! You read them and think, "That is how the gospel should be received by a congregation." Yet how many evangelical sermons these days are more like commentaries than the words of Paul? Our preaching must not just be words but as in Thessalonica, they must be offered with the sincere prayer for the power of the Holy Spirit to be at work in them, and for deep conviction in listeners as the word is preached.

- Some needed to mature in faith. Paul tells the church at Ephesus, "That he would grant you, according to the riches of his glory, to be strengthened with might by his Spirit in the inner man; that Christ may dwell in your hearts by faith; that ye, being rooted and grounded in love, may be able to comprehend with all saints what is the breadth, and length, and depth, and height; and to know the love of Christ, which passeth knowledge, that ye might be filled with all the fulness of God" (Eph. 3:16–19). The church at Ephesus had the truth, the Spirit, and Christ, but Paul wanted them to have more. He wanted them to have spiritual growth, not in the ways some of us perceive growth—in increasing numbers of people at our evening service or new faces in Sunday school—but that they would be rooted and established in the love of Christ, which passes knowledge.

Likewise, we are to pray for growth in our own congregations based on the work of the Holy Spirit. We must repent of our cold hearts and cry to God for help. Doesn't our Lord tell us of a congregation that left its first love? Doesn't Christ describe one church as being neither cold nor hot but lukewarm? If the Lord Jesus appeared in our pulpit today and told us we were guilty of base attitudes, would we respond as the Corinthian believers did? Would we exhibit such earnestness, indignation, alarm, longing, and concern? Surely that is exactly what Christ is saying to many of us today. Are we alarmed? Are we changing?

A CONGREGATION IN TRUE REVIVAL

Stephen Rees of Stockport, Manchester, describes the consequences of the Spirit's coming upon a church in true revival in the following ways:[1]

1. God is present in our meetings. At times God's Spirit descends upon a meeting, and everyone senses that God is present. The unseen world becomes terribly, wonderfully close. At those times, preaching is transformed. The preacher speaks with boldness and authority that is obviously supernatural. Listeners forget the preacher and hear the voice of God speaking to their hearts. Familiar truths become real.

Those who listen tremble at the thought of God; they shake with fear as they are made aware of their sins, they are overwhelmed with wonder as they hear about the cross of the Lord Jesus, and they are filled with a joy that cannot be put into words as they are reminded of heaven to come. Singing is transformed as people realize the wonder of the words that they're singing and become conscious that God is listening. Praying

---

1. Stephen Rees, a letter to the congregation from the manse of Grace Baptist Church, Stockport.

is also transformed as God's people pray with confidence, earnestness, and the wrestling spirit which says "I will not let thee go, except thou bless me" (Gen. 32:26). Many of us remember meetings like that. But we want *all* our meetings to be like that. We want to know that God is among His people whenever they meet.

2. *People are filled with the Holy Spirit.* If we are filled with the Spirit, we will have a great sense of the love of God toward us. We would say, "The love of God is shed abroad in our hearts by the Holy Ghost which is given unto us" (Rom. 5:5). We would also love the Savior with a warm, steady love and long for the day when He comes again. We would want to serve Him with all our strength. If we were filled with the Spirit, we would love one another more warmly, more affectionately, and more practically. We would pray for one another more consistently. We would commit ourselves to the life of the church more thoroughly. We would be eager to be with our fellow believers and do everything in our power to be at church meetings. We would look forward to being at the Lord's Supper to feed on Christ. If we were filled with the Spirit, we would avoid anything sinful or even dubious. We'd turn away from worldly entertainments and distractions. In every situation we would ask, "How can I honor God?" not, "What do I want to do?" We would deal with our problems, especially our disagreements with other church members, in a biblical way. We would pray in church prayer meetings. We would not let dislikes or grudges fester in our hearts. We would apologize and be straight with people. We would talk to people who offend us, not talk about them behind their backs. The life of the church would be sweeter and happier.

3. *Many would be converted.* Members of our families that we have long prayed for would change their attitude to our Lord if the Holy Spirit came upon our congregations. Young people, who had professed faith as teenagers but have since fallen away, would come back to church. Husbands whose wives have prayed over for years would end their rebellion and bow the knee to Christ.

We do witness the conversion of students and the children of church members, but what about people wholly outside of Christ? What about utterly indifferent Muslims, policemen, professors, fishermen, jewelers, clergymen, Jehovah's Witnesses, journalists, car dealers, bank managers, and scientists—what do they know of Christ? The doors of heaven are open to everyone. During times of spiritual awakening, many people are given boldness to share their faith with whomever Providence brings them. They grow weary of materialism and television and sports as they consider the greatness of God. Even if people they witness to are not converted, the fear of God might fall on them.

When the Spirit comes, He convicts the world of sin, righteousness, and judgment, for He honors and magnifies Jesus Christ as the Son of God. And He changes lives forever. People who have served sin come to the Savior when the Spirit falls on them. Let us cry to God that He would generously pour the Holy Spirit on us, through Jesus Christ our Savior.

CHAPTER TWENTY

The Authority of the Holy Spirit

How much authority should the Bible have in your life? We answer that question first by examining the attitude of God's Son to Scripture. Jesus said Scripture cannot be broken because Scripture is the Word of God. Jesus overcame Satan's temptations in the wilderness by quoting passages from the Old Testament, prefacing each quotation with "It is written." Christ specifically cited the creation of our first parents, Adam and Eve; Noah's redemption from the flood; Lot's salvation from the destruction of Sodom and Gomorrah; and Jonah's freedom from drowning by being swallowed by a great fish. Jesus says the Bible is the written Word of God. Thus the Word of God must have complete authority over our lives.

Now let us consider how much authority the Holy Spirit has over us and how we may show that we are under the Spirit's authority.

MARKS OF THE HOLY SPIRIT'S AUTHORITY

The three words that best describe the work of the Holy Spirit seem rather cold, intimidating, and cerebral, but behind those words *revelation, regeneration,* and *sanctification* are the loving authority of God. Here is how each works.

1. Revelation. The church learned of the Holy Spirit's authority by how the Spirit revealed the Word of God to the prophets and the apostles. The apostle Peter wrote, "For the prophecy came not in old time by the will of man: but holy men of God spake as they were moved by the Holy Ghost" (2 Peter 1:21). The prophet Jeremiah didn't drum up some bright ideas that he passed on to anyone who would hear him. As Peter said, Jeremiah was carried by the Holy Spirit when he wrote and delivered his prophecies. What the Holy Spirit said, Jeremiah said.

Later in his epistle, Peter says of the apostle Paul's writings: "As also in all his epistles, speaking in them of these things; in which are some things hard to be understood, which they that are unlearned and unstable wrest, as they do also the other scriptures, unto their own destruction" (2 Peter 3:16). Peter puts Paul's writings in the same category as other Scriptures, such as Jeremiah's, which he says were "given by inspiration of God" (2 Tim. 3:16). So we submit to the Holy Spirit, first, by submitting to His revelations in Scripture. We are under moral obligation to do that.

2. Regeneration. The Holy Spirit's authority is evident in His work of repentance in the hearts of people. The Spirit is the only one who can add people who are being saved to the church. He does so by His sovereign work of regeneration. Church growth is His special sphere of activity. Just as divine revelation is of the Spirit, so also is salvation. As John 3:8 tells us, "The wind bloweth where it listeth, and thou hearest the sound thereof, but canst not tell whence it cometh, and whither it goeth: so is every one that is born of the Spirit."

The Spirit of God takes the initiative in converting sinners. He does this first by stirring a person's conscience, using various influences to touch their hearts, showing them the glory of God in creation, and, most of all, by bringing the truth of Scripture to them in reading and listening to the preached Word.

Second, the Spirit calls unbelievers by His effective and invincible grace. The Spirit illuminates the dark recesses of people's hearts, giving them understanding and renewing their wills. The Holy Spirit invariably uses Scripture as the tool for regeneration, but regeneration is also the result of His internal, effectual, and irresistible grace. The regeneration of Christians is sealed with the Holy Spirit. He is the stamp of divine authority on them. When we call a Christian "brother," we are acknowledging the authority of the Spirit in saving him. Each Christian can testify to the Spirit's authority in these words of Charles Wesley:

> Long my imprisoned spirit lay
> Fast bound in sin and nature's night:
> Thine eye diffused a quick'ning ray;
> I woke: the dungeon flam'd with light;
> My chains fell off, my heart was free—
> I rose, went forth and followed Thee.

3. Sanctification. Just as God's truth to man is by the authority of the Spirit, and unbelievers are changed to believers through the authority of the Holy Spirit, so too the change of sinners into the likeness of Christ is by the authority of the Spirit. For who but the Spirit can take a depraved person and make him Christlike?

The Spirit does this in two ways. First, He does this by mortification. Romans 8:13 says, "For if ye live after the flesh, ye shall die: but if ye through the Spirit do mortify the deeds of the body, ye shall live." The Spirit gives us power to strangle any remaining sin in us, which is indispensable to triumphing over our lusts. We must do this killing work to our own sinful nature. We may not sit back and expect the Spirit to do it. We must wage war against sin, for only then can we live.

The gospel lays that work upon us. Putting to death any remaining sin is proof of the Spirit's authority over us. The highway of holiness is the only road that leads to heaven. Some of you may complain that you increasingly feel the power of sin in your lives. That is because you are more conscious of your inward corruptions than you used to be. Tenderness to sin is a mark that the Holy Spirit is working in you. George Verwer said, "I am a terrible slave to my emotions: in the course of a single day I can go up and down as much as twenty-five times. If any of you lean a bit towards a similar instability then I can tell you that there is still hope: I have found it necessary to be ruthless with my feelings, to dominate my gut-level reactions. It is not easy, but the reward is great."[1]

Second, the Spirit transforms us by fixing our minds on the glories of Christ. As 2 Corinthians 3:18 says, "But we all, with open face beholding as in a glass the glory of the Lord, are changed into the same image from glory to glory, even as by the Spirit of the Lord." Every Christian is in the process of being transformed. We are constantly being changed into the likeness of Christ, with ever-increasing glory. Robert Murray M'Cheyne, in his twenties, already showed that Christlikeness. Likewise, we know some elderly men and women in whom we see much of heaven. The Holy Spirit produces such life transformation by turning a believer's eyes upon Jesus over and over again.

I have just referred to two great themes that are found throughout the Bible: repentance and faith. Through repentance we are sanctified by the Spirit. This is evident in our continual mortification and constant trust,

---

1. George Verwer, *No Turning Back* (Waynesboro, Ga.: Authentic Media, 1983), 107.

which become evident as we continually look to Jesus. When these graces are evident in us, so is the authority of the Holy Spirit in sanctification.

If you want to know God, seek that knowledge through the Holy Spirit in revelation. If you want to love God, you do that through the work of the Spirit in regeneration. If you want to become like God, do that through the work of the Spirit in sanctification.

SUBMISSION TO THE AUTHORITY OF THE SPIRIT

The Holy Spirit is sovereign over us, so we must live under His authority in everything we do. In every choice we make, whether in great things or small, the Spirit has authority over our lives. As the children of God, we are led through life and into eternity by the Holy Spirit. How do we show our submission to His authority?

1. Not by hunch but by Holy Scripture. Some people talk incessantly about sensing the authority of the Spirit in what they do. They say, "The Spirit told me...the Spirit showed me...or the Spirit led me to do this or that." Their language encourages other Christians to talk this way as well. But I wonder: Are we to expect immediate guidance by the Spirit for every decision we make? If we note some striking coincidence or some new insight into a verse in the Bible or some intrusive thought that hooks our minds and won't go away, do we immediately conclude these things are from the Holy Spirit? Two things may result from such thinking. The first is pride, elitism, or a sense of superiority in those who claim to have constant nudges or whispers from the Holy Ghost. The second is anxiety and depression and paralysis of action in those who do not get such hunches from heaven.

So how do we properly show submission to the authority of the Holy Spirit? We sit under the authoritative Word of the Spirit-given God each week. The Word constantly teaches us, "Live like this...believe these truths...be this kind of father...be this kind of church member...be this kind of neighbor...treat your enemy like this" and so on. In such truths, the Spirit of God is connecting with us. He personalizes and particularizes the Word that is preached week by week so that we grasp the will of God for us while at college or in the kitchen or in a retirement home. The result of sitting under systematic, expository, experiential preaching is not so much that we get little messages from God every Sunday. Rather, we are built up in how to think, how to make judgments, and how to grow in discernment. We are progressively established as Christlike men and women. That is the work of the Spirit.

We hear wisdom from God every Sunday, and then, quite imperceptibly, God's wisdom increasingly becomes ours. We begin to see it as the Spirit's gift to us week after week. It renews our minds so that we start to reason and behave as God desires. The mind of our Lord Christ Jesus also increases in us. Because we are constantly sitting under Spirit-led ministry of the Spirit-inspired Book, we are less and less under the authority of our age. Our minds are being renewed by the Spirit day by day.

Of course the Spirit of God can offer us flashes of insight in extraordinary, direct, and immediate ways. God can do that. I won't deny it. But we have no business expecting to be led that way all through our lives when God has gone to such pains in providing His Scriptures to us as well as calling and gifting ministers to preach the Bible to us. So let us live under the authority of the Holy Spirit, not by hunches but by understanding and obeying Holy Scripture.

2. *Not by despair but by repentance.* The Holy Spirit's plan for the world is to convict and make alive everyone the Father and Son gives to Him, to change them into the likeness of God, and to take them safely to heaven. That plan was given to the Spirit by God the Father and the Son. We know God's plan, but we don't know all the names that are in that plan.

Some religious people think they are no longer part of the Spirit's plan. They once happily started out on the journey to Christlikeness, but somewhere they missed the way by committing some folly. Maybe they married the wrong person or lost their sense of calling at work or were attracted to non-Christian beliefs. So now they think their spiritual lives are ruined. All that's left for them is a second-best, substandard Christian life. They aren't on the scrap heap, but they're certain they're on the shelf, and their usefulness to God is gone.

That evaluation is all speculation. You don't know that you are on the shelf. I think the devil wants to tell many Christians they're over and done for. If he can get Christians to believe that, he has done a very clever thing indeed, for it is all guesswork. Nothing in Scripture supports such a morbid idea.

God may permit us to fall to humble us. For example, Peter in denying he knew Christ learned lessons that he couldn't have learned any other way. Even though what Peter did was absolutely wrong, he eventually became a better man for it. Likewise, can't God put you back on track after you have wandered away?

It is true that bad choices have bad consequences. Jacob had to live with a limp after fighting with God at Jabbok, and David had to live with family troubles after committing adultery with Bathsheba. But the idea that God cannot or will not forgive transgressions, even when we confess our folly and repent of sin, or that the rest of our service will be shelved is contrary to God's Word. We are still under the authority of the Spirit after we fall.

Many of God's servants made grievous mistakes. Jacob beggared his brother and fooled his father. Moses killed an Egyptian and ran off to hide in the backside of the desert. David counted his people, and Peter boycotted Gentile Christians at Antioch. Yet none of those men was demoted to a second-class status. God didn't say, "The salt has lost its savor. Throw it on the road and trample it down." The Spirit did not tell these believers that they were no longer under His authority. If God restored David after he slept with Bathsheba and killed her husband and showed His love to Peter after the disciple's threefold denial of Christ, we should not doubt God's readiness to restore Christians who acknowledge that they have sinned. It's blasphemous to think that after we have gone to God in repentance and confessed our sins in the name of Jesus that God will refuse to forgive us. We show we are under the authority of the Spirit by repenting of our sins.

3. Respecting the holiness of the Holy Spirit. If we are under the authority of the Spirit, we do not want to grieve Him by doing something contrary to God. The Father is God, the Son is God, and the Holy Spirit is God; and these three are one God. So anything that is anti-God or anti-Christ will grieve the Holy Spirit. That is evident in Ephesians 4:30, which says the Holy Spirit is the "holy Spirit of God." This Spirit comes from God the Father and God the Son to work in the lives of the people whom God loves. Anything opposed to God or Christ will deeply grieve the Holy Spirit of God. So we are to avoid taking the name of the Lord in vain, using God's name as a curse, or being careless in referring to our heavenly Father or the Lord Jesus Christ. Grieving God also grieves the Holy Spirit.

The Holy Spirit is the Spirit of truth, so anything contrary to the truth as revealed in the Scriptures will grieve the Holy Spirit. We must not indulge in deceit, a lying tongue, a half- truth, a studied silence, or errors contrary to the word of truth, because the Holy Spirit is the Spirit of truth. He inspired men of old to write the truth for our instruction and edifica-tion. Anything in our hearts that rebels against the truth of the Scriptures or defies the commands of the Bible grieves the Holy Spirit of God.

Anything contrary to the spirit of love also grieves Him, for the Holy Spirit is the source of our love. The Holy Spirit enables us to love our neighbors as ourselves; He gives us grace to love our enemies, to do good to those who despitefully use us, and helps us live in harmony with other believers. Ephesians 4:2–3 tells us, "With all lowliness and meek-ness, with longsuffering, forbearing one another in love; endeavouring to keep the unity of the Spirit in the bond of peace." If hostility, scorn, and impatience are allowed in our relationships, the Holy Spirit will surely be grieved. Division, strife, bitterness, and impatience have no place in the body of Christ. They grieve the Holy Spirit of God. If we are under the authority of the Spirit, we will not want to grieve the Holy Spirit of God.

4. *Not quenching the Spirit (1 Thess. 5:19).* If you are under the Spirit's author-ity, you will avoid doing anything that quenches the Spirit. Putting the two words *grieve* and *quench* together suggests something dark about the word *quench*. It sounds threatening, like extinguishing something that was alive, blowing out a flame, or shooting foam on a fire to quench it. So if grieving the Spirit lessens the Spirit in our lives, quenching the Spirit causes the cessation of the Spirit in our lives. We not only grow cold spiri-tually, but we also turn our backs on the Spirit and His comfort.

We behave as though we can do without the Spirit and no longer have to be under His authority. In response He says, as it were, "Very well, see how you do on your own." Quenching the Spirit causes the Spirit's influ-ence to die down in our lives. That results in spiritual disaster. If we have not been startled by the word *grieve*, we should be painfully hurt by the possibility of *quenching* the Spirit.

What quenches the Spirit is willfully persisting in a sin or defying God in lovelessness. If we do not genuinely repent of such sin and turn from it, the next stage in our backsliding will be quenching the Spirit. I believe that if a person persists in opposing the Word of God in a life of unholiness, he or she is in grave danger of quenching the Spirit.

Satan tries to inject evil into our lives by encouraging us to belittle evil, to defend it, and to rationalize it as well as to justify ourselves and excuse ourselves. Eventually that can so deaden our conscience that we quench the Spirit. One of the greatest grievances that can happen to believers is to fear that they have quenched the Spirit. They think there is no hope for them. They are in an iron cage from which there is no escape. Scripture tells us the way of transgressors is hard, but that way is impossible for anyone who is exercised about it. We cannot be under the authority of the Spirit if we willfully continue the sin that grieves or quenches the Spirit. But if we are under His authority, we will be in such anguish about grieving the Spirit that we will beg Him for forgiveness and submit to His will for us.

5. Being filled with the Spirit (Eph. 5:18). Those who are in danger of quenching the Holy Spirit consider the ways of holiness an awful drag. They consider it a drag to pray or go to worship services or read the Bible. There is a dark, cold, deadness about their spiritual lives; they certainly will not be doing what the next verses in Ephesians 5 tell us about speaking to one another in psalms and hymns and spiritual songs and making melody in our hearts to the Lord.

The apostle Paul asks, "How can I sing songs of praise if I'm not praising God? How can I sing hymns of prayer if I am not praying to God?" We are to beg God to fill us with the Spirit. Have you ever prayed to be filled with the Spirit? You need to do that if you have grieved the Spirit, especially if you are close to quenching the Spirit. Plead with the Lord to be merciful to you and to fill you with His Spirit. Only then will you come under the authority of the Spirit.

It is also right to seek a fuller measure of the Spirit's authority over your life. Surely all of Scripture points you in the direction of seeking a fuller measure of the Spirit's influence in your life. So you might pray, "Lord, let me know more of the power of the Holy Spirit in my life by filling me with the Spirit. Help me to count for Thee. Deliver me from going through the motions of religion. Kindle a flame of sacred love on the mean altar of my heart. Fill me to the brim with the Holy Spirit."

What evil do you tolerate in your life: angry words, impatience, depressing thoughts, envy, jealousy? Did you go to a service because others dragged you there? You were too embarrassed to turn back and go home, yet not at all inclined to go to church because of where you've been and what you've felt and done. You feel like a hypocrite. The devil torments you, saying, "How dare you ask to be filled with the Spirit?" He argues with you about this because he knows the more you experience the authority of the Holy Spirit in your life, the greater will be Satan's defeat.

"Be filled!" Paul commands us. "Be filled with the Spirit!" When you were unconverted, your life was filled with all sorts of things. You were under the authority of the god of this world and under the lordship of sin. You were compelled to seek worldly pleasures. But now that you have a new life, you must be filled with the Spirit! You'll discover what it means to be attracted to what is approved by the Spirit of God.

So pray through your temptations, saying, "Lord, sinful and unworthy as I am, I long to be filled with the Spirit. I want to be forgiven, I want a closer walk with God, and I want to be filled with the Spirit." Cry out to God, asking to be filled with the Spirit. Then you will find fresh joy in worship, in psalms, hymns, and spiritual songs, and making melody in your heart to the Lord. Your singing will be different. Listening to sermons will be different, as will prayer. You will find the presence of Christian friends delightful. You will live in the joyful presence of God under the authority of the Spirit.

6. *Setting your mind on spiritual things (Rom. 8:5).* What is your mind set on right now? What do you really care about? What most occupies your mind, your attention, your ambition, your desires, your plans, and your longings? If you want to be under the authority of God's Spirit, your mind will be concerned about the things of God. You will seek first the kingdom of God and His righteousness. They will become the principal things in your life.

To be spiritually minded is life, says the apostle Paul. So when you are filled with the Spirit, you will feel more liveliness in your singing and in hearing the Word preached. You will no longer be a mere spectator, and your Christian testimony will be more authentic. The things of God will be more central in your life when you are spiritually minded.

A life of grieving the Spirit is not peaceful, especially if you are a child of God. Your conscience will grieve you if you are grieving the Holy Spirit of God. To be spiritually minded is life and peace because when we are spiritually minded and the Holy Spirit is exercising His authority in our lives, we have a deeper relationship with the Lord, and we experience peace with God through our Lord Jesus Christ.

Being under the authority of the Spirit affects your walk with God. It affects your church life and your relationship with other believers. If you presently find relationships with other believers difficult, you should pray for the unity of the Spirit in the bond of peace, saying, "Lord, make me so spiritually minded that I can live at peace with this person who is so difficult to get along with. Make me spiritually minded, keep me humble, and keep me resilient so I can accept what is happening. If others want to throw things at me, let me be quiet and calm about it. Let me pray for them." Those under the authority of the Spirit pray like that. So by constant obedience to Scripture, by repentant restoration, by neither grieving nor quenching the Holy Spirit of God, by being filled with the Spirit, and by minding the things of the Spirit, you will know and your life will show that you are under the Spirit's authority.

CHAPTER TWENTY-ONE

The Spirit and Ministry

People of God have always recognized the need for Jesus Christ to baptize His pulpits with the fire of the Holy Spirit. J. K. Popham in 1912 described the time preceding World War I as "dark, discouraging and painful." He said ninety years ago, "There is a lack of unction, life, and power in the ministry. I suppose no ministerial brother present would deny that. Each will for himself be continually, as exercised, confessing and mourning over that sad fact and, as led and helped, be seeking fresh and increased supplies of grace and power, that he may be eminently useful in the ministry. No good ministry without Christ; no unction without him; no power or authority without Christ." What would Popham think of the ministry today?

Edward Donnelly in *Peter: Eyewitness of His Majesty* included a chapter titled "Spirit-filled Preaching," in which he described how the Holy Spirit might affect the pulpit today. He wrote, "Most true preachers have had experience of this marvellous enabling. Its coming is unpredictable, often unexpected. Suddenly the minister's heart is aflame and his words seem clothed with a new power. The congregation is strangely hushed or moved. There is a palpable sense of the presence of God. The Spirit exercises a melting, penetrating influence, so that all are aware that momentous issues are before them.... Such an experience is unforgettable, addictive, a day of heaven on earth. Once a preacher has known the richness of God's enabling, he can never again rest satisfied without it."[1]

---

1. Edward Donnelly, *Peter: Eyewitness of His Majesty* (Edinburgh: The Banner of Truth Trust, 1998), 91.

THE NEED FOR SPIRIT-FILLED PULPITS

All gospel preachers recognize the need for the Holy Spirit to come upon them when they preach. They sometimes refer to this coming as a "baptism of the Holy Spirit." Their concern is that the church should also be seeking more supplies of grace and power. Who can deny that? At times they use intemperate language, and their theology is not always as biblical as it should be, but, like us, they are concerned about the Holy Spirit's influence on preaching. Donnelly wrote, "That preacher is in a pitiable condition who can continue year after year without the breath of God upon his ministry. He is not alive enough to know his own deadness. He knows too little of preaching to realize that he is not preaching. His lack of concern is his condemnation. God spare us from that awful futility!"[2]

Being filled with the Spirit is not the prerogative of preachers alone. An aged Christian lady who died last year spent her life loving God and working for His church. As a young believer she yearned for a closer walk with God, a deeper knowledge of Him, and more of His fullness so she could be a more courageous and useful witness for Him. God abundantly answered that longing. The woman spent her life serving the gospel and laboring to advance God's kingdom.

When I think of how many Christians in our congregations seem so satisfied with a low level of attainment, I yearn for them to experience some of this woman's dedication by being filled with the Spirit of God. Will a special word in a sermon have a transforming effect on a person's walk with God? It can happen. A pastor can preach something that the Spirit uses to convict and awaken a person. Sometimes it takes an earthquake to open doors and break chains. Other times the quiet and gentle dove does His work through words of comfort. Whether the Spirit works imperceptibly or comes like a mighty wind makes no difference. Our prayer is simply that He would come to us and bless our pulpits so that our congregations may be blessed with new consecration and seriousness about living under the authority of the Holy Spirit.

ERRONEOUS THOUGHTS ABOUT SPIRIT BAPTISM

There are a number of mistaken approaches to the ministry of the Spirit. Here are four of them.

---

2. Donnelly, *Peter*, 92.

1. *Romanticizing the New Testament church.* The book of Acts describes the extraordinary growth and vitality of believers who responded to a handful of men who preached to them about Jesus. Starting with Jerusalem, the disciples carried the good news of Jesus' resurrection to people all over the world. There was no need for them to first take seminars on evangelism. They knew what Jesus wanted them to do.

By contrast, the Christians in Corinth weren't told to leave their homes to bring the gospel to the world. Rather, they were told to remain where they were when God called them (1 Cor. 7:20). That was because Christian men and women, old and young, slave and free, were going around the city and out from Corinth taking the gospel of Jesus Christ everywhere, while neglecting their family life and financial obligations.

These were days of the growth and zeal of a new movement under the blessing of the Spirit. Yet these were also days of confusion, immorality, and immaturity. In Corinth, believers were not convinced about the resurrection of the body. Paul needed to spell out in fifty verses what would happen to our bodies after death.

Meantime, some male believers in the church at Corinth were keeping "virgin wives," with whom they had no sexual union. Another man in that same congregation had taken his father's own wife. What a scandal!

In Galatia, the church quickly fell into the legalism of insisting on circumcising new converts and making them follow Old Testament food laws. In Colossae, some believers were worshiping angels. In Thessalonica, men stopped working so they could await the second coming of Christ. In Asia Minor, congregations were growing lukewarm about the gospel. They were also listening to teachers who turned them against Paul's preaching. They tore the church apart with contentious issues.

Prominent people in the Philippian church argued with each other. People lied and blasphemed against the Holy Spirit, even in the Jerusalem church, which was under the authority of apostles. So, the first-century church with its problems was not much different from the congregations of our day. It was hardly a church to be upheld or imitated as a Spirit-filled church.

2. *Denigrating the church today.* Today an estimated six hundred million evangelical Christians worship Christ in several million gospel churches. A single generalization about the state of the twenty-first-century church is virtually impossible. However, what we do know is that this is the

church that Jesus Christ built. All of His elect have been saved, and every one of them has been regenerated by the Holy Spirit. Christ has taken the responsibility of sanctifying them and keeping them so that not one of them is lost. He has been and is preparing them for heaven.

In this age, the gospel has gone into the entire world. Hundreds of tribes now have the Bible in their own language. Men and women have dedicated their lives to serve in countries far from the ones in which they were raised. Tens of thousands of believers have lain down their lives for the Savior. Christian publishing houses have produced countless books. Thousands of seminaries and Bible schools filled with dedicated staff are training men for the ministry. Millions of Christian homes have raised children to know and love the Savior. All this is being done without a twentieth-century awakening. Father, Son, and Holy Spirit have chosen to adopt this manner of building the church in our age. Let us not disdain the bride of Christ in our day. He loves her passionately and eternally.

3. *Downgrading individual Christians.* As Christians, we have been blessed in the heavenly realms with every blessing of the Holy Spirit in Christ (Eph. 1:3). That is the undeniable privilege of every believer, from the youngest lamb in the flock to the oldest. All have received the blessing of the Holy Spirit. Isn't that what the Word of God teaches?

Every Christian was chosen by God in love before the foundations of the world were laid. The sins of every Christian were atoned for by the Lamb of God so that all is well between us and God. Every Christian is given a new heart that replaces his old stony heart. Every Christian has been made a new creation in a birth from above. Every Christian is indwelt by the Holy Spirit so that his heart and mind and affections and body are touched by the Spirit. Every Christian learns to know a reconciled, smiling Father.

Every Christian has been adopted into the family of God and made joint heirs with Christ. No Christian is under the dominion of sin but is seated in the heavens in Christ. Christ intercedes for every Christian at the right hand of God, and the Father receives His intercession so that each one is saved to the uttermost. Christ has purchased persevering grace for every believer, and this is sealed to every Christian by the Holy Spirit so that no one can take a single Christian out of the Father's hand. God supplies the needs of every Christian according to His riches in glory in Christ Jesus.

That is what God does for every believer. Not every Christian realizes everything that has happened to him at the moment he made a simple confession of faith, such as, "God help me never to sin again." Yet God dealt with them more graciously than they could ask. They didn't know they needed regeneration, justification, imputed righteousness, adoption into God's family, union with Christ, termination of the reign of sin, and glorification. God didn't wait for them to realize all of this; they bowed before Christ and confessed their need for Him, and they were flooded with this grace.

A long golden chain was forged in Christ's body and soul as He hung in the flame of God's rectitude on Golgotha. God has joined each of His people to one end of this chain, and the other end to His own heart. These are just some of the spiritual blessings of those immutable links. There are many more and others we will appreciate only on the great day. As Robert Murray M'Cheyne wrote, "Then, Lord, shall I fully know, not till then how much I owe."

Any doctrine of the comings of the Spirit upon the Christian must begin by a growing wonder at the untold glories of what God has already done for us by the Spirit through Christ. Along with the apostle Paul we must say, "Blessed be the God and Father of our Lord Jesus Christ, who hath blessed us with all spiritual blessings in heavenly places in Christ" (Eph. 1:3). God knew all about us; He knew our secret sins, our prayerlessness; our grudges and bitterness of heart, and how prone we were to wander and leave the God we loved. He still blesses us. Our uselessness and failure are not because of any inadequacy on God's part. We cannot say we had some cause for living as a sub-Christian. No such Christian exists. Any doctrine of the baptism of the Spirit must honor what the Word of God teaches us about the glorious redemptive achievements of Christ and the glorious redemptive applications of the Holy Spirit.

All of God's people are given every spiritual blessing. Nothing that happens subsequent to regeneration can compare to what happens to every Christian in the new birth. Of course, the marvel of God's blessing is that for some Christians the working of regeneration is so secret that they are not aware of when the Spirit gave them new life. They were passing through this enormous change and were blessed with every spiritual blessing in Christ, and yet they were not aware of what was happening to them. They had no memory of when regeneration occurred. Future experiences were more stirring, yet their significance pales compared to being put in Christ. Not even glorification is as great a change as being put in Christ.

Sadly, many Christians have never heard about the blessings of the new life. Even sadder, some Christians live with their pulpit's refrain of what they don't possess and what they might get some day if they agonize enough. If they haven't gotten these blessings, it is not because they fail to be earnest. Their sanctification diet is the problem. How different is that fare from the grace that God bestows on every believer.

This glorious primary blessing bestowed on all the people of God is described throughout the Acts of the Apostles. "And when the day of Pentecost was fully come, they were all with one accord in one place" (Acts 2:1). The Spirit came to rest on each of them, says Acts 2:3–4. "They were all filled with the Holy Ghost." The Spirit came to rest upon every single believer and filled them all. They had different backgrounds and different experiences of Christ, with various levels of piety and seriousness, but each was filled with the Holy Spirit. Peter tells the thousands of listeners to repent and be baptized, "and ye shall receive the gift of the Holy Ghost" (Acts 2:38). He does not tell them to agonize and keep crying until they have this blessing. No. They must simply repent and be baptized, and the blessings will come.

That is the pattern throughout the book of Acts. When the apostles went to Samaria, they laid their hands on believers, and every one of them received the Holy Spirit. The Spirit was not selective in baptizing one Samaritan here and half a dozen Samaritans there. When the apostles laid their hands on believers, the apostolic blessing immediately came on each one. Not a Christian in Samaria was left without the Spirit.

It was the same in Cornelius's household. The gospel had moved outside Jerusalem to Samaria and then to the home of Cornelius, a Gentile. People packed into the house to hear Peter preach. Acts 10:44 tells us that while Peter was still speaking, the Holy Spirit came on all who heard the message. He did not come just on the leaders or the most prayerful believers or the most mature. No. The Spirit came upon *all* of the believers.

It was also so of twelve men in Ephesus who had been baptized by John but had never heard of the Holy Spirit. They received the Spirit after Peter told them about the Holy Spirit. They were then on a par with other Christians in Ephesus who had been baptized into the Holy Spirit. There is no account in Acts of the Spirit bypassing some Christians while falling upon others. Acts is in perfect harmony with the New Testament definition of what a Christian is: someone who is blessed in the heavenly realms with every blessing of the Holy Spirit in Christ.

We therefore do not push for the spiritual quickening of the church by a special blessing of the Holy Spirit. Rather we take great care that we do not slight the work of the Spirit. Think of a penniless beggar who has been taken from the streets and adopted by a multimillionaire lord who cancels all his debts and pays all his fines. The beggar lives in unimaginable splendor with every need satisfied because he has been adopted as a son into a family and is heir to all the lord owns. What would you think if this person then complained that even more blessings had not been given to him? You would call him an ungrateful wretch.

So it is with us. When we say we need more of the unction and empowering of the Holy Spirit, we must always begin by reminding ourselves of all that God has already accomplished by His Son Jesus Christ for us, and applied to us by the Holy Spirit that is in us. We must continually thank God for the privileges of being forgiven. We honor and glorify Jesus Christ because of this and in this we know that we are cooperating with the work of the Spirit.

Not a single believer who has been redeemed through the accomplishment of Christ is denied the blessings of the Holy Spirit, for all of God's children are joined to Christ, and God the Father loves them the same way that He loves the Son. Each believer is complete in Christ. According to a recent newspaper article, Mohammed Ismail, age sixty, of Bangladesh, asked the Bangladesh Telephone and Telegraph Board in 1976 for a telephone line. He was finally connected in 2003. Ismail said, "It was a frustrating experience. I needed the telephone very badly twenty-seven years ago."[3] No preacher ever needs to ask God the Father for some essential grace to effectively glorify Christ, then has to wait for twenty-seven years. No one who appears before Christ on the day of judgment will need to complain, "Why didn't you give me the Spirit?" He who believes already *has* the Spirit and His gifts.

4. *Failing to distinguish levels of maturity.* First, the Bible describes a beginner believer as "a novice" (1 Tim. 3:6). This believer is not blessed with instant maturity. His understanding of everything is inadequate. God veils the full power of remaining sin in a believer, or he would be crushed.

---

3. *Times,* June 25, 2003.

A preacher recently spoke of his nine-year-old son who earnestly witnessed in his South Wales school about Jesus Christ. The boy was tormented by some children for this witness. One day he was so upset that he came to his mother for help. She got out her Bible and read verses from John 15, in which Jesus tells His disciples that, as He was persecuted, so they would be persecuted for telling the truth. Gareth listened, then said, "You mean it is always going to be like this?"

Yes it will. One of the early lessons a new convert learns is that he will need courage to take a stand for Christ. He will always need to battle remaining sin, always need to grow in knowledge of the Scriptures, and always need to grow in evangelistic earnestness. Every believer begins as a novice. But he does not begin without the Holy Spirit. We progress spiritually as we do physically—by inches. We become mature people of God through the means of grace as we grow in communion with God.

Second, the spiritual gifts of the Holy Spirit vary. The church is described as a body in 1 Corinthians 12, in which believers with different kinds of gifts from the same God work together (1 Cor. 12:4–6). We are told, "God set the members every one of them in the body, as it hath pleased him" (1 Cor. 12:18). Some parts seem weaker, while others are less honorable, but all are designed and given by God.

Is everyone in the body a teacher? No. Does everyone speak in tongues? No. God plans diversity in every congregation. The gifts of the Spirit make us different from one another so that we can minister to one another and receive ministry from one another in different ways. Yet, the fruit of the Spirit makes us like one another, and the chief of those fruits is love. Paul never says a particular gift of the Spirit is necessary for a believer to know he has the presence of the Spirit. A New Testament congregation in which every person spoke in tongues would have been like one enormous nose rather than a body of various complementary organs. So too extraordinary preaching is not the infallible mark that a man is full of the Spirit and an heir of heaven. Paul says, "Though I speak with the tongues of men and of angels, and have not charity, I am become as sounding brass, or a tinkling cymbal" (1 Cor. 13:1).

Third, there is a difference in talents. Some Christians are strong, while others are weak. Jesus tells a parable in which the master is preparing to go on a long journey. Before he leaves, he gives five talents to one servant and tells him to use these talents until he returns. He gives another servant three talents, and another, one.

The number of talents and their bestowal was up to the master, not the servants, but each man had to put his talents to use. They were later judged according to what they did with those talents; if they multiplied those talents, they were rewarded, but if they buried them they were punished. Likewise, some Christians have been called to be preachers and pastors. That is their gift from the Holy Spirit. Yet there are different degrees of gifts; some are given five talents for preaching; some, three; and some, one. For example, Martin Luther had a great gift of teaching. So did John Bunyan and Cornelius Van Til. The grandeur of those men was their persevering use of those talents throughout their lives. There was no let-up in their efforts.

Those men are our examples and we should seek to copy them, but we should not fret that we will never accomplish what they did. Most preachers are one-talent men, and that is enough for them to answer to God in the great day how they have employed that one. Were they steadfast and always abounding in the work of the Lord with the talent God gave them?

No special empowering of the Spirit will change one talent into five. A baptism of the Spirit will not turn a John Bunyan into a John Owen. We need John Bunyan and John Owen just as they are. We ourselves will never be transformed into a Jonathan Edwards, but we will need the Holy Spirit to enable us to work with one talent just as he helped the five-talent William Tyndale to labor.

When I get to heaven, the Lord will not ask me, "Geoff, why weren't you a Tyndale?" Rather, He will ask me, "Geoff, why weren't you the Geoff I gifted and blessed?" The pulpits all over the world are filled with men of one or two talents who, by the ministry of the Spirit, have used their gifts for the Lord and have been greatly used by Him. If there is one evident pattern for the twenty-first-century church, it is that there are few hyper-preachers in our day but thousands of faithful servants working by the Spirit's enabling to advance God's kingdom.

However, let no Christian excuse his own laziness and cowardice and prayerlessness by saying, "My name is not George Whitefield." That may be true, but you can go to the same God as Whitefield's and ask for the same strengthening of your heart and soul in the Lord's service. Let us dedicate the talent we have to God and seek the strength of the Spirit to employ it until the Savior comes. As Edward Donnelly wrote, "We must seek unction. We must forsake every sin which might grieve or quench the Spirit. We need to feel, as never before, our utter dependence upon

God. Without the power of the Holy Spirit, our preaching is ineffective. How often have we spoken lifelessly and coldly about the most glorious realities in the universe! Or perhaps we have entered into the pulpits with warm hearts and high expectations, only to be chilled and depressed by an indifferent audience. What a stale, unprofitable thing it is to preach only in our own strength or to apathetic people! How exhausted and miserable it makes us."[4]

Robert Murray M'Cheyne wrote, "Master, help!" on his sermon manuscripts. Surely nothing is more important than praying for God's help in preaching the gospel. Whatever talents we are given, we need the Holy Spirit's help to use them as they should be used.

Fourth, the gifts of members in every congregation vary. The members of a cult are like postage stamps; the dark-suited, white-shirted Mormons are the same all over the world. Members of Christ's church are far different. In a church, no true Christian is like his brother or sister. He is different physically, psychologically, economically, and racially. He is different in age and IQ and personality. Christians gather together in different blends and proportions. They reflect the manner of their conversion and the ministry they are sitting under. Perhaps the angel of each of the seven churches in Asia Minor is a symbol of the corporate personality of each congregation. Each differs from one another in terms of weaknesses as well as virtues. None is without the Holy Ghost; all are part of the body of Christ, elect of God, part of the fellowship of the Spirit, and pillars of the truth, but each is in a different stage of maturity. Each needs to be filled with the Spirit. The mighty church in Ephesus was blessed in the heavenly realms with every spiritual blessing in Christ, but it needed more of His gifts, His love, His morale-boosting ministry, and the strength to mortify its sinful natures and the courage to stand up for Jesus.

There is no perfect congregation, but some have been more pervasively affected by the sword of the Spirit and thus more fully reflect the grace of Christ. Few churches have or need more than one pastor-preacher. Few churches have leaders with the gifts of theologians or of church planters. There is no secret, either, that can open up a church to the full presence of Christ. Each congregation must be aware that it can be so busy or so dead that Christ is left outside knocking to be let in. That is what happened to the church in Laodicea.

---

4. Donnelly, *Peter*, 92.

So each Christian in the church must constantly be asking Christ to come in. Every Sunday we must say, "Welcome, Lord. We are honored to have Thee here again. Thou art the hub of our lives. Welcome to our assembly." Then things will begin to hum as we experience true worship and holy sermons.

THE RIGHT APPROACH TO SPIRIT BAPTISM

Scripture uses the phrase *baptism of the Spirit* to describe the first definitive work of the Spirit in giving birth to the New Testament church, or to emphasize an aspect of regeneration at the beginning of spiritual life in a believer. All people of God worldwide have been baptized by the Spirit because Christ has rent the heavens and poured forth His regenerating Spirit upon them. So to be biblical, we should be reluctant to use the phrase *baptism of the Spirit* in asking for the unction of the Spirit in the preaching of the Word.

Perhaps it would be better to use the plural form of the phrase. We then may talk about Christ abundantly pouring out His Spirit on men and churches as He has done at various times in history to revive a declining testimony. I long to hear that somewhere today Christ has visited a congregation by sending His Spirit to revive it and save many. We are always listening for such news, yet we confess we are sceptical about reports of revival in places that are faraway and difficult to verify.

Let me once more describe a church of revival, so as to whet your appetite for such a blessing so that you may long for better days for the church. Stephen Rees of Stockport, Manchester, wrote in a recent church letter about some of the consequences of the Spirit's blessing. He describes two effects:

1. The felt presence of God in church meetings. "There are times when God's Spirit descends upon a meeting, and everybody knows God is present," Rees says.

> The unseen world becomes terribly, wonderfully close. At those times, the preaching is transformed. The preacher speaks with a boldness and authority that is obviously supernatural. Hearers forget the preacher and hear only the voice of God speaking to their hearts. Familiar truths become real as they are preached. Those who listen tremble at the thought of God; they shake with fear as they are made aware of their sins, they are overwhelmed with wonder as

they hear about the cross of the Lord Jesus, they are filled with a joy that can't be put into words as they are reminded of heaven to come.

The singing is transformed. People sing as they've never sung before, realizing how wonderful the words are that they're singing, and conscious that God is listening. The praying is transformed. God's people pray with confidence, earnestness, and with the wrestling spirit which says "I will not let you go unless you bless me." All of us, I hope, can remember meetings when we've had a taste of that. But we want all our meetings to be like that. We want to know that God is among his people whenever they meet.[5]

2. Every member of the church is filled with the Holy Spirit. "I am not talking about one great crisis experience," Rees says.

I am saying that every one of us ought to be brim-full of the life of God every moment. If we were filled with the Spirit, we would have a great sense of the love of God towards us. We would be able to say, "Because the love of God is shed abroad in our hearts by the Holy Ghost which is given unto us" (Rom. 5:5). And we on our side would love the Savior with a warm, steady love. We would long for the day when he comes again. We would want to serve him with all our strength. If we were filled with the Spirit, we would love one another more warmly, more affectionately and more practically than we do. We would pray for one another more consistently. We would commit ourselves to the life of the church more thoroughly.

We would be eager to be with our fellow-believers, listening to God's Word, so we would do everything in our power to be at the meetings. We would look forward all month to being at the Lord's Supper and feeding on Christ there. If we were filled with the Spirit, we'd be very careful to avoid anything sinful or even dubious. We'd turn away from worldly entertainments and distractions. In every situation our first question would be 'How can I honour God?' not 'What do I want to do?' We'd deal with our problems—especially our disagreements with other church-members—in a biblical way. We would be praying in the various church prayer meetings. We'd never let dislikes or grudges fester in our hearts. We'd learn to say sorry. We'd learn to be straight with people. We'd learn to talk to

---

5. Rees, a letter to the congregation.

people who offend us, not talk about them behind their backs. The life of the church would be sweeter and happier."[6]

That is such a useful description of what occurs when Christ pours out His Spirit on His people. Tongues, we have said, couldn't have been the mark of a Spirit-filled New Testament Christian because speaking in tongues was one of those gifts by which Christians differed from one another. One person was given that spiritual gift while another person was not.

That twofold description is also useful because it clears up misunderstandings regarding a so-called second blessing of the Spirit. Fred Mitchell, a devout Christian pharmacist from Bradford, England, was killed fifty years ago in Calcutta. Mitchell was a godly man who became chairman of the Methodist convention in Keswick. He believed that by an act of faith and dedication the Christian could enter a more victorious life. He could move from the life of defeat in Romans 7 to the life of victory in Romans 8 by an action he chose to take. In such an act you entrusted yourself to God again. Mitchell's biography includes the account of a young nurse who longed to know how she could be filled with the Holy Spirit. She talked to Mitchell about it. He told her about the full consecration of keeping nothing back from God.

> "Before I left the room I was quite clear that as soon as a full consecration was made, God was waiting and willing to bestow the Gift I was seeking," the nurse wrote. "In the wisdom God gave him, Mr. Mitchell didn't press me to take the step of faith right then. Whether he discerned that there were yet reserves, I do not know. He didn't probe—he wasn't one of those who try to do the Holy Spirit's work for him! He had pointed the way, given me his testimony, which was confirmed by the testimony of his life, and he left it at that.
>
> "During the days or weeks that followed, the Holy Spirit himself showed me what was hindering his taking full possession of me," the nurse continued. "One day, while I was waiting for a friend, I let go of the last hindering thing I knew of. God's answer was immediate. I knew 'He had come to His temple.' A group of us nurses came into this blessing about the same time in different ways. There followed a period of blessing and witness, not only in the hospital, but in various chapels and missions in the town, which I shall never forget."[7]

---

6. Rees, a letter to the congregation.
7. Phyllis Thompson, *Climbing on Track* (London: China Inland Mission, 1954), 83.

No one can fail to be moved by such an account. A growing desire to live a more obedient Christian life is a mark of new birth, and laying aside darling sins to serve more zealously the Lord is surely needed in all of us. But the Keswick view of full consecration does not fully understand the definitive nature of the work of God in every single Christian so that we increasingly die to the reign of sin. Paul teaches in Romans 6 that every Christian must die to the dominion of sin and live henceforth to serve righteousness.

The Keswick second blessing is often a rather clinical step. The blessing is named and claimed by an act of faith, without any reference to the affections; it is a bare decision. People are invited to come to the front of the church where they bow in prayer. They are then told that they will get entire sanctification. The Bradford nurse's description of the blessing she received is different. It has a ring of truth and humility about it. She wanted more of God, and she describes her experience according to the theology she was given. She talked about her new zeal as a life of service. As she labored for God, she knew more of God's grace and love than she had known before.

It is impossible to give three conditions for a Holy Spirit baptism. It would be as impossible as suggesting three ways to regenerate your unbelieving husband or teenage son. We may only say that God may grant this regeneration, in His grace, and your duty is to live a wise and loving and holy life before your loved ones day by day, so that they may be won by your meekness and graciousness. Meantime, do not stop praying that the Spirit will come into their hearts, and do not doubt that God may save them if He chooses.

Consider how the Lord Jesus preached and performed miracles in unrepentant Korazin and Bethsaida. There was no revival in those places, no outpouring of the Holy Spirit, but still Jesus thanked God, saying, "I thank thee, O Father, Lord of heaven and earth, because thou hast hid these things from the wise and prudent, and hast revealed them unto babes. Even so, Father: for so it seemed good in thy sight" (Matt. 11:25–26). Jesus bowed before the sovereignty of God. He pleased His Father in all He did, He resisted sin, loved His neighbor as Himself, and preached to the people that God had given Him. Yet no nights of agonizing prayer or months of fasting could guarantee that Korazin or Bethsaida would receive the outpouring of the Spirit in revival.

D. Martyn Lloyd-Jones both edified and surprised me in a sermon on the great words of Paul, who says, "I can do all things through Christ which strengtheneth me" (Phil. 4:13). Lloyd-Jones said,

> No subject is discussed more often than power in preaching. "Oh, that I might have power in preaching," says the preacher, and he goes on his knees and prays for power. I think that that may be quite wrong. It certainly is if it is the only thing that the preacher does. The way to have power is to prepare your message carefully. Study the Word of God, think it out, analyze it, put it in order, do your utmost. That is the message God is most likely to bless—the indirect approach rather than the direct. It is exactly the same in this matter of power and ability to live the Christian life. In addition to our prayer for power and ability, we must obey certain primary rules and laws.

In summary, Lloyd-Jones said,

> The secret of power is to learn from the New Testament what is possible for us in Christ. What I have to do is go to Christ. I must spend my time with Him, I must meditate upon Him, I must get to know Him. Paul's ambition to know Christ teaches me that I must maintain communion with Christ and I must concentrate on knowing Him.
>
> I must also do exactly what He tells me. I must avoid things that would hamper my walk with Him. If we don't keep the spiritual rules we may pray endlessly for power but we'll never get it. There are no short cuts in the Christian life. If in the midst of persecution we want to feel as Paul felt, we must live as Paul lived. I must do what he tells me. I must read the Bible, I must exercise, I must practice the Christian life, I must live the Christian life in all its fullness. In other words, I must implement all that Paul teaches.
>
> I must abide in Christ. I may do this, Paul says, if Christ infuses His strength into me. What a wonderful idea. Paul proposes a kind of spiritual blood transfusion. Nowhere does one experience it more than in the Christian pulpit. I often say that the most romantic place on earth is the pulpit. I ascend the pulpit stairs Sunday after Sunday without knowing exactly what will happen. I confess that sometimes I expect nothing; but suddenly the power is given to me. At other times I expect much because of my preparation; but, alas, I find there is no power in it. Thank God it is like that. I do my utmost, but God controls the supply and the power.
>
> He is the heavenly physician, who knows every variation in my condition. He sees my complexion, He feels my pulse. He knows

my inadequacies in preaching, He knows everything. As Paul says, "Therefore I am able for all things through the One who is constantly infusing strength into me."

"That, then, is the prescription," Lloyd-Jones said. "Do not agonize in prayer, beseeching Christ for power. Do what He has told you to do. Live the Christian life. Pray, and meditate upon him. Spend time with Him and ask Him to manifest Himself to you. And as long as you do that, you can leave the rest to Him. He will give you strength: 'as thy days, so shall thy strength be' (Deut. 33:25). He knows us better than we know ourselves, and according to our need so will be our supply. Do that and you will be able to say with the apostle: 'I am able [made strong] for all things through the One who is constantly infusing strength into me.'"[8]

---

8. D. Martyn Lloyd-Jones, *The Life of Peace: Studies in Philippians 3 and 4* (London: Hodder and Stoughton, 1990), 225–27.

Scripture Index